Images Below

Images Below

A MANUAL OF UNDERGROUND AND FLASH PHOTOGRAPHY

Chris Howes

Images Below

Images Below

A manual of
underground
and flash
photography

Chris Howes

WILD PLACES
CARDIFF

WILD PLACES PUBLISHING
51 TIMBERS SQUARE, ROATH
CARDIFF CF2 3SH, UK

First published 1997

By the same author, a companion volume:
To Photograph Darkness. The history of underground and flash photography

All photographs by the author.

Caves, mines and other underground sites are inherently dangerous and should not be entered without appropriate training and experience; you should become a proficient caver or mine explorer before taking up underground photography. Some techniques described in this manual involve chemical means of producing artificial light or adaptations to standard photographic equipment. Caution should be used where appropriate and no responsibility is accepted by the author or publisher for any injury, accident or loss, however caused.

Distributed in the USA by Speleobooks, Box 10, Schoharie, NY 12157, USA

British Library Cataloguing in Publication Data
A catalogue record for this book is available from the British Library

ISBN 0 9526701 1 9

Design and origination by Wild Places Publishing, Cardiff
Film output by Radstock Reproductions, Midsomer Norton
Printed on Precision Smooth, a paper manufactured from sustainable sources
Printed and bound in Great Britain by Butler & Tanner, Frome

CONTENTS

PREFACE

I N 1968 I 'discovered' caving by the simple expedient of being told by my father that I was not to venture underground; with a collier in the family it was obviously 'far too dangerous'. The opportunity to cave first arose during a school-based residential course, and I quietly enjoyed the experience. During successive years I wandered between mountain walking and rock climbing, through surfing, canoeing and skiing, but always returned to cave photography. The distinction is important: photography was always the motivating force.

In 1978 a whim led to the purchase of a cheap enlarger and, that evening, a makeshift darkroom was created from black plastic bags taped over a bathroom window. There was no safe light (a torch, painted with red nail varnish, sufficed), and prints were developed in a sink and fixed in the bath (which promptly lost its ceramic coating). Printing in black and white added another facet to controlling and producing an image. The first night's stumbling, self-taught results were awful, but the cave photographs taken over the next three years gained a Fellowship of the Royal Photographic Society.

As I experimented and gained experience, friends suggested that I should write down my techniques as, at that time, there were limited sources of 'modern' information about cave photography. *Cave Photography. A practical guide* appeared in 1987.

It proved invaluable as, once the book became widespread, cavers contacted me with questions and initiated many a photographic discussion. However, it was a basic guide and, though I initially envisaged a companion volume covering advanced techniques, time rushed by and other commitments grew. The end of the 1980s saw the culmination of my research into early cave photography with the publication of *To Photograph Darkness*. Then, when *Cave Photography* sold out, it was time to consider its replacement.

The result is *Images Below*, a manual which would not have been written without the constructive comments, help and encouragement of fellow cavers and cave photographers. In many ways it is the volume I would have liked to have written ten years ago, but is stronger today for not having been so.

I, as all photographers, am still learning the craft, something I hope to continue. If this manual encourages a new generation of cavers to take up the challenge and expand this distillation of techniques, it will have fulfilled its function. Within the pages of this manual I sincerely hope that there are words which encourage and photographs which will help you along your own, enjoyable road towards the perfect picture.

Chris Howes
May 1997

ACKNOWLEDGEMENTS

C AVE photography requires careful planning, preparation and, more than anything, the aid of fellow cavers. This extends beyond the obvious: arranging access to a cave, accommodation while you travel, or simply talking through a problem. To mention everyone who has helped in these diverse ways is impossible; nevertheless, I must record my gratitude to these unnamed friends.

In addition, a huge number of people have provided direct help in taking these underground photographs, so much so that omissions are inevitable. I can only apologise for anyone I have inadvertently missed. Cavers featured in the photographs and linked with their production include:

STEVE Ainley, Christine Airey, Richard Aldham, Evan Anderson, Nigel Atkins, Graham Barrett, Hazel Barton, Rod Beaumont, Djuna Bewley, Peter Bolt, Dave Bunnell, Olaf Buskens, Ian Caldwell, Alan Calford, Judith Calford, Angela Cave, John Cliffe, Pete Cloke, Alice Crook, Sophie Crook, Andy Deeley, Isobel Fairclough, Tim Fewster, John Finch, John Forder, Steve Fowler, Rob Franklin, Rob Frowen, Alastair Garman, David Gibson, Ivan Gibson, Pete Glanvill, John Gray, Glenn Hasbrouk, Graham Heslop, Linda Heslop, Rhian Hicks, Chris Hurley, Sue Hutchins, Ruth Jacobs, Greg Jahn, Robin James, Huw Jones, Liam Kealy, Andy Kendall, Judith Kings, Steve Kings, Paul Kirkwood, Denise Knibbs, Sarah Knibbs, Tony Knibbs, Alex Laxton, Bruce Levitan, Tim Long, Ben Lovett, Simon McKinna, Nick Milton, Jane Mitchell, Alan Morgan, Dave Morris, Kevin Munn, Gavin Newman, John 'Jox' Oxley, Art Palmer, Peggy Palmer, Rob Palmer, Huw Parsons, Hugh Penney, Barry Phillips, Chrissy Price, Graham Price, Chris Printz, Shaun Puckering, Simon Raven, Karen Rees, Hugh Rice, Fran Rose, Bill Roughton, Phil Sandercott, Susan Sanders, Theo Schuurmans, Tom Sharpe, Karen Sinyard, Clinton Small, Chris Smart, Richard Stevenson, Malcolm Stewart, David Stuckey, Andy Tyler, Cyndie Walck, Jane Wallace, Kevin West, Clive Westlake, Fiona Whitaker and Dave Whiteside.

Many cavers have helped design and make sometimes esoteric pieces of cave photography equipment. In recent years these include, in particular, Andy Bell and David Gibson. Particular thanks are due to David for permission to include his slave unit circuit in this manual, to Nigel Lovell for the loan of modified electronic flashguns and to Mike Bedford for the use of his experimental cascade flash assembly.

The photographs would not have been achieved without the team spirit, time, effort and unstinting help offered by all those involved and this manual is dedicated to the many cavers who have made this project possible. In the USA, Emily Davis Mobley has supported publication, and from Australia David Stuckey offered valuable advice concerning stereo photography. Tim Long, Ben Lovett and Malcolm Stewart went far beyond the call of duty in producing many of the 'technique' photographs.

In particular, Judith Calford must be credited for her patience and involvement in every stage of this manual's production, from acting as a flash assistant and model to checking the draft of the text. My gratitude and thanks for her hard work and support are recorded here.

PRODUCTION NOTES

THE majority of the photographs presented in this manual were taken using a Rollei 35 LED, Olympus OM1N or OM2N, or a Practica L2. Most pictures were taken with a 35mm lens – a Zuiko on the Olympus bodies and a Pentax lens on the Practica; the Rollei bears a fixed 40mm lens. Other focal lengths include 50mm, 28mm, 24mm and 17mm. Underwater photographs, and some taken under extreme in-cave conditions, were taken using a Nikonos III or V with a 35mm lens and, on occasion, a supplementary 16mm adaptor.

Colour transparencies, some of which are reproduced in black and white, were taken using Fuji Velvia, Fuji Sensia or Kodachrome 200 film. Black and white photographs were taken almost exclusively on Ilford FP4 Plus and developed in Paterson's Acutol, Acuspecial or Kodak HC110, although Pan F was also used for fine-grained close-up photographs. Prints were made on resin-coated Slovenian graded papers or on Ilford's Ilfospeed range, processed in a machine-grade MQ developer with, on occasion, an added quantity of metol to adjust the characteristics of shadow development.

During reproduction the photographs have been scanned from negatives, prints and slides. Pictures which demonstrate photographic techniques are reproduced without alteration; where enhancements have been made during printing these have been achieved using traditional darkroom techniques such as dodging and burning.

Common photographic terminology makes use of different measurement systems in various parts of the world. For example, film sensitivity is properly measured using an ISO rating but some countries still use the older ASA prefix; this manual uses the numerically identical ISO system.

Photographers, by convention, may be more used to working in metric (metres) or imperial (feet) measurements, a difference which directly affects the concept of guide numbers for flash photography. The techniques described in this manual are valid for any system of distance measurement and, to aid the reader, attention has been given to converting from one unit to another. Nevertheless, standardisation is required and, unless otherwise stated, the guide numbers in this manual are based on metres.

Caving terminology also has its differences, particularly between the UK and US where a number of equivalent terms can be misleading or

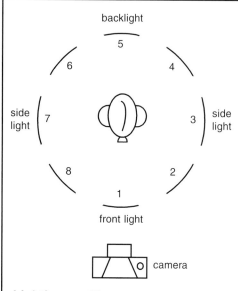

Lighting positions

To enable lighting positions to be easily described a code system is used throughout this book. These codes locate a flash position relative to the camera, using a designation of E and B to indicate the use of an electronic flash or flashbulb respectively. An electronic flash fired from the camera is therefore E1, while a flashbulb used to light the subject from behind but to one side is B4 or B6.

The Candlewax Formations, Dan yr Ogof, were lit using two flashes behind the caver. The designation (E6, B4) indicates their nature and position: an electronic flash from position 6 to help rimlight the formations and add detail to the face, with the main lighting from a flashbulb placed at position 4.

These designations are used throughout this manual to describe the angle of lighting relative to the camera position

not readily understood. Examples include tackle sack/cave pack, torch/ flashlight and electronic flash/strobe. Areas of potential confusion have been avoided where possible or kept to a minimum (flashgun terminology, for example, could not be avoided and the European 'electronic flash' has been used). In cases where difficulties might arise the terminology is defined in the text, with cross-referenced explanations in the glossary.

INTRODUCTION

Iɴ 1866 Charles Waldack was already familiar with the problems of underground photography when he wrote: 'You will agree with me that photographing in a cave is photographing under the worst conditions.' Since then, equipment has improved and new techniques have been established, yet the production of pictures in the utter darkness found beneath the earth is still considered one of the hardest forms of photography to master.

Many cavers regularly take pictures on the surface, but find that the world below their feet presents different problems. When their efforts are processed, all too often they are faced with a roll of film containing little more than misty, poorly exposed pictures. When occasional successes are achieved, they are difficult to repeat. What was done on this occasion that was not done before? Why did this picture work, but not the others?

Every cave photographer, experienced and novice alike, wants to improve both the success rate and quality of the final pictures. By using this manual, both of these aims can be achieved. It will shorten the learning process and minimise the difficulties encountered. There are many pitfalls, not always obvious to the inexperienced, which can readily be avoided.

The cave environment is an unforgiving one. While cavers revel in darkness and water, cameras and flashguns have to survive far greater hazards than their designers ever intended. Dirt and mud conspire to clog contacts, water shorts out high-voltage circuits, and delicate mechanisms do not survive long. Choice of equipment can often determine success or failure, so the first three chapters are devoted to what to use and how to modify and protect it. Here, as in successive chapters, the emphasis is on the practical production of photographs; theory is discussed as a part of the techniques to use, but only where it will aid understanding and enable a wider range of pictures to be tackled. The stress remains on practical matters.

There is no one method of taking pictures underground. Cave photographers, using different equipment in vastly different situations, have independently evolved their own, individual techniques, something that you also will have to accomplish in order to produce an original style. This manual is therefore a guide, a 'how-to-do-it recipe book', which greatly expands upon the advice given in its predecessor, *Cave Photography. A practical guide*. It

The Score, Ogof Draenen (E1, B5)

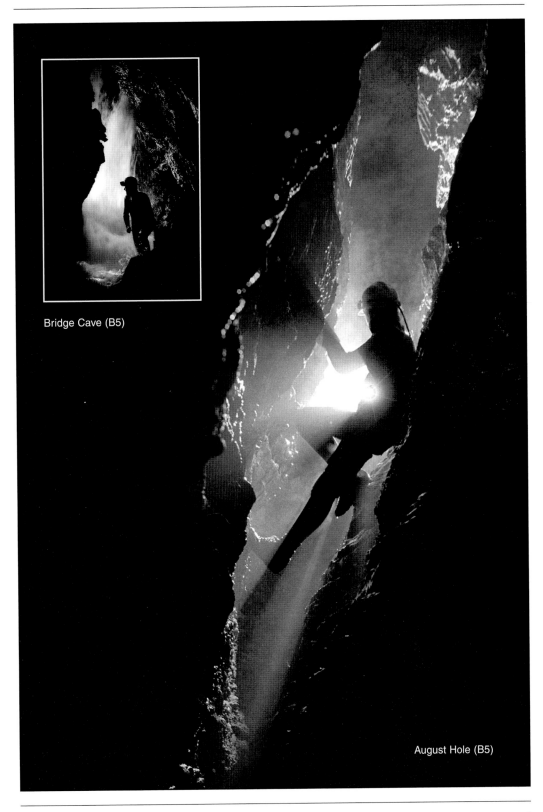

Bridge Cave (B5)

August Hole (B5)

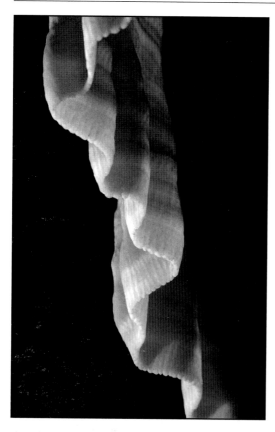

Ogof Ffynnon Taf (E7)

is divided into four sections covering equipment, basic techniques, advanced techniques in specialist areas such as close-up photography, and finally a general section which includes composition and how to assess and learn from your work. If you follow and build upon the instructions, your success rate will rise.

Details with each photograph indicate how it was taken; study the pictures and add your own ideas. Each is given a notation linked to the type of flash and where it was positioned relative to the camera; consult the diagrams on p.viii or p.89 to interpret the code.

Experiment with the suggested procedures and concepts described in this manual, changing or modifying them to suit the available equipment or to obtain a particular effect. There is certainly no need to purchase more than a few essential items of equipment in order to get started. By working with the techniques presented here you will learn faster, but walk before you can run. Make sure you understand basic techniques before moving on to advanced uses of multiple flash – there is far more that can be accomplished with a single flash than is generally recognised, and simplicity is often the key to success. Then, as new ideas occur to you, you will begin to establish your own standards and style.

Cave photography is, if anything, an exercise in problem solving and ingenuity: think of an effect or picture, and find a way to take it. Experiment: boldly go where no cave photographer has gone before, to coin a misquote. An equally important adage is to 'Leave nothing but footprints, kill nothing but time, take nothing but photographs.' Caves are not only awesome, demanding places, they are also delicate. A careless foot, tilt of a head or swing of a tripod leg can be enough to ruin the very subject that you and others have come to experience. It is therefore assumed that, before you begin taking underground pictures, you have already become a competent caver and will respect the environment you work within. In effect, do not even leave footprints.

Waldack persevered with his pioneering photography, and achieved success. With care and thought, you too can record this special environment. I hope this will prove as enjoyable for you as it has for me; above all, that is what counts.

Chapter one
CAMERAS AND LENSES

I used Rollei cameras a lot, although they weren't especially robust. On one occasion, the camera set up ready, I was balancing a flashgun on a ledge when I heard a thud. I looked round. A tripod leg had fallen off, leaving the camera swaying, balanced on the two remaining legs.

Time stood still, but the camera did not. A wobble and a sway and the lens impact-tested on Welsh rock. I rushed over, to hear another thud behind me as the flashgun joined the camera in oblivion.

Ogof Ffynnon Ddu

THE correct choice and preparation of equipment helps increase the success rate of underground photography. While nothing is ideal for underground work, some cameras and flashguns are more suitable than others and yet more are totally unsuited to the cave environment.

Caving conditions, as here in Ogof Cynnes (E8), do not mix with photographic equipment

Problems can be further minimised by modifying standard photographic equipment, searching out second-hand apparatus, or by constructing specialist items that are not commercially available.

If you already own a camera you will naturally want to press it into immediate use, but it is probably better to buy a camera solely for use underground. Modern, sophisticated cameras and flashguns are readily

The Burren, Co. Clare

available off the shelf, but they are unlikely to prove the best choice in the long run. In the conditions of high humidity and grinding dirt found in caves and mines, delicate electronic apparatus will not survive forever. The cost of cleaning expensive cameras may outweigh the price of something which was cheaper and more suitable in the first place. In addition, while developing your techniques you may form preferences for certain camera features, and upgrades to your equipment can then be made with the benefit of hindsight.

There are many different approaches to underground photography. A general caving trip might require a small, compact, lightweight set of equipment for incidental work, while a special photographic session could demand a wide range of cameras and flash-guns. In either case, acquiring a special set of equipment which permits a flexible approach is worth serious consideration.

Cave photography need not be an expensive hobby. The most suitable items are often available second-hand and, indeed, many out-of-date cameras are better than modern ones for taking underground. With these factors in mind, the first three chapters of this manual give advice on the photographic equipment required and the features to avoid.

CAMERAS

The choice of camera is the cave photographer's greatest source of frustration in the search for something ideal. Unfortunately, no perfect caving camera has ever existed, and probably never will; some features make a camera suitable for a certain type of shot, and less useful for another. When choosing a camera there are a series of features which should be considered.

APS film (left), 120 roll film and a 35mm cassette

Format

The first step is to match your requirements to the camera's format – in other words, to the size of film it uses.

The smallest commonly available film format is the cassette-loading 110 cartridge, used in Instamatic cameras. These cameras have no control over aperture or shutter speed, the negative is too small to permit good enlargements, and there are limitations in the way that flashguns are fired. While Instamatic-type cameras may be suitable for taking quick record photographs of a specific location such as a dig (they are, after all, easy to transport and are cheap and light), their restrictions are so great that they cannot be seriously considered for underground work. Instant-picture, Polaroid-type cameras share many of the same reservations, with the additional drawbacks of a large size and relatively expensive film.

At the other extreme, medium and large format cameras use roll or sheet film, giving a much larger negative or slide. This will yield better quality prints, all other factors being equal, as the film does not have to be enlarged as much to obtain a particular size. Interchangeable backs permit pictures to be taken on different film types while only using one camera body. Using Polaroid film, an instant picture can be taken to check lighting angles and exposure before switching to the final film. This ability to switch backs may offer a distinct advantage for a professional photographer.

However, there are drawbacks to medium and large format cameras: they are heavy, bulky and expensive. Some publications may demand these formats but, if you do not have a specific need for this size, the far commoner 35mm camera is more convenient and yields perfectly acceptable results.

Introduced in 1996, APS (Advanced Photo System) films can be changed in mid-roll without losing frames and, as there is less handling involved, the risk of scratching the film is reduced. Different shapes of pictures (landscape, panoramic, classic 35mm) are possible on the same roll, if the camera supports this feature.

The price of using an APS system is one of automation: for nearly all cavers, manual 35mm cameras are the best choice as they are relatively cheap and small, and second-hand models are common. This manual therefore concentrates on using 35mm cameras, although the techniques it includes can be applied to any camera and film format.

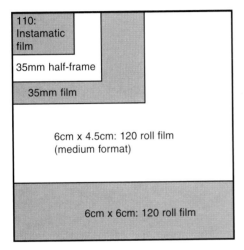

110:
Instamatic
film

35mm half-frame

35mm film

6cm x 4.5cm: 120 roll film
(medium format)

6cm x 6cm: 120 roll film

Larger film sizes allow greater enlargements without a loss of quality. For many cavers, 35mm cameras are a good compromise for camera size and weight against the final picture. The diagram shows the actual size of miniature and medium format films

Exposure control

Any 35mm camera *can* be used underground, but some features are useful while others should be totally avoided. Obviously, any model that appears too delicate or which might allow mud or water to enter the mechanism (usually through gaps around the aperture ring or where the lens and body join) should be rejected. With a wealth of cameras on the market, the following factors can only be pointers; it is impossible to list every make and model. Look for one that possesses as many of the following features as possible.

The lens is of paramount importance as it determines picture quality. A cheap lens may introduce distortions or defects, so that crispness and contrast in the resulting photograph are never acceptable. In this respect the lens is more important than the camera body; for cave photography most 'modern' camera features are not required.

Light entering the camera is focused by the lens onto the film, which is 'exposed'. Accurate focusing is therefore important: some cameras are manually focused, while others (in the main, more expensive SLR and compact cameras) are automatic. Underground, automatic systems can be fooled and produce poor results; as a generalisation, manual control (with a clearly engraved scale of distances on the barrel of the lens) is more useful.

In 'normal' photography on the surface, the quantity of light permitted to reach the sensitive film emulsion is controlled by a combination of the shutter speed and lens aperture (when using flash the exposure depends on a combination of the flash intensity and aperture). The slower the shutter speed (in other words, the longer the shutter is open) or the larger the aperture – determined by the iris – the more light is admitted.

Water rushes over a lip in the August/Longwood System (B7)

Fully automatic cameras control both the aperture and shutter, while others use an aperture-priority or shutter-priority system. In an aperture-priority system the aperture is set manually and the camera selects a matching shutter speed to produce a correct exposure. The same system is used in reverse in shutter-priority cameras, where a shutter speed is selected manually with the camera's electronics selecting a suitable aperture. For cave photography, manual control of both aperture and shutter speed is required: manual cameras are preferable to automatic models.

Some cameras have electronic linkages between the camera body and lens, or a shutter which is electronically rather than mechanically triggered. With the high humidity found underground and the risk of getting equipment wet, cameras that rely on electronic controls do not generally survive as long as mechanical ones. The camera's exposure meter (lightmeter) is usually but not always battery powered. As a working meter is not required for flash photography (though it is useful in cave entrances), 'broken' (and therefore cheap) second-hand cameras can sometimes be found. The shutter on many cameras, even some with manual control of the aperture and shutter speeds, will not operate if the battery is dead or removed: check before you buy.

Opposite: Ogof Ffynnon Ddu streamway (B5). Cameras are being carried in an ex-army ammunition box

Flash synchronisation

The camera's shutter must synchronise with the flashgun and only fire the flash when the shutter is fully open. Electronic flash usually synchronises at 1/60 second on an SLR camera, although faster speeds are possible on some models, and at least one speed of 1/30 second, or slower, is required to make the best use of flashbulbs.

In cave photography flashguns may be fired some distance from the camera. One of the easiest techniques of doing this, in total darkness, is to lock open the shutter using a 'B' (Bulb or Brief) or 'T' (Time) setting, a technique known as open flash. The flash can then be fired manually while the shutter is open, so a B or T setting – marked on the shutter speed control or the lens itself – is obviously useful. Although it is an anomaly to refer to a 'bulb' setting now that the heyday of flashbulbs is long past, the B designation is the commonest.

The camera can be hand-held on B, but it is more usual to fix it on a tripod. When B is used, the shutter release button has to be held down, usually by attaching a cable release to the shutter button. In each case check that the fitting is present: a screw-thread tripod bush underneath the camera, and a threaded hole in the shutter button or some other, inbuilt, locking device.

Flash synchronisation was once only possible using B, but modern models use a hot shoe or pc cable connection. The flashgun's pc cable (sometimes called a sync cable) is inserted into a matching pc socket on the camera, while a hot shoe uses two or more contacts which directly connect with the base of the flashgun; often, both cable and hot shoe connections are present. Check the hot shoe on older cameras as some were made with 'cold shoes' which only supported the flashgun without making electrical contact. Two-contact shoes, the commonest sort, use a central contact plus the main body of the shoe itself. More sophisticated, dedicated flash systems may bear three or four contacts, presenting information in the viewfinder and controlling the flash output. Underground, a pc cable/socket is the weakest point in the flash system as the socket is prone to shorting out or becoming clogged with mud, and the matching cable is fragile: hot shoe connections are preferable.

Different settings, normally found on a switch near the pc socket, are used for flash synchronisation: an X setting is essential.

A hot shoe (lower) has at least one central contact. Cold shoes, such as found on the Nikonos, have no flash contact and are used to support but not fire a flashgun

The almost universal pc connector is unsuited to wet, muddy conditions; hot shoe contacts are more reliable

Viewing the scene

Some viewfinders are easy to see through and include a large, bright eyepiece – in particular those on waterproof cameras intended for diving. Unfortunately, the majority of camera viewfinders (particularly on compact cameras) are difficult to use in the dark, where the extremities of the finder blend into the blackness of the cave.

When choosing a camera, place the edge of the picture in deep shadow: is there an adequate difference between the finder and the image? In a darkened room, is it easy to bring the viewfinder directly to your eye, or are you left puzzling whether you are looking through the finder or only

Flash synchronisation

Leaf shutters are found in compact cameras. They open like an iris and snap shut when the exposure is completed. As the shutter is always fully open before a picture is taken, this type of shutter can synchronise with electronic flash at any speed.

Focal plane shutters, found on SLR cameras, consist of two spring-loaded blinds. When the shutter is cocked (the film is wound on) both blinds are tensioned. When the shutter is pressed one blind is released, opening the shutter. After a pre-set delay (dependent on the selected shutter speed) the second blind is released, closing the shutter and covering the film.

This mechanism places an upper limit on flash photography. At 1/60 second (on some cameras, slightly faster) the first blind completes its travel before the second blind is released and there is an instant of time when the complete area of film can be exposed by a flash of light (top left). At faster shutter speeds the second blind is released before the first has completed its travel, effectively exposing the film with a moving slit of light. At 1/125 second the slit covers half the area of film at one time (top right), at 1/250 second a quarter of the film, and so on.

A flash used at high shutter speeds therefore only exposes a portion of the film, the rest being covered by the shutter. Flashbulbs emit light for 1/30 second (or longer, for example FP bulbs) so, even if synchronisation is possible at higher speeds, 1/30 second synchronisation is needed to use all the light. If flashbulb-lit pictures are underexposed, check the shutter speed as well as exposure calculations. Black portions of film indicate too high a speed, that the shutter is sticking during its travel, or that the wrong synchronisation setting was used.

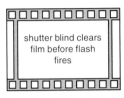

shutter blind clears film before flash fires

1/60 second: complete frame exposed

blind part way through traverse, covering film

flash exposes half the frame

1/125 second: flash pictures partly exposed

Surveying in Ogof Draenen. Because the image which exposes the film is inverted, in most cameras the right-hand portion of the picture is missing when the shutter speed is too high

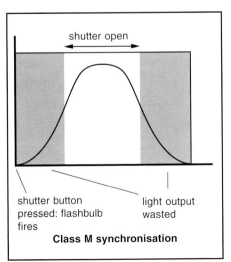

shutter open

shutter button pressed: flashbulb fires

light output wasted

Class M synchronisation

There are three forms of flash synchronisation: X, M and FP. Class FP is used with specialist, slow-burning FP (focal plane) bulbs. Class M is used with 'normal' flashbulbs. In both cases the flash is fired *before* the shutter opens, wasting some of the bulb's output in an attempt to reduce shutter speeds and therefore the risk of blurring.

Class X synchronisation is used with electronic flash, which is fired *after* the shutter is opened. To obtain the maximum light from a bulb, class X is therefore used for all cave photography. Ensure your camera's X synchronisation is operational.

Further information on synchronisation and flash characteristics appears on pages 65 and 85–7.

at the back of the camera? A large, bright viewfinder which permits easy framing can make all the difference to a successful picture.

As well as manual control of aperture and shutter speed, flash synchronisation, a bright viewfinder and a good quality lens, the 'ideal' manual caving camera should also be small, rugged, light and waterproof. It is probably evident that this combination of features will not be easily found – the previously vast range of cameras on the market has been reduced to almost zero. The final choice will be primarily determined by availability as well as personal preferences and cost.

There are three basic designs of 35mm camera available: underwater, compact (sometimes referred to as rangefinder or viewfinder cameras), and single lens reflex (SLR). Each has its advantages and disadvantages.

Underwater cameras

Many cavers assume that an underwater camera is an ideal choice for cave photography. However, while they are often robust, prices are high and the design may not be suited to underground work.

'All weather' cameras from Canon, Fuji, Minolta, Nikon and Vivitar are useful as they are totally sealed against the elements, but are restricted to shallow depths when diving; fully fledged diving models are typified by those from Sea & Sea and Nikon. Many underwater cameras do not possess a B setting (or, if they do, there is no locking mechanism), and most have no manual control of aperture or shutter speed. Fewer still have a fitting to attach a supplementary flash, although there is normally an integral flash. These are usually too weak to be genuinely useful in caves and, for general use, these cameras are not ideal.

The Nikonos range, with interchangeable lenses and sealed flashguns, is one of the best known underwater systems, but the system is heavy, comparatively large, and costly. The Nikonos IV-A has a limited manual shutter speed (1/90 second) and both it and the Nikonos V have a B setting but no lock. In addition, although the Nikonos V has a manual shutter speed of 1/30 second, its advanced electronic circuitry makes using a

In extremely wet or muddy conditions underwater cameras become highly useful, as here in Bridge Cave (E8, B5)

The Nikonos V (left) is an example of a rugged underwater camera, but the obsolete Nikonos III is more suited to cave photography. The Canon A11 is typical of automatic cameras with no manual override

bulb flashgun unwise as it can damage the printed circuit boards when the capacitor discharges. The Nikonos RS is an SLR model, but is far too bulky and expensive for regular underground use.

One exception is the Nikonos III, introduced in 1975 and still available second-hand. An exceptional camera, it is smaller and lighter than the Nikonos V and relies totally on mechanical controls. The earlier Nikonos II

Charterhouse Warren
Farm Swallet (E2, B6)

is also mechanically reliable, but suffers from flash synchronisation problems and irregular frame spacing; if you use a Nikonos II it is better to have film processed and returned uncut than to risk an automated lab cutting into the picture area. There is full manual control of the shutter and aperture on early models, and bulbs and 'normal' (non-dedicated) electronic flash can be fired using an adaptor, though this may be difficult to obtain and is not waterproof.

In general, specialist diving cameras are less suited to cave photography than 'normal' designs, although in extremely wet conditions their restrictions become more acceptable.

Compact cameras

The main advantages of manual compact (viewfinder) cameras lie with their light weight and (usually) small size compared with an SLR. Disadvantages include the small and dim viewfinder many of them bear, and a fixed lens.

There are two basic types of compact camera: an older, manual model with control of all features, and a modern, automatic design. The latter is far from ideal, but, as automatic cameras are so prevalent in the market-place and are probably owned by many cavers, chapter eight covers

The Paxette (left) and the Rollei 35B (centre top) are examples of manual compact cameras which are suitable for cave photography. The Taron (right) is also manual, but far larger and heavier than the others, while the Olympus Mju typifies many modern, fully automatic cameras

techniques for their use. Further discussion of automatic compact cameras is left until that point, although it should be stressed that manual cameras are far more versatile and form the better choice.

While an SLR viewfinder shows exactly the same image that will be recorded on film, a compact camera has a separate viewfinder which, as it is physically separated from the lens, provides a slightly different image. This difference, termed parallax, causes problems in close-up photography, where it interferes with accurate framing and composition; in any case, close focusing is not usually possible. For general photography a compact camera can be highly useful but, if you wish to take close-up pictures, choose another design.

A rangefinder is sometimes fitted in the viewfinder. This forms two images of part of the subject, normally in a small central portion of the viewfinder. When the lens is correctly focused the images coincide. Unfortunately, the system is virtually useless in the dark as the images are hard to see, and a knock may make it inaccurate. It is better to rely on judging distances by eye and setting the lens by hand; most manual rangefinder cameras have a suitable engraved scale.

If the camera's viewfinder is difficult to use, buy or make a sports finder. This example is produced for the Nikonos camera and is fitted to its cold shoe. When the central holes are in line, the view is correctly framed. With practice, sports finders are extremely fast and accurate to use

The most suitable designs for cave photography are no longer manu-factured and, to obtain a manual model, searching the second-hand market is the cave photographer's only recourse. While it is impossible to cover every design, and every cave photographer will have a favourite model, it is worth mentioning the diminutive Rollei 35 range. Beginning with the 35B and 35 LED, all the essential features are present, including a shutter speed of 1/30 second, a B setting, cable release attachment, manual

Manual compact and SLR cameras provide the control required to take backlit silhouettes. This picture, in St Cuthbert's Swallet (B5), was taken on a Rollei 35LED

Many older SLR cameras are manually operated and excellent for cave photography. The Praktica L2 (left) is fitted with an obsolete Pentax lens, making the combination very affordable. The Olympus OM1 has proved rugged and is the first choice of many cave photographers

aperture and focus controls, and a hot shoe. More advanced models are fitted with a higher quality lens, although the lens quality on the cheaper versions is more than acceptable. Against the camera is its delicate nature, yet its small size and light weight have been favoured by many cavers.

It is also worth looking out for 'collector's cameras' such as the Paxette. Often superbly built, older models usually use a pc fitting rather than a hot shoe for flash synchronisation (a few possess both), but otherwise come close to being ideal cameras for cave photography. A leaf shutter is built into the lens, which enables electronic flash synchronisation at any speed, even above 1/60 second. Cheaper and more rugged, though heavier, is the Russian-built Zorki range, which has an inbuilt shutter lock for using B. The Olympus RC and Ricoh SP500 are both well designed; suitable cameras were also made by Konica, Minolta and Yashica. However, when searching out second-hand cameras it is more important to look for useful features than to be dogmatic about locating one of these models.

Single Lens Reflex cameras

A Single Lens Reflex (SLR) camera is the first choice for most cave photographers. It is easy to focus, uses interchangeable lenses, is suitable for close-up photography, and is readily obtainable in manual designs (second-hand, at least). In general, it is more versatile than other formats. Against this can be a high price and a larger size and weight compared with compact models.

Light entering the lens is reflected by a mirror through a prism and into the viewfinder. This aids accurate framing with what is usually a large, bright viewfinder, but a major disadvantage is introduced. When a picture is taken the mirror must flip up to enable light to reach the film, thereby cutting the viewfinder out of the system. This makes little difference in daylight, where the scene can be examined with ease just before and after the picture is taken. In darkness this is not possible, as the viewfinder is blacked out at the crucial moment when the flashes are fired.

This disadvantage should not be under-estimated. Seeing flashes through a viewfinder permits evaluation, fine tuning and repositioning the camera or flashguns for subsequent pictures. Flare caused by flashes inadvertently aimed directly at the lens can be immediately detected. There is a thrill in seeing exactly what

The ideal caving camera

An ideal caving camera possesses as many of the following features as possible:
- Full frame, 35mm format
- Good lens quality
- Small, light, rugged and 'cave proof' with minimum electronics
- Manual aperture control
- Manual focusing in feet or metres (rather than distance symbols)
- Manual shutter speed, including 1/30 second or slower and a B setting
- Hot shoe flash synchronisation
- Tripod bush and cable release attachment
- Bright, easily usable viewfinder
- Low cost

Points to consider:
- Auto-only cameras are extremely limiting
- Medium format is bulkier than 35mm
- Most underwater cameras are unsuitable for general cave photography
- If interchangeable lenses are not required, a manual compact camera is well suited to underground work
- An SLR is best for close-up photography
- A dedicated flash system is useful for close-up photography

Devonshire Cavern (E8, B4)

you are creating which is lost with an SLR; indeed, it is sometimes difficult to even tell if the flashes have fired.

Very basic SLR camera bodies can be coupled with expensive, higher quality lenses; you need little more sophistication in the body than a film transport mechanism and flash synchronisation. As before, the following specific suggestions for suitable cameras are by no means exclusive.

In 1972 Olympus introduced the OM1, a superb, manual camera that combined light weight with a small size. It grew to be many cave photographers' favourite camera and, though no longer made, it is still in widespread use. The OM2, with its dedicated and accurate flash exposures, is also a sturdy workhorse.

Olympus has not proved the exclusive choice of cave photographers. Nikon's Nikkormat series and the Pentax SP500, K1000 and MX cameras are reliable and excellent for underground use, though some are heavier than the OM1. If price is the limiting factor, many cheaper models are available, such as those from Practica or the Zenith range. For example, a Practica L2 body fitted with a second-hand 35mm Pentax lens forms a cheap system as it relies on outdated screw-thread lenses. If in

Lake of the Clouds, Carlsbad Caverns, New Mexico (E6)

doubt about what to choose, look at any of these models and compare others with them: the list of cameras favoured by different cave photographers is almost endless.

PREPARATIONS

A camera is an extremely delicate item which is prone to physical damage during both transport and use. Electronic systems suffer the ravages of high humidity and the effects of water; mechanical linkages fail with the ingress of mud or dirt. Minimising the potential for harm will increase the camera's working life.

Cases

A case made from wetsuit neoprene provides good protection against physical damage. Neoprene is light and waterproof, and can be glued with contact adhesive and sewn for added strength. Use a paper pattern

Ogof Ffynnon Ddu. The photograph takes advantage of the wide spread of light produced by a flashbulb (B5)

Lake of the Clouds, Carlsbad Caverns, New Mexico (B5). The light in the foreground has been reflected from nearby formations

based on a leather camera case, if possible including a flap over the lens as an added safeguard.

Cover any camera controls which are not required, but design the case to maintain muddy-finger access to other parts. The hot shoe on Rollei cameras is located underneath the camera body and the lens can be collapsed into the body, so designing a complete case is difficult. When operated, the lens system inevitably pumps mud and moisture into the mechanism. It is better, for the camera's longevity, to leave the lens barrel permanently out and cover it with a tube of neoprene: even small parts of a camera will benefit from being cased.

A neoprene bag is useful for carrying compact cameras, which are often 'streamlined' with no protruding parts. Fully automatic models can be covered with cling film and totally enclosed in neoprene, with controls operated through the case. If the shutter release button is threaded, add an accessory to make it easier to press through a case or with gloved hands. The additional button is commercially available, or can be made by gluing a toothpaste tube cap onto the screwed end of a cable release.

A container is needed to transport the camera equipment; a discussion covering hard and padded cases appears in chapter three.

Housings

To protect a camera from excessively muddy conditions attach a polythene bag around the lens using an elastic band or tape or, as in this illustration, with a second filter with the glass removed

A commercially available, waterproof camera housing offers perfect protection against mud and water. Unfortunately, housings are expensive, cumbersome and fragile, and controls tend to be incomplete or difficult to use; they are better suited to the ocean than a cave.

A polythene bag is useful in excessively muddy or wet situations, although operating controls can be frustrating. A large bag is easier to use than a small one, with the opening taped to the lens filter. Alternatively, remove the glass from a second filter and grip the edge of the polythene with the ring or a rubber lens hood, which also helps protect the lens against knocks. Fix the bag to the viewfinder with a push-fit eyecup containing plain glass or a prescription lens.

Flash synchronisation

The camera's flash synchronisation may be fixed, with no options available to the photographer, or selectable between X, M and FP. The switch is normally located near the pc socket; a B or T setting is found separately on the lens or shutter control. The X setting is used for cave photography; the M or FP synchronisation can produced exposure errors. So that it cannot be accidentally altered, fix the switch at X using silicone, which can be peeled off when the camera is serviced.

LENSES

Light is focused onto the film by the camera lens which is, arguably, the most important part of the system. Compact cameras have fixed lenses which cannot be changed, while SLR lenses of different focal lengths can be fitted to suit the situation. Most SLR cameras are sold with a 'standard' 50mm lens, while fixed lenses are usually around 40mm focal length.

The focal length of a lens indicates the amount of the scene it will include: a 35mm wide-angle lens 'sees' more than a 50mm, and a 28mm covers a greater area than a 35mm lens would. In a cave, where there is often a restriction on moving the camera away from the subject so as to include more of the scene, a wide-angle lens is therefore of real benefit. Assuming that the subject fills the frame a wide-angle lens will place the camera closer to the subject than a standard lens would; by implication,

The ideal caving lens

- High quality, from a reputable manufacturer
- Focal length of 28mm or 35mm (or a zoom lens encompassing these lengths)
- Maximum aperture of f2.8 or better
- A clearly inscribed distance scale for manual focusing
- Fitted with a protective filter

As well as the manufacturer's name, lenses are marked with their maximum aperture and focal length. This 35mm lens has a maximum aperture of f2.8

Focal length

The focal length of a lens indicates its angle of view: a 'standard' 50mm lens has a narrower angle of view than a 35mm or 28mm lens. The photographs in Ogof Ffynnon Ddu (E8, B7) were taken with the camera and flash at the same point using (left to right) a 50mm, 35mm and 28mm lens.

Wider lenses include more of the scene from the same viewpoint, an advantage if it is impossible to move back from the subject. In the diagram the 50mm lens includes the caver but not the stalactites (S), while the 35mm and 28mm lenses include both. For a constant subject size a wide-angle lens decreases the camera-to-subject distance and this, in turn, allows flashguns to be moved nearer to the subject.

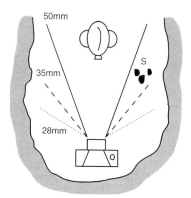

the flashgun is also moved closer and in turn this enables a smaller aperture to be selected: maximum benefits are derived from the available light.

A zoom lens covers a range of focal lengths. When it is not possible to move the camera closer to the subject, which is perhaps down a shaft or a stalactite high above, framing is made easier. However, zoom lenses are usually larger and have a poorer maximum aperture. Although it is easier to frame the subject using a zoom lens, lighting may be problematical: if the camera cannot be moved closer, neither can the flashguns. While a zoom lens appears an attractive option that may be useful on occasion, most cave photographers use a single focal length lens.

As the angle of view of a lens widens it progressively introduces distortion to the image, particularly with close subjects or when the lens is tilted up or down. Many cave photographers find that a 35mm lens is convenient, versatile and offers a good compromise between standard and wider-angle lenses, although other cavers prefer a 28mm; much depends on the specific nature of the cave and the style you develop.

Aperture

A correct exposure only occurs if a predetermined level of light reaches the film. In daylight this is determined by an aperture/shutter speed

combination, but in flash photography only the size of the aperture is important (the duration of the flash replaces the shutter speed control): a large aperture admits a lot of light, while a small aperture admits less. The aperture is controlled by an iris, which in cave photography must be manually controlled to accommodate the light from different flashguns.

The aperture's size is represented by a series of numbers, termed f-stops, engraved on the lens. A small number such as f4 represents a large aperture, while a large number such as f16 represents a small aperture. A lens set to its maximum aperture is termed 'wide open', while moving to a smaller f-stop is called 'stopping down'.

Each time the lens is stopped down by one f-stop, the area of the aperture is halved: a change from f4 to f5.6 admits half the light. Be wary of the numbers at either end of the scale, as these may represent intermediate f-stops such as f1.8. The international sequence of full f-stops is f1, f1.4, f2, f2.8, f4, f5.6, f8, f11, f16, f22 and f32.

A wide maximum aperture would, on the surface, match a fast shutter speed for a correct exposure: the factors are inextricably linked. 'Fast' lenses have a wider than normal maximum aperture and admit more light, a boon in the dark as the viewfinder image is brighter and each flash has more effect. In large chamber shots, where important parts of the image

The aperture and f-stop relationship

The size of the aperture, controlled by an iris (also known as a diaphragm), determines the amount of light which enters the lens. A lot of light can enter a large aperture, less in a small one. Different apertures are used to suit changing light intensity, for example when using flashguns at different distances.

Apertures are measured in f-stops. A small number, for example f2.8, indicates a large aperture. As the number increases, each f-stop in the sequence halves the area of the aperture, and therefore halves the amount of light admitted. Changing from f4 to f5.6 halves the light admitted through the lens and able to reach the film, while moving from f11 to f8 doubles the light reaching the film.

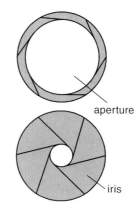

aperture

iris

In the upper diagram the iris is shown almost fully open, perhaps to f4 on a lens with a maximum aperture of f2.8. The lower diagram shows the iris closed to f11

---

are far away and every photon of light is needed, fast lenses are valuable. The disadvantage is that wide apertures produce a shallower depth of field (the amount of the picture in focus in front of and behind the subject), and such lenses are expensive.

For most cave photography an f-stop scale beginning around f1.8 or f2.8 is perfectly adequate, but reject any lens with a maximum aperture worse than f4 (f5.6 and above); some zoom lenses fall into this category.

Filters and lens caps

A filter protects the front element of the lens. It is easier to clean than a lens and, if scratched, can be discarded and cheaply replaced. It is exceedingly poor economy not to fit a filter and be prepared to replace it often, although this may not be possible on a compact camera.

The filter can be clear (UV) or, more commonly, tinted (skylight). To reduce flare, caused by internal reflection of light, a coating is applied. A standard coated filter is sufficient for cave photography as, although a multi-coated filter is more efficient, its coating is more susceptible to scratching due to frequent cleaning.

The filter is traditionally protected with an opaque lens cap, but there are several advantages if this is transparent. In extremely wet or dirty conditions the photographer can compose the picture while the filter remains clean and protected, only removing the lens cap just before pressing the shutter. There are several options, including fitting a second filter. Continually using a threaded filter is frustrating, so purchase a push-fit filter or adapt a plastic lens cap by cutting out the centre and gluing in a filter glass.

Two difficulties can arise. Condensation may gather in the trapped airspace, which lingers while the photograph is taken: leave sufficient time for the lens to reach the same temperature as the cave. Secondly, while concentrating on setting up a shot it is easy to forget to remove the lens cap, resulting in a degraded image and darkened corners to the photograph where the edge of the cap intrudes. Draw a line with a marker pen across the lens cap's glass as a visible reminder.

In the upper photograph the glass has been unclipped from a filter and glued into the centre of a push-fit plastic cap. A line drawn across the filter acts as a reminder to remove it before taking the picture. A transparent lens cap can protect the lens while setting up a shot in extremely muddy or wet conditions, such as in West Kingsdale Master Cave (B4)

Chapter two
FLASH

Sometimes, just sometimes, you hear the crackle of flashguns and see the chamber light up, silhouetted figures against an ink-black background. The image sealed into your memory perfectly matches what you intended. The rest of the squalor recedes: you don't have to wait until you see the results, you know it's there, a transient scene captured forever on film. You've got it!

Ogof Draenen

THERE are many similarities between cave and studio photography. In both cases the photographer creatively controls the quality, power and direction of light. The nature of the flashgun and the flash it produces are crucial as their characteristics will do much to dictate the appearance of the final photograph.

Power

The power of a flashgun is indicated by a guide number: the higher the number, the more light energy the flashgun produces over a given area. To enable different flashguns and flashbulbs to be compared, manufacturers normally quote a guide number based on a 'standard' set of conditions, though it is not uncommon to find inaccurate guide numbers that make a gun appear more powerful than it really is. A guide number can be calculated using imperial (feet) or metric (metres) measurements, the latter being normal with modern guns. When considering older flashguns, or some sold in North America, check whether the guide number has been calculated using feet; numerically, this can make it appear more powerful in comparison with a guide number calculated in metres.

It matters little which system is used, as long as it is consistent. If no guide number is marked on an older flashgun, check the exposure table or dial on the gun itself. Set the film speed to ISO 100 (the flash may be marked with the older term, ASA) and choose a convenient distance, say 10m. Read the aperture off the scale and multiply it by the distance to obtain the guide number. If the result is much below 30, look for something with more power. More information on determining guide numbers appears in chapter four.

At first thought, a flashgun cannot be considered too powerful. At the expense of size and weight, high-power guns which exceed a guide number of 30 are available, but are not necessarily more useful. Depending on the type of photography you are interested in, most situations benefit from a number of guns of reasonable power rather than fewer flashguns of higher power: two weaker guns are often more useful than a single powerful one.

At ISO 100 (numerically, an ISO figure is the same as ASA) a picture can be taken with this flashgun at 4m (13ft) distance using an aperture of f8; the flashgun has a guide number of 32 (determined by multiplying the distance by the aperture, giving 100 using imperial measurements)

Flashguns are not always physically linked to the camera, and might be fired manually by assistants – a technique which only requires basic equipment. Alternatively, using an electronic device termed a slave unit, flashes can be fired remotely yet remain under the control of the photographer, even though there is no physical connection. For on-camera use, check that the flashgun's firing circuit is compatible with the camera's, either via a pc cable or hot shoe; many flashguns will possess both. If no test button exists to fire the flash by hand, the gun can be modified.

ELECTRONIC FLASH

Electronic flash is typified by a short-duration, high-intensity burst of light that is useful in freezing motion. Readily purchased, some design features are unnecessary while others are useful.

The physical shape of the flashgun is important. Bulky, oddly shaped guns are difficult to transport without wasting limited space. Large brackets or handles, flashing lights and illuminated screens are superfluous; avoid these and other unwanted features. Choose the most compact, regular shape possible as this will probably be the most durable and makes waterproofing easier. You will probably require several electronic flashguns to produce a range of lighting effects. To have one gun with a bounce head is useful, but not essential.

Manual-only flashguns with reasonable power are no longer manufactured in a portable form, so the second-hand market again becomes the cave photographer's hunting ground. Some older flashguns, in particular from Metz and Rollei, originally contained integral rechargeable batteries that are probably now useless. Unless you know the history of such guns, they are best avoided. Replacing the battery is probably expensive and troublesome, and when the battery is flat there is no option other than resorting to a mains charger – hardly viable within a cave.

Automatic flash circuits

Modern electronic flashguns may be operated manually or with an automatic 'computer' sensor. In this simplified diagram, switch (S) turns on the charging circuit and the battery (B) charges the capacitor (C) through a resistor (R). The capacitor discharges through the flash tube (F) when the flash contacts (FC) are closed. The flash contacts are part of a low-voltage trigger circuit, protecting the user from the power stored in the capacitor.

Some of the light is reflected from the subject and detected by a photocell sensor (P). When enough light has been received for the aperture to correctly expose the film, a quench tube (Q) triggers a holding switch (H), preventing the production of more light. In older flashguns the unused electricity in the capacitor was wasted; in modern flashguns a thyristor saves the energy and permits faster recycling times.

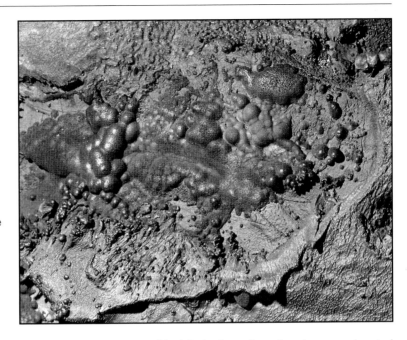

Mud formations, Ogof Draenen (E6). Close-up photographs which fill the frame are ideal subjects for automatic electronic flash lighting

Most flashguns use removable AA size batteries; when they are exhausted it is easy to replace the batteries and continue using the gun.

Automatic control

Modern electronic flashguns are invariably fitted with an automatic 'computer' sensor. This detects light being reflected back from the subject, quenching the flash when the exposure is theoretically perfect. Different f-stop settings are usually present, normally using a small grey filter or smaller aperture over the sensor which affects the light output. However, there are pitfalls in what is otherwise an excellent theory.

The automatic system must, by default, make certain assumptions about the photograph being taken. As manufacturers consider most flash pictures will be taken in the confines of an 'average' room, with well-painted, reflective walls, the exposure is easy to predict and the auto-system is designed for these conditions. A subject close to reflective walls occurs less frequently underground, sometimes resulting in vast errors in exposure with auto-flash.

Consider a caver or formation within a chamber. Light reflected back to the flashgun's sensor will only come from a small portion of the overall scene; the rest of the light disappears into the distance. As the sensor assumes an 'average' wall is present, the flash continues to output light until the sensor determines that the scene has been correctly exposed – yet all this light was reflected from the subject alone, which is overexposed and 'burnt out'. The larger, black area of background adversely affects the exposure when using automatic flashguns.

Flashguns are usually hand-held or left unattended in the cave, as opposed to being attached to the camera, so the sensor's position relative to the flash tube is important. Hold the flashgun in a natural position and

The light tones of the caving gear contrast heavily with the dark lava in Hopkins Chocolate Cave, a lava tube in northern California (E8, B4). The large dark area would fool an auto-flash system so the electronic flash was set to manual

21

note where your fingers lie. The manufacturer assumes that the gun will be fitted to a camera, and some models are difficult to hold without also covering the sensor. If introducing a potential source of user error is easy, bearing in mind that assistants may be holding the flashgun, select a different model.

Dedicated flashguns are more sophisticated. These link to a specific camera; for example a T32 flash uses sensors built into an Olympus OM2N

The limitations of auto-sensors

Automatic flashguns assume that most parts of the scene reflect light evenly. In an 'average' room this is often true; a person near a wall (left) will closely match the manufacturer's criteria and the exposure is accurate.

However, a caver in a chamber (right) represents only part of the scene and a lot of light is lost in the background. The flashgun emits more total light than necessary in order to receive its anticipated, preset amount of reflected light from the subject alone: the caver is therefore overexposed. Uneven or absent reflective surfaces mislead auto-flash sensors.

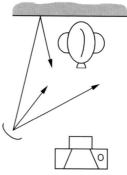
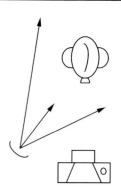
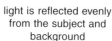

light is reflected evenly from the subject and background

most light is wasted and the subject is overexposed

Flashguns require a minimum of two contacts, one within the groove which fits onto the hot shoe and the other centrally on the foot of the flash (upper gun). Dedicated flashguns have supplementary contacts; the lower gun has two of these plus a catch to ensure it seats properly

camera body. This TTL (Through The Lens) system is highly accurate, as it measures light entering the lens rather than light reflected back to the flashgun. Underground, however, it is prone to the same problems as automatic flashguns. While dedicated flash is highly useful for close-up photography, the high cost of camera/flash combinations and an increased reliance on electronics is enough to dissuade most cave photographers from TTL flash, at least when they are learning their craft.

Automatic flash control is not possible when two or more flashes are fired together, as light from one gun can affect the auto-sensor of another and cause underexposure. While one auto-flash which offers a range of camera apertures can be a boon in some situations, the other guns in the set need only be manually operated. It may prove impossible to buy a manual-only electronic flash but all auto-flashes have a manual override to produce a full power output. In any case an auto-sensor can be covered with opaque tape; if no light enters the sensor it cannot shut down the system. Two or more flashguns with variable power settings may also be useful as their light output can be manually balanced with respect to each other, a valuable though not essential feature for fill-in flash techniques.

Electronic flashgun circuits are powered by charging a capacitor from a battery. The energy in the capacitor is discharged through a xenon tube, producing a flash of light. When automatic flashguns were introduced in the late 1960s, only part of this power was used in light output; when the flash was quenched by the sensor control the rest of the energy in the

Auto-flash

Automatic flash sensors have limitations as they can easily produce an incorrect exposure. However, when the subject fills the frame or the exposure error is predictable and can readily be compensated for, using auto-flash avoids having to calculate flash values and speeds up photography.

These pictures, taken using auto-flash, are from Ogof Dan-y-Lleuad Wen (left: E8, fired from below the camera position) and Little Neath River Cave (bottom right: E8, B5). The remaining two photographs were taken in Going Square in Ogof Draenen (below: E8; bottom left: E8, B5).

capacitor was wasted. In the early 1970s a thyristor was added as a power-saving device, retaining the unused energy in the capacitor. This shortens recycling times and produces more flashes from a set of batteries. In addition, a thyristor-controlled flashgun left switched on does not waste as much energy as a non-thyristor gun. Modern flashguns are normally thyristor controlled, but older ones may not be.

Bounce heads

Many flashguns possess a tiltable 'bounce' head so that a flash fixed in a hot shoe can be aimed to indirectly light the subject by bouncing the flash off a wall or ceiling. In a room this produces a less harsh, diffuse light which softens shadows, but it is of limited use in a cave where the gun is often hand-held and can be aimed wherever required.

Electronic flashguns are made in a huge variety of shapes, sizes and power. The small Kinoluxe on the left is suitable for triggering infra-red slave units, while the others have a guide number of around 30 and can be used as main flashguns. The Sunpak 3000 (top left) and Vivitar 283 (top right) both have bounce heads, the Sunpak being a more convenient shape. The National PE-2850 (right), in common with the Vivitar, has a removable sensor. The centre gun, an Olympus QA310, is reasonably compact for its power

Bounce heads can be cumbersome and take up valuable space, but do have one use. With a slave unit, flashguns can be left unattended and yet still remain under the photographer's control. Trying to find pebbles or mud to prop up an unwieldy gun is both time-consuming and haphazard, whereas a bounce-head gun can be placed in a stable position with the flash reflector swivelled to aim at the subject.

A further refinement is a diffusing filter or lens system fitted over the flash. These additional items focus the flash into a narrower beam (zooming) or spread the light over a wider area (diffusing). In a cave, zooming a flash is unlikely to be used often as it is easier to place the flash closer to the subject; the mechanism adds to the flashgun's bulk and can be more of a hinderance than a help. A diffuser is sometimes useful to match the field of view of a wide-angle lens, although a similar effect can be produced by moving the flash further away. The trade-off is power: when light is spread over a larger area, its intensity decreases.

Final choices

As well as the flashguns which form the mainstay of your set of equipment, one or two weaker flashguns are useful as fill-in flashes to help remove hard shadows, and to fire slave units. Light, compact, low-power flashguns with a guide number around 10 or so are ideal and are readily and cheaply available.

The final features to check, especially when purchasing second-hand flashguns which may have been manufactured before 'modern' designs were developed, are that there is a test button for manual firing and a neon ready light to indicate that the gun is charged. On most flashguns the ready light glows when the capacitor is only 90 per cent charged, producing a correspondingly lower flash output. Check that the light is operational and, to achive maximum output, allow a few seconds after it comes on before firing; the difference between two photographs taken with fully or partially charged guns is noticeable.

Any or all of these features – bounce heads, zoom control, variable power, TTL flash and so on – might be of benefit to a cave photographer. More practically, you need to assess how *often* they will be used, and if this makes additional expense and carrying the added bulk worthwhile.

Suggesting a specific flashgun is not easy, as there are conflicts between reasonable power and a convenient, small shape. The Vivitar 283 is far from an ideal shape, yet it is readily available and many cave photographers have found that it stands up well to the rigours of caving. This model has a removable sensor, which is mounted on the camera and increases the accuracy of the auto-system as it measures light reflected towards the camera rather than the flash. Its linking cable is thicker and substantially better than the normal thin and easily damaged pc cable. The National PE-2850 shares this feature, with a more convenient shape than the Vivitar but retaining the same power. A bounce head, thyristor control and reasonable power with manual adjustment are also found in Sunpak's Autozoom 3000. There are many other suitable, older, guns from companies such as Braun, Metz, Sunpak and National, and this short list is not intended to be exhaustive.

The sensor on a Vivitar 283 can be mounted on the camera's hot shoe. The sensor on auto flashguns, in this case just below the word 'thyristor', is covered by a grey filter which restricts the amount of light detected by the sensor. Different densities of filters are used to match different apertures on the camera; covering the sensor forces the flash to produce its maximum output

---

The ideal electronic flashgun

- High power, with a guide number around 30 (ISO 100, in metres) or 90 (ISO 100, in feet)
- Compact shape
- Low cost
- Test button for open flash, and ready light
- Hot shoe and/or pc cable, as required by the camera
- Thyristor control
- Changeable batteries, preferably AA size
- Even coverage of light over an area at least equivalent to a 35mm lens

Points to consider:

- How many guns you require
- Only one auto flashgun is required in the set; the rest can be manual only
- A bounce head may be useful, but is bulky and is far from essential
- Variable power (with a manual setting) is useful for fill-in flash
- A weaker, and therefore smaller, infra-red gun can fire slaves
- A dedicated TTL flashgun is used with some cameras

PROTECTING ELECTRONIC FLASHGUNS

Cameras and flashguns are expensive items and prone to damage. Work spent on protection before taking them underground can greatly extend their reliability and useful life span. While nothing can be made 100 per cent reliable, and what works on the surface inevitably fails at a crucial moment within the cave, reducing potential problems improves efficiency and produces a better success rate. Designing and protecting specialist equipment is vital. It is not an exaggeration to state that the majority of successful pictures are only accomplished because due care was given to this groundwork.

Never switch on a wet flashgun

In particular, electronic flashguns are probably the most sensitive items in the cave photographer's arsenal. Being dependent on high voltages and usually being poorly sealed against the ingress of water, even highly humid air can cause a flashgun to fail. The principal objective is to prevent water entering the gun, but if this protection fails and the flashgun is soaked, *never* switch it on. The voltages involved are dangerous; when wet, discharging the capacitor could damage both the flashgun and the photographer. Outside the cave, opening the gun and allowing it to dry usually results in a fully functional flash and a fully functional caver – but only if it has not been switched on in the meantime. A basic warning must be given: electronic flashguns and water do not mix; underground, use all flashguns with care.

Physical protection

A flashgun's shape dictates much of what can be done externally to protect it. Hammerhead and bounce-head flashguns are harder to deal with than older, square-shaped designs. If the flash is only used off-camera, and no hot shoe is required, modifying the flashgun is easier.

For physical protection make a neoprene case. To help seal the gun against water cover the flash and its controls with cling film or tape all joins with plastic PVC tape; both techniques are highly effective. A flash–slave combination can be protected inside two layers of zip-lock polythene bags. With some air inside, the flash is sealed well enough to float if dropped by mistake and, with care, can be hand-held with the reflector just underwater for special lighting effects. If a rigid container is needed cut a clear, plastic soft drinks bottle in half, insert the flash and slave and tape the two parts together.

This flashgun has been opened to fit an infra-red filter under the reflector cover. Before the gun is closed and sealed with PVC tape the circuit board will be sprayed with varnish

Internal modifications

The reliability of an electronic flash can be increased with internal adjustments, but high voltages are involved and if you are not comfortable with electronics or you are not sure *exactly* what you are doing, these modifications are best left alone. Flash circuits are delicate and, if you make changes, it is *entirely at your own risk*. Neither the author nor publisher can take responsibility for any problems which may arise, and any manufacturer's guarantee will become invalid. It is up to the individual how many and which, if any, suggestions are acted upon. None are obligatory, but in humid caves most flashguns will operate for a longer period if internal alterations are made.

There are four types of modification that can increase reliability under caving conditions: removal of parts that are prone to damage or shorting out by water, improved sealing of circuit boards, internally sealing joins, and replacing wires or connectors with cables that are more suited to the caving environment. Permanently attaching a slave unit is also an option.

Before beginning, check the flashgun's capacitor is fully discharged. With the gun switched off, 'fire' the gun several times on a manual setting to ensure a total discharge. Even if the ready light is not glowing, a capacitor can hold a charge for several hours and may still be dangerous. Remove the batteries, open the flash and find the large, cylindrical capacitor. Do not accidentally touch the terminals (normally both sited

This flashgun is being modified. The pc cable has been removed and its two wires joined together. The two wires from the hot shoe will be soldered to its replacement, a miniature bnc connector. The hot shoe will then be removed, the hole blanked off and all connections (with the exception of the battery compartment and switch) coated with varnish before sealing internal joins with silicone

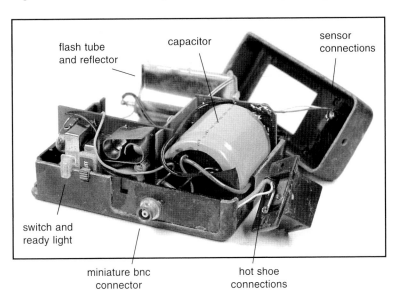

flash tube and reflector

capacitor

sensor connections

switch and ready light

miniature bnc connector

hot shoe connections

on one end of the capacitor): shorting these out can release a huge surge of electricity. Cover the contacts with PVC tape as a safety measure.

Circuit boards are normally sprayed with varnish by the manufacturer, but sometimes areas remain unprotected. A further coat of varnish helps seal the board against water. Latex rubber, used for modelling, is also suitable and can be peeled off later if necessary. Do *not* coat the xenon flash tube, reflector, battery or switch contacts (including those to the hot shoe and pc connector). Any other part of the gun can be coated, including soldered cable connections. In wet conditions the operational life of the gun should be considerably enhanced.

The flashgun will bear either a hot shoe or pc cable, or both. The cable and its connector is probably the single most common cause of failure in electronic flashguns. This part of the trigger circuit is at a lower voltage than the capacitor and flash tube, sometimes only a few volts, and even minuscule amounts of moisture in the connector can short out the gun. Replacing the pc cable with something more substantial is easy and of

Goyden Pot (E8, B5)

enormous benefit. The best option is to use twin core wire or thin co-axial cable. Drill out the hole in the flashgun case until the new cable will pass through and, to prevent it being pulled out, grip it with a nylon cable tie before feeding the cable through the hole from the inside. Finally, solder the two wires to the old contacts and seal the hole with silicone or 'hot glue' from a gun.

An alternative is to remove the pc cable and replace it with a suitable socket. This adds versatility to the system: heavier cables of different lengths and fittings can be attached when required. The socket must be small, reliable and prevent the cable from pulling out. Miniature bnc connectors are a good choice: they have a positive, bayonet action and function well even in damp conditions. The standard size bnc connector may appear more robust, but in practice its greater bulk can be hard to fit into a flashgun's cramped confines; the miniature connector should not cause any difficulties. Fit a protective cover when the socket is not in use.

Flashguns and slave units are likely to become wet and muddy. It is essential that equipment is protected against the worst ravages that the cave can offer

When installing a replacement socket, transfer the two wires from the existing terminals or hot shoe to the bnc connector. If either the pc cable or hot shoe will not be used, remove them. This reduces bulk, streamlines the gun for packing and removes points of potential failure due to damp.

Hot shoe and pc cables are often interconnected, switching the hot shoe out of the circuit when the pc cable is used. This avoids shocks through the shoe's contacts when the flash is fired. Although the connector and hot shoe are at low voltage in modern flashguns, older ones may carry an appreciably higher voltage. The pc cable is sometimes stored in a groove in the flashgun body, with the pc connector pushed onto a metal pin. This completes the circuit and makes the hot shoe operational: if the gun will not fire and the hot shoe is dead, check the pc cable is properly shorted out and that the cable does not have an internal break. Leaving the cable hanging free may disconnect the shoe. In other systems the centre pin of the hot shoe has to be depressed to complete the circuit.

Check your flashgun carefully to ensure the circuit is kept intact when removing parts or installing a new connector. If your gun fails to fire after modifications have been completed, check whether the two wires from the removed component should be wired together to complete a circuit, or vice versa. If in doubt, obtain specialist help.

Seal joins in the plastic case, especially where there are inserts such as the ready light panel, with latex rubber or silicone sealant used for aquarium construction; if the need arises these materials can be peeled off later. A thin smear is sufficient, with a thicker layer where cables exit through the case. As with varnish, do not coat switches or battery contacts.

Silicone releases a small amount of acetic acid while it sets, and may conduct electricity before curing is complete. Home-made equipment is sometimes totally encased or 'potted' with special compound; if silicone is used near electrical components, build up the coating in layers to form a solid block. Do not operate the flashgun until the silicone is fully cured.

Finally, check the flashgun for open-cell, foam rubber. Small pieces are often used to prevent the circuit board or capacitor from moving. Open-cell foam absorbs water, so replace any that is found with non-absorbent, electrically non-conductive material such as neoprene.

Easter Grotto, Ease Gill Caverns (E8, hidden in the foreground; B6)

None of these modifications are essential and unmodified guns are commonly used underground. Again, wet conditions and electronic flashguns were never intended to mix: take adequate care in these situations.

FLASHBULBS

Long superseded, the lowly flashbulb remains invaluable for underground photography. Bulbs are light, small and are generally even more powerful than high-intensity electronic flashguns. A combination of electronic and bulb flash is often an excellent way to light a scene. In particular, flashbulbs emit a long-duration flash which helps portray moving water.

Against these advantages, bulbs are not reusable and therefore can be expensive. Literally hundreds of types have been marketed since their introduction in 1929, including flashcubes, flashbars and a range of fittings. A surprising number still appear for sale through specialist outlets, and older camera shops often have a supply of unsold bulbs gathering dust in an attic. Faced with an unusual make or fitting of flashbulb, if the price is not prohibitive cave photographers are best advised to make the purchase and construct a flashgun later.

Flashbulbs are not essential for cave photography, and most lighting angles given in this manual can equally be used with electronic flash. Indeed, some top cave photographers use electronic flash exclusively and produce stunning pictures. However, flashbulbs possess a subtle quality of light that is unmatched by other sources. A cascading series of electronic flashes can simulate the unique nature of a flashbulb, but current designs do not offer the power, compact nature or quality of flashbulbs. Using a flashbulb, rather than electronic flash, for specific effects or when large chambers must be lit is worth serious consideration. Cave photographers should make their own experiments and determine whether bulbs will be part of their evolving photographic technique, to be used alongside electronic flash, or if electronic flash alone will be used.

Bulb design

All flashbulbs share the same basic design: aluminium foil is contained in a low-pressure oxygen atmosphere, enclosed by a thin glass capsule. Two wires are attached to terminals, joined by a filament. When a current passes through the terminals this heats up the filament, which melts, breaking the circuit. The heat ignites an explosive paste and fires the flash. Only a very few early flashbulbs contained magnesium, despite popular belief.

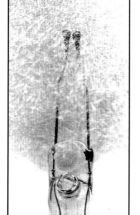

Flashbulb terminals are connected by a thin filament that heats up and fires an explosive paste which, in turn, ignites the surrounding aluminium wire

During manufacture, bulbs were coated with clear lacquer to help prevent injury if a bulb exploded when fired. Clear (or 'white') bulbs were used with black and white film, where the colour quality of the emitted light was not important. However, clear bulbs produced a reddish cast on colour film (see p.171) so, to alter their emission to a daylight balance, they were coated with blue lacquer and given a 'B' designation: AG3 bulbs are clear, while AG3B bulbs are blue.

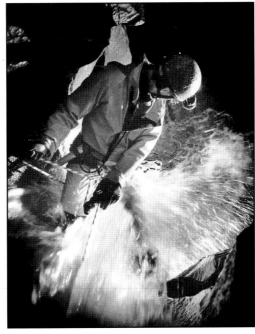

Lighting effects

These photographs, of a waterfall in Lower Long Churn Cave, were taken using a single flash from position 4, behind and lower than the caver. The electronic flash (top left) is extremely directional, casting hard shadows and, with its short duration, freezing the flowing water. The flashbulb (top right), with its larger reflector, provides a softer light and, as a bulb burns for around 1/30 second, moving water blurs and appears more fluid.

The third photograph (left) was taken with an experimental cascade flash assembly. Six electronic flashguns were fired a few fractions of a second apart. Each weak flash has produced an image which, cumulatively, gives a correct exposure. The inset photograph shows the results in detail, where individual droplets of water can be seen. The overall effect simulates a flashbulb's long duration flash; angling the flashguns with respect to each other can produce a wider lighting angle but with an overall loss in intensity in any given area.

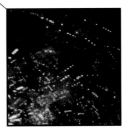

The Score in Ogof Draenen (B1, B6). Flashguns must be simple to operate as they will often be manually fired by other cavers

Clear bulbs can be used with colour film by using a blue conversion filter on the lens, adding a layer of blue lacquer to the bulb, or by dying the existing coating of lacquer. Obviously, blue bulbs can be used for black and white photography, where the colour balance of the light does not matter, but only at the expense of a loss in intensity. The blue coating itself absorbs as much as half the flash's output, and thereby reduces the guide number.

After manufacture the wires in the base of older bulbs, in particular PF types, soon tarnished or rusted so they were protected with lacquer. This had the side-effect of preventing a good electrical contact, but when the bulb was inserted into a gun the lacquer was scraped off and contact was made. However, after many years in storage the coating hardened and the surface is now not easily broken, a common cause of misfires. Additionally, some bulbs may be faulty. To detect cracks in the glass, flashbulbs contain a small blue spot of cobalt chloride as a safety warning. If moisture enters the bulb the blue spot turns pink, indicating that it is prone to misfire.

Check all bulbs before a caving trip. Ensure the warning spot is blue and discard it if a pink colour is present. Scrape the contacts with a knife to bare the metal, and check the circuit with a testmeter (also known as a multimeter, available cheaply from electrical shops). Set the meter to read resistance (ohms) and touch the two probes together; the scale will show a high reading. The bulb should give a similar reading, indicating that a circuit is present and that it is functional. To test a lot of bulbs, attach the contacts from a bulb-holder directly to a meter. Failure to carry out these checks is the biggest cause of bulb misfires in cave photography.

For safety reasons transport bulbs in their original packing. Carrying unprotected bulbs may be dangerous; a crushed bulb ignited due to friction could fire the rest, with disastrous consequences.

Bulb types

For cave photography some bulb types may be more convenient than others. It is a myth to believe that powerful bulbs are always more useful than weaker ones; situations exist where either may hold benefits or disadvantages. Bulbs were made in a range of sizes, fittings and power; carrying the greater bulk of a high-intensity PF60 to use in a small passage is pointless, when a cheaper and smaller AG3 would suffice. On the other hand, powerful bulbs may be more convenient during an expedition where large voids are anticipated. If you have a choice, match the bulb to the situation. For most situations the smaller PF1 and AG3 bulbs (and others of similar size and output) are ideal.

Flashbulb classification and power

This list of commoner bulbs compares manufacturers' ratings and guide numbers (based on using the full light output of the bulb at 1/30 second or slower, with ISO 100 film).

Edison screw

PF/M capless

AG capless

bayonet

centre cap

A collection of Edison screw-fit bulbs

Bulb type	Guide number (ft)	(m)	Fitting
Philips Magicube/flashcube	100	30	cube
Flashbar/flipflash	100	30	bar
Wotan XM1B	120	36	PF capless
Atlas AG3B	125	38	AG capless
Philips AG1	130	40	AG capless
Philips PF1B	130	40	PF capless
Mazda MF1	140	42	PF capless
Sylvania AG3B	145	44	AG capless
General Electric SM	160	48	bayonet
Hanimex AG3B	170	52	AG capless
Westinghouse 5B	200	61	bayonet
Philips PF5B	210	64	PF capless
Wotan M3	220	67	PF capless
Philips PF5	260	79	PF capless
Sylvania Floodflash 33B	340	103	Edison screw
Bowens M22B	360	110	Edison screw
Flashbar (5 bulb) fired together	360	110	bar
Philips PF60	440	134	Edison screw
Sylvania Floodflash 33	470	142	Edison screw
Philips PF100	560	170	Edison screw

Notes:

- Guide numbers are dependent on the reflector as well as the light output of the bulb, and other tables may include different values. A modified guide number related to caving conditions and specific equipment must be determined. A fan-fold, dimpled reflector may give more than one f-stop less light than a smooth, polished reflector. In caves the guide number is generally lower than the manufacturer's figure. These figures are based on the use of an 'average' reflector.
- For comparative purposes, the popular Vivitar 283 electronic flash has a guide number of 28 (metres), although it illuminates a smaller area than a bulb.
- Cubes, flipflash and flashbars are similar to, but weaker than, AG3B bulbs. Due to their characteristics, they may be more reliable at firing slave units than 'normal' bulbs. Hi-power cubes have roughly twice the light output of flashcubes.
- Flashbulbs codes were many and varied. A 'B' suffix indicates a blue bulb. 'SM' stands for Speed Midget, while 'PF' indicates a Photoflux (a designation of the Philips corporation, though PF also represents Photo Flash and Push Fit) and 'SF' means Super Flash. X, M and FP give the synchronisation characteristics of the bulb, based on total duration and the time to peak emission. Philips' bulbs are numbered /97 (blue) or /98 (yellow, for tungsten lighting).
- The Sylvania Floodflash is a slow-burning bulb which emits light for 2.5s, allowing the flash to be moved during exposure to soften shadows or light a wider area.
- A blue coating can reduce a bulb's output by one f-stop or more.
- Use B or X synchronisation at 1/30s or slower with all classes of bulb.

The bulbs in the top row (left to right) are: an early foil-filled Sashalite, a PF60 and an M22B plus a flipflash and flashbar. The bottom row contains a variety of fittings: PF capless, two bayonet bulbs, a centre cap and a Flashcube and Magicube. At the bottom right are two makes of PF1B and a diminutive AG3B flashbulb

This synchronisation switch can select X and FP. In addition, class M synchronisation is often found on older cameras

There are three types of flash synchronisation: X, M and FP. Class X is intended for electronic flash, where the shutter is fully opened and then the short-duration flash is fired before the shutter closes again. A flashbulb's characteristics are somewhat different. A flashbulb builds up its light output slowly, which means that in the early and late stages ambient light may have more effect on exposure than the bulb does. To reduce this problem, class M synchronisation fires the flashbulb just before the shutter is opened, enabling a shorter shutter speed but sacrificing a portion of the bulb's output: only the central peak of intensity reaches the film. Class FP stands for 'focal plane', for synchronising with a special type of slow-burning flashbulb at fast, focal plane shutter speeds.

For cave photography all light is at a premium; it is pointless to waste any by misunderstanding the synchronisation settings on a camera. Select M or FP settings and, at best, only a portion of the light output from the bulb will reach the film. At worse, no light at all is received. *Always* use the X synchronisation for both bulbs and electronic flash to receive maximum light. All classifications of bulb can be used for cave photography, though FP bulbs are uncommon.

BULB FLASHGUNS

Commercially produced bulb flashguns are collectors' items. Even when found in old, dusty shops they are unlikely to be pressed directly into service as most require an obscure, redundant 15½V or 22½V battery.

The best flashguns for cave photography accept a single type of bulb fitting. Some guns, with a so-called 'universal' fitting, fire both PF and AG bulbs. These have a higher chance of misfires because the design uses a number of sprung metal plates which sometimes fail to make good contact.

Even though working bulb guns are scarce, redundant guns can be easily modified to alter their battery requirements or, with a little ingenuity, new ones made from first principles.

Circuit design

A bulb gun possesses only five components: a bulb-holder, capacitor, battery, resistor and a switch. At its most basic the capacitor and resistor are dispensable, while more sophisticated designs may include a test light to check that the capacitor is charging and the flashbulb is correctly seated. Others can accept more than one bulb for multiple or sequential firing.

The classic bulb–capacitor (bc) circuit uses a battery to charge a capacitor through a resistor, which limits the current so that the bulb does not fire. The capacitor can only charge when a bulb is in place, avoiding unnecessary current drain. The flash is fired by shorting out two contacts,

Flashbulb circuits

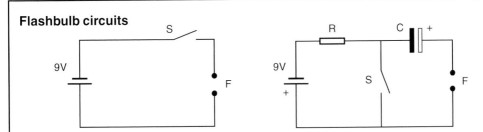

A simple series flashbulb circuit (left) uses a rechargeable (nicad) battery. A 9V PP3 battery is a convenient size, though lower voltages may be sufficient to fire some bulbs. When the switch (S) is closed (manually, or via a slave unit), the battery is short-circuited through the flashbulb at (F).

A capacitor and resistor are added to make a capacitor circuit (right). The resistor (R) restricts the current flowing through the flashbulb (F) so that it does not prematurely fire while the capacitor (C) is charging. Closing the switch (S) discharges the capacitor through the flashbulb. As a high discharge from the battery is not required, a standard (non-rechargeable) 9V battery can be used.

Component values vary greatly: a 1200 ohm, 0.25W resistor and 470mF, 16V capacitor are suitable. Raising the resistor value increases the capacitor recharge time; the bulb will fire immediately it is inserted if the value is too low. A larger capacitor increases the time to full charge, but its greater surge of power may fire multiple bulbs more efficiently. There is a trade-off between component values, and an acceptable average is required which protects the bulb yet permits the capacitor to charge within a few seconds.

Notes:
- The capacitor can only be charged if a bulb is inserted. The battery, therefore, is only drained when a bulb is in place.
- The battery is protected against short circuits by the capacitor.
- Commercial circuits operate at 18V or more. High voltages charge the capacitor faster, but a 9V battery produces an acceptable compromise between recharge time and battery availability.
- As battery voltage drops during use it may become too low to charge the capacitor.
- An LED, placed between the battery and resistor, indicates that a current is flowing when a bulb is inserted. It dims while the capacitor is charged; when it goes out the gun can be fired. If the LED does not light, the flashbulb is poorly seated, faulty, or the battery is flat. Use fresh batteries.
- Test a bulb gun with a 6V, 0.1A torch bulb, which will glow momentarily when the gun is fired; this avoids wasting flashbulbs.

A vast array of flashguns can still be purchased second-hand. The left-hand gun accepts bayonet fittings or, with the adaptor beside it, push-fit PF1 bulbs. To the right of centre is a combination gun which fires a flashcube or single AG3 bulbs

which might be an 'open flash' test switch or button, through a hot shoe or pc cable, or by connection to a slave unit. When the contacts are closed the capacitor's stored energy is released, igniting the flashbulb.

The capacitor is included to ensure a sudden, high discharge of electricity is produced, but this can also be supplied by a rechargeable, nicad battery. The capacitor and resistor dispensed with, a simpler series circuit only requires a battery, bulb and switch. When the contacts are closed the battery is momentarily short-circuited through the bulb, which fires. Short-circuiting the battery will, technically, damage it. However, the short circuit only lasts for an instant as the wire filament in the bulb then melts, breaking the circuit; keeping a switch depressed will have no effect on the battery.

However, even though the surge of electricity is momentary and unlikely to damage the battery, a home-made series circuit gun fired by a camera or slave unit might damage the synchronisation contacts or components. Firing this type of bulb gun with a modern camera is **not** recommended. Careful experimentation with a slave unit is required to ensure that its components are not damaged.

A series circuit is simple to make. There is no delay while a capacitor recharges; as fast as a bulb can be replaced, it can be fired. Nominally rated at 9V (though actually producing about 8.4V), a nicad PP3 battery should fire any bulb. If only a single bulb type is used, experiment with a smaller battery as it may prove equally suitable and have less bulk. Using a nicad battery is essential as, when shorted out, it has a greater discharge rate than disposable batteries due to its low internal resistance; a non-rechargeable 9V battery will not consistently fire some types of PF1 flashbulbs.

This photograph, in Llygad Llwchwr, was lit with a single flashbulb (B6) held just beneath the surface of the water

Capacitor circuits can be powered by an alkaline battery (which, being disposable, can be replaced during expeditions where recharging nicad batteries is unpractical), firing is consistent, and it is easy to add a test light. An LED in the circuit confirms that the flashbulb is in good condition and making contact, reducing the possibility of misfires, as well as indicating the quality of the battery.

Flashguns are normally used by an assistant, and the design should bear this in mind. It is easy to rig a switch or press-to-make button to fire the flash, and any gun must be self-contained and foolproof in operation.

The battery and capacitor do not have to be located within the flashgun. An Oldham or Wheat lamp battery, normally used to run a helmet light, can be readily adapted for firing a flashgun; if there are charging contacts on the rear of the headpiece and the flash is fitted with a standard charging plate, a direct connection can be made. This system has been successfully used to photograph large chambers with PF60 flashbulbs. The weight and bulk of flashgun batteries are removed, and the gun itself is reduced to a reflector and switch (the capacitor is not essential, but can still be present). Ingenuity counts for a lot in cave photography!

Flashbulbs are individually sealed, waterproof units. By separating the battery from the bulb with a length of wire, the bulb can be placed underwater while the battery is kept dry. Flashbulbs will fire underwater (it does not matter if the contacts are wet): water lit from above appears black, but a submerged bulb introduces greens, blues and warm, peaty colours (see p.167). To help the bulb sink, add an attachment point for a karabiner or maillon, or include a small lead weight in the design.

Bulb-holders

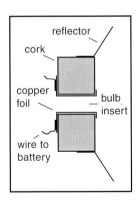

If no commercial gun is available a simple and positive method of holding a bulb must be found. Temporary solutions include attaching crocodile clips to the wires on the bulb; using rubber-coated clips, such as found on testmeters, avoids the possibility of the clips touching each other. Clothes pegs fitted with copper terminals work well with the spade-like base of AG3 bulbs.

Push-fit capless bulb-holders used with instrument lights in some cars are also a perfect fit for AG3 bulbs; a visit to your car dealer or electrical component shop may be fruitful. Edison screw-fit reflectors and bulb-holders are still manufactured for household light fixtures. If all else fails, drill a hole through a wine cork which will grip the bulb when it is inserted. Insert two strips of thin copper foil and solder the wires directly on. A little thought will reveal many other options.

A piece of cork, drilled to grip a flashbulb and lined with copper foil (shown here in section), can readily be fitted with an aluminium reflector

Firing bulbs together

Multiple bulbs can be fired by both series and capacitor circuits. It is usual to wire the bulbs one after the other, in series, and all bulbs should be the same type. Although, logically, when the first bulb fires it breaks the circuit and the other bulbs should fail, in practice there is a short delay while the filament heats up and all the bulbs fire. Bulbs can also be wired in parallel with roughly the same length of cable to each bulb; if there is a significant difference there may be a delay or failure in firing. A parallel arrangement avoids the need for shorting plugs to bridge unused contacts: if one bulb is faulty it does not prevent others from firing.

A capacitor circuit is recommended for multi-bulb set-ups as, with a massive discharge from the capacitor, it is more predictable. High-energy circuits with larger capacitors, using modified circuitry from an electronic

Firing multiple bulbs

Two bulbs wired in series (top) can be fired by a 9V battery; component values for a series multi-bulb capacitor circuit are given in the table. Bulbs in parallel (bottom) do not require a voltage increase, but to maintain consistent firing make each bulb's circuit approximately the same length. Do not mix bulb types within one circuit.

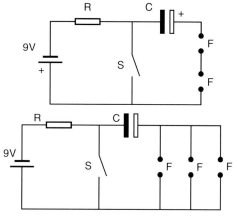

Number of bulbs	Capacitor mF, V	Battery V	Resistor ohm, W
1–2	470, 16	9	1200, 0.25
1–4	100, 25	18	2500, 0.25
1–6	100, 35	27	2700, 0.5

NB: Values are approximate. Experimentation may be required with specific bulbs. Slave units can be damaged by high currents; add a resistor to one of the wires leading to a slave to protect it, although this may decrease the number of bulbs which can be fired. Do not fire multiple bulbs with a camera shutter, as the currents involved may damage camera semiconductors or synchro-nisation contacts.

flashgun, can overcome a greater resistance due to dirty bulb contacts. Old photographic manuals indicate that, for bulbs in a series circuit, around 4.5V (with a minimum of 3V) should be allowed for each bulb. Whether from a battery or capacitor, more power equates to less chance of misfires.

The heat from one bulb can be used to fire others which are attached to it using transparent tape. This simple method of producing a single, high-intensity flash is a useful technique to fall back upon during expeditions or when greater light output is unexpectedly required. The flash duration will be extended and a shutter speed slower than 1/30 second is required.

Cubes and multiple bulbs

In the 1970s the flashcube, Magicube, flashbar and flipflash were intro-duced, each containing more than one bulb. Cube flashes were normally used with Instamatic cameras, where a mechanism rotated the cube by one face as the film was wound on; the flashguns were often built into the camera, although some were made separately.

A flashcube carries four flashes, essentially AG3B bulbs set in their own reflectors with two wires extending through the base of the cube. To fire more than one bulb at a time, twist the wires together in parallel. If the reflector assembly is removed the four bare bulbs can be fired together in front of a large reflector, effectively producing a guide number of about 80 – as with other guide numbers, this is dependent on the reflector as well as the light source, and in practice some light output is lost with respect to calculated values.

A Magicube is similar to a flashcube, but is not fired with a battery. A hole below each bulb contains a sprung wire which, when pushed upwards, is released to strike a firing paste and ignite the bulb. Any object pushed

Flashcubes are easy to take apart if the individual (effectively AG3) bulbs are required

Flashbulb adaptors.
Left to right: a flashcube adaptor for four AG3 bulbs, Edison screw to bayonet-fit, and a PF1 bulb to bayonet-loading gun (a bulb is fitted to the foreground adaptor).
On the right are two components for making flash fittings: a computer connector which fits flashbars and a bulbholder from a car dashboard which accepts AG flashbulbs

into the hole (thick wire, a bent paperclip, a trimmed and shaped guitar plectrum) will operate it.

To reduce the problems of red-eye (the reflection of light from eyes, producing a red colour in the photograph), an extender which increased the distance between the flash and lens was sometimes used. This can be adapted for hand-held operation but, as with flashcubes, the easiest way of firing a Magicube is to use an old Instamatic camera, which is treated as no more than a flashgun. To cut down on bulk, remount the flashgun components in a suitable plastic box. The potential uses for Magicubes in cave photography are therefore endless, as this percussion system can be manually fired in extreme conditions, in air or underwater, with minimal equipment and few failures.

Flashbar and flipflash designs contain one or two banks of bulbs, usually in sets of 4, 5 or 6. The inbuilt circuit ensures that each fires in succession. Again, this opens up areas of experimentation for cave photographers, as it is possible to rewire flashbars to fire more than one bulb at once if a greater light output is desired. For expedition use, in particular, this may offer a means of reducing bulk compared with transporting large M22B bulbs, and retains versatility. A computer component (such as an RS232 connector) may form a suitable bulb-holder which can be pre-wired to fire multiple bulbs.

While flashbars are similar in construction to a rack of 'normal' bulbs, a flipflash has only two contacts. The firing sequence is controlled internally by a series of thin metal strips which melt as each flash is fired by a high-voltage piezo-electric spark, altering the circuit. There is no

Multiple bulbs

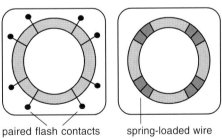

common contact

Flashbar

paired flash contacts

Flashcube

spring-loaded wire

Magicube

Flashbars with five bulbs have six contacts – one for each bulb plus a one common to all (some flashbars have six bulbs and seven contacts). Bulbs are fired using the common contact and one other. By soldering contacts together more than one bulb can be fired; a 'jump' wire may be needed to bridge the common contact.

The diagrams of cubes, viewed from underneath, show the difference between a flashcube and a Magicube. Flashcubes have four pairs of wire contacts, each pair firing one bulb. A Magicube has no electrical contacts, the bulbs firing when a spring-loaded wire is pushed upwards and released to strike an explosive primer.

filament in the bulb, so it is not possible to test the circuit with a meter and flipflashes cannot readily be fired by a 'normal' flashgun. The simplest method is to use a design based on an original camera mechanism.

Reflectors

Repackaged electronic flashguns. The left-hand gun has been remounted in a plastic box with a clear cover over the flash tube; a press-to-make switch on the top fires the gun, or it can be connected to a slave using the miniature bnc connector.

A bulb flash reflector has been added to the right-hand gun. The flash tube has been remounted inside a film cassette container. Both guns give a wide spread of light, at the expense of the manufacturer's original guide number

The useful output of any flashgun, bulb or electronic, is dependent not only upon the raw power of light emitted, but also on its reflector. A bare bulb or flash tube emits light in all directions, in 360 degrees. Under normal circumstances this means that the majority of light is wasted as much of it illuminates areas not being photographed, so a reflector is used to concentrate the flash in one direction.

Electronic flashgun manufacturers assume that the flash will be used on or close to the camera and it must cover the field of view of a 'standard' 50mm lens. In fact, the reflector is usually shaped to cover a 35mm lens but not that of a 28mm lens. A bulb gun reflector is shallower, casting the light over a wider area – typically producing up to 180 degrees of light. This is useful in cave photography to illuminate passage shapes, in situations where the narrower beam of an electronic flashgun would not suffice. In an attempt to simulate flashbulbs, some electronic flashgun manufacturers produce a 'bare bulb' flash head, without a reflector. A similar effect can be created by removing a flash tube from an electronic gun and remounting it in a flashbulb reflector – an effective and cheap bare bulb flashgun. U-shaped tubes will usually fit inside a transparent film container, which affords a measure of protection.

A diffuser screen will also spread light over a wider area. Diffusers are pieces of moulded plastic or glass which clip onto the flashgun. As a greater area is covered by the flash a wider-angle lens can be used but, as with a bare bulb flash head, the light in any one area is at a lower intensity and requires a wider aperture on the camera; diffusers cannot enable an electronic flash to match the light output and spread of a flashbulb, but are sometimes useful to produce a softer light in close-up photography.

Some flashguns have a lens system which acts to 'zoom' the flash into a narrower beam; the converse is now true and the intensity is higher, being more suited to a telephoto lens. A zoom lens on a flashgun is unlikely to be used often, and is probably not worth the added bulk unless a particular picture demands it.

Using a home-made reflector means that almost anything which weighs little and is shiny can be pressed into service: an aluminium pie dish, old car headlight, carbide lamp, torch or flashlight, half an aluminium drink can, or even aluminium cooking foil. Thin materials can be bent and shaped as required, or hinged and folded flat for transport; pie dishes have helped to make a number of photographs in this manual.

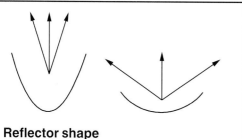

Reflector shape

A parabolic reflector (left) gives a more intense beam than a wide, shallow flashbulb reflector.

Electronic flash	Bulb flash
Reflector nearly parabolic	Reflector shallow
Small reflector	Large reflector
Narrow beam	Wide beam
High-contrast: 'harsh'	Low-contrast: 'soft'

The wide spread of light provided by the bulb flashgun's reflector has helped highlight the caver in Gilwern Passage, Ogof Draenen (B5). A narrow beam of light from an electronic flash would have picked out the figure, but would not have lit the roof and floor so effectively

The reflector must be kept clean. Dirt on a reflector absorbs light, and as much as two f-stops (equivalent to using a film with a quarter of the ISO rating) can be lost due to a dull surface. Dimpled reflectors produce a more diffuse light over a larger area, again at the expense of intensity.

If the reflector is poorly designed, particularly in electronic flashguns, light will not be spread evenly and the centre of the photograph may receive more illumination than the edges. In theory, a reflector should produce constant illumination across the whole of a flat surface, but even with commercial flashguns there is often a 'hot spot' in the centre with the corners receiving as much as one f-stop less light. A one f-stop difference is considered an acceptable standard by some manufacturers, but check that this is not exceeded. At night, take a photograph of a wall with the flash on camera and inspect the resulting picture for variations in illumination. Large differences should be addressed by using a modified reflector. This test can be coupled with checking the quoted guide number.

WATERPROOFING

Bulb flashguns will benefit from the same protective measures as for electronic guns. When home-made devices are involved, protection can be built into the system.

Magicubes can be fired underwater with no protection to any part of the mechanism, as they require no battery. Flashbulbs are also waterproof, leaving only the battery and electronic components to deal with. For a temporary, though surprisingly workable solution, a coating of candle wax melted over the circuitry is excellent for excluding water. Alternatively, the gun can be totally sealed with resin, silicone or (preferably) electrical potting compound, and the gun replaced when the battery is dead. The components cost little and the system is effective.

Small containers made for the diving and mountaineering market, such as canisters used to keep matches, films or keys dry, can be adapted for home-made guns. Electrical circuits are sometimes mounted in plastic boxes with rubber seals, available cheaply from hobby shops. Plastic plumbing components are ideal for larger containers, with a 'stop end' to seal the end of a pipe. Even film cassette pots can be pressed into service. Some pairs of film containers, from different manufacturers, will tightly push-fit together to make an ideal housing for slave units or bulb guns, with a PVC tape seal over the join.

Youd's Level (B6)

Switches always present a problem when waterproofing electrical items. Magnetic reed switches will operate through a plastic box, but can cause misfires if a flashgun is jolted (use two at right angles, both operated by the magnet, to reduce this risk). A mercury switch will fire a flash when it is tilted. The most reliable solution is to use an internal switch, turning the gun on for the duration of the trip.

There have been several documented instances of low cost, underwater cameras literally exploding under caving conditions. The cause seems to be a build-up of hydrogen gas within the sealed, plastic body, which ignites when the integral flash is discharged; every recorded instance of explosion has occurred as the shutter was pressed. There are two possible explanations for a build-up of hydrogen: batteries releasing hydrogen when under load, and

Waterproofing is essential to maintain equipment in working order, as in the Ogof Ffynnon Ddu streamway (E8, B5)

electrolysis of water trapped within the camera producing an explosive mixture of hydrogen and oxygen. Any dry-cell battery has the potential for releasing gas, hence the vent plugs built into most sealed battery packs.

Some diving torches contain a 'hydrogen absorber', a platinum catalyst on aluminium oxide. This absorbs hydrogen and oxygen and converts these elements into water which is absorbed, in turn, by the pellet or a sachet of silica gel. The pellet is sold under the name of Hy-Stor, and is available in platinum concentrations of 0.5 per cent and 1 per cent; according to the documentation the weaker (and cheaper) option appears sufficient to deal with problems of this nature using 1 pellet per AA cell or two pellets per C-cell.

The basic problem of hydrogen production applies to all electronic equipment where a total seal around a battery has been made, trapping any gas produced and allowing pressure to build up. It is particularly applicable to home-made flashguns. For safety reasons, as well as including an absorbent in any sealed container there are several pieces of practical advice which are worth remembering:

- Ensure all electrical equipment is completely dry before sealing and that it is switched off when not in use
- Before storing a sealed camera or electronic flash, turn the power off and fire the flash several times (even after there is no more light produced, especially if there is a thyristor control) to completely discharge its capacitor. Remove the batteries. This eliminates the risk of long-term hydrogen production if humid air has been trapped

- Never fire the first frame of a sealed camera or flashgun near your face. Even an hour is enough to allow hydrogen to build up: waste the first picture by pressing the shutter at arm's length

Although the risks are slight, you should be aware of them and take appropriate safety measures if building or using totally sealed electrical equipment.

TESTING AND FINAL ADJUSTMENTS

All flashguns must be tested carefully before each caving trip, preferably with more than one flash in quick succession to determine the minimum time that must be allowed between flashes for the capacitor to recharge.

When flashbulbs are involved this can become expensive, so a test bulb is required. Make a holder for a 6V, 0.1A torch bulb which will fit the bulb gun or be attached using rubber-coated crocodile clips. When the flash is fired the capacitor discharges through the test bulb, which glows briefly and indicates a good circuit. In a series circuit the test bulb stays lit and should therefore be matched to the battery's voltage; a higher voltage test bulb, or one in series with a resistor, offers greater safety against damaging an attached slave unit.

If there is no test button on a commercially made gun, there may be a metal stud near the cable clip which is used to short out the pc connector and complete the circuit. A temporary (though crude) solution is to insert the end of a ballpoint pen or nail. It is better to remove the cable, replacing it with a bnc connector. This allows a range of firing mechanisms to be attached, such as a slave unit or a press-to-make button which can be used remotely at the end of a cable. If you insist on taking the easy course, tape a bent paperclip to the pc cable to ensure a means of shorting out the connector is always to hand.

Finally, after testing any flashgun, bulb or electronic, commercial or home-made, it is useful to attach a table indicating its guide number, aperture and the distance most commonly used underground with a particular film speed, bulb and reflector. The actual values will depend on your system and experiments. With a clearly marked guide number the chance of error is reduced and time is saved while taking the photograph.

Sell Gill Holes

Chapter three
ACCESSORIES

The camera box seemed heavier than usual. Deep in the cave it was opened to take the first photo, to find cameras, flashguns and a sodden towel. The box was half full of water stained with dye leached from the infra-red filters. It fluoresced in our helmet lights. The box had flooded in the lakes near the entrance; we had carried a couple of litres of water for three hours. Everything was written off. It doesn't matter how many times gear is checked or how much care you take: sometimes nothing, absolutely nothing, goes right.

Dan yr Ogof

Most manufacturers of photographic equipment never intended their equipment to be taken into the extreme conditions found underground and, indeed, might be surprised at how many of their products survive. However, as with bulb flashguns, many diverse items must be adapted for cave use or be home-made. Some are essential tools, while others are highly desirable because they speed up the photographic process. Whatever final selection of equipment is made, some or all of the following items will be required.

TRIPODS

The traditional method of taking a picture is by mounting a camera on a tripod, locking the shutter open on B and firing flashes where and when required. To save time and resources more than one camera can be used with a single set of flashes, and tripods are invaluable near entrances where ambient light is involved. Although heavier and larger than a slave unit, a tripod is cheaper and enables a photographer to work with limited resources.

Design features

A ball-and-socket head (right) is smaller and more versatile than a pan-and-tilt head

Choosing a caving tripod has always required a compromise between size, weight and stability. A large, heavy tripod is sturdier than a small, light one and is better able to withstand the rigors of the cave environment. It is easier to use, but harder to transport. Small tripods which fit into a tackle bag or camera box are lighter and more straightforward to carry, but infuriating or impossible to employ. They can be better than nothing, but not by much; if a tripod shakes when water flows past a leg, it is useless. Heavier cameras demand sturdier tripods; ensure your choice can support your camera.

Most tripods are supplied with a three-way pan-and-tilt head. This is useful for cine and video work, but is far from ideal for cave photography.

Levelling the head is difficult; if this is not perfect, when the camera is turned it will tilt. A ball-and-socket head is considerably easier and faster to control and permits all movements with a single locking lever.

Extendible tripod legs are locked using spring-loaded pins, twist rings and clamps. Different systems allow legs to be locked at any height or only at preset intervals. Spring-loaded pins are unsuitable because leg extensions are restricted and the pins soon clog with mud and rust. Some twist ring locks are hard to turn with cold hands and may slip on wet or muddy tripod legs. Locking clamps are preferred.

Some tripod designs use a central column linked to each leg with a bar, which adds stability but forces each leg to open by the same amount. Confined spaces may require an uneven splay of legs; tripods with independent legs which can be individually locked at any height are the most useful.

Before making a purchase, mount a camera on the tripod and simulate using it, especially with the camera positioned close to the floor. Choose an alternative if the tripod is too short to see through the viewfinder when the camera is aimed upwards; there will not always be a convenient boulder to add height in the cave. Check that the head is interchangeable – some are not – and that the camera can swing vertically for upright photographs. Some heads do not easily allow all orientations.

When they are wet and muddy some locks will not grip efficiently. Clamps, as in the two centre tripod legs, are preferable to rings and spring-loaded pins

As a final check, place a glass of water on the head and lightly tap one of the legs. When a camera's shutter is fired there will inevitably be some vibration; similarly, a tripod in a streamway vibrates due to the moving water. The vibration transferred to the camera is indicated by ripples in the glass of water. Obviously, use the tripod which has the least movement for the shortest time.

Ultimately, your choice of tripod depends on the techniques you use – plus your determination to carry it.

Tripod modifications

Tripod modifications should only be made to increase stability or versatility. The centre column or a central leg support (which limits the splay of legs) can be removed, allowing a greater range of leg positions but potentially making it less stable. Change a pan-and-tilt head for a small ball-and-socket head.

The ideal tripod

- Sturdy and rigid
- Collapses to a transportable size, but is high enough to allow easy viewing when erected
- Lockable legs at any height
- Clamps which are not susceptible to mud
- Legs can be swung independently of each other, at any angle
- Fitted with a ball-and-socket head

Points to consider:
- Large tripods are difficult to transport in small passages
- A pan-and-tilt head incorporating a spirit level is suitable for video and/or cine work
- A ball-and-socket head mounted on a camera box is a lightweight alternative
- Stability can be increased using a weighted bag

A ball-and-socket head mounted on the camera box

Heavy tripods are steadier than light ones, so adding weight produces a firmer camera base. A small nylon bag filled with sand, rocks or spare equipment such as karabiners or flashguns, suspended by a loop of string from the central column or tripod head, makes the tripod more stable. If necessary, fix a hook on the centre column to act as a suspension point.

A rigid container used to transport the photographic equipment, such as an ex-army steel ammunition box, can be drilled and fitted with a tripod bush made from a ¼in Whitworth bolt. A small ball-and-socket head carried in the box and attached when required forms an adequate if not perfect tripod replacement. Place the bolt near the edge of the box so that the camera can swing over the side for upright shots, seat it in silicone to maintain waterproofing and cover the end with a cap to prevent damage during transport.

CABLE RELEASES

A cable release attaches to the shutter release and helps avoid camera shake while the camera is mounted on a tripod. In cave photography it is used to lock open the shutter on B.

Despite the simplicity of its design, being little more than a flexible, sleeved cable, there are certain types of release to avoid. When it is pressed

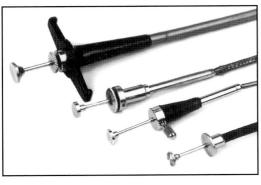

a pin extends from the release and trips the shutter. The pin must be long enough to reach the shutter mechanism, a point easily overlooked. Some pins will not operate a Rollei 35 camera, for example; check your camera for compatibility before buying a cable release.

To lock the shutter on B the cable release is clamped down, usually by small knurled screw or a spring-loaded collar. A screw is difficult to operate with cold hands and inevitably breaks off with continued use – a spring-loaded grip is better. The cable itself runs in a tube made of

A plastic-coated cable release (top) is more durable than metal-braided or cloth-covered cables

braided metal, cloth, or plastic. The latter is preferable as the others degrade when wet, sometimes becoming slack so that the sleeve stretches and the pin can no longer fire the shutter.

In total darkness it is easy to fumble with a cable release and close the shutter too early, wasting a frame. Check that the release is easy to operate and lock in the dark.

SLAVE UNITS

A reliable slave unit is a boon. Tripods are made redundant, the flash is synchronised with the camera shutter, helpers have less to operate and, most important of all, the photograph can be taken quickly and efficiently. A good slave system allows more adventurous pictures to be taken.

A slave unit can be connected to a flashgun either by its pc cable or hot shoe. It detects a pulse of visible or infra-red light from a flashgun and acts as a switch, firing the second flash. If the first flashgun is fired by the camera, the slaved flash fires in synchronisation without the need for a physical connection such as an extension cable. Avoid trailing cables at all costs: in the cave environment they inevitably fail. Slaves are the only reliable way of synchronising with off-camera flashguns.

Basic slave operation

There are two basic designs of slave unit. The first, available cheaply through photographic stores, is intended for home use and is set to trigger if a pre-set threshold intensity of light is reached. The manufacturer assumes that some light will already be present, and the slave will fire if *additional* light is detected. If the unit is made more sensitive it becomes unstable and prone to misfiring or not firing at all, as ambient light alone may pass the threshold level of illumination. Usually small and encapsulated in clear plastic, other than over short distances of two to three metres, these slaves are virtually useless in caves. It is pointless generating light merely to reach a threshold illumination.

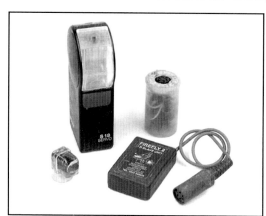

Slave units may be incorporated into a flashgun or attached via the pc cable or hot shoe. The encapsulated unit (left) is powered by the flashgun's batteries, but is relatively insensitive. The slaves on the right are caver designed and extremely sensitive, one being incorporated into a film container

A better design measures the speed of change of light. If the light intensity changes rapidly, as it will when a flash is fired, this is detected and the slave triggers a second flash. The sensitivity is pre-set so that minute changes in illumination – as long as they are rapid – are sufficient. These slaves are invariably battery powered, unlike 'threshold' designs which rely on the flashgun battery; this difference can be used to identify the type of slave.

Slave units are made with either visible light or infra-red sensors. Infra-red slaves can be fired by either an infra-red or visible flash; 'ordinary' flashguns emit close to 50 per cent of their power in otherwise wasted infra-red light and this is detected by the slave's sensor. A dedicated infra-red flashgun is more versatile, however, as daylight-sensitive film does not react to infra-red light. Cave photographers can therefore attain full synchronisation when taking silhouettes and sidelit photographs, without a visible flash from the camera position.

Some electronic flashguns contain an integral slave unit but, underground, these designs have serious shortcomings. Normally, these slaves are relatively insensitive and in a fixed position, often facing in the same direction as the flash. As a cave photographer you will control where to aim the flashes; to be restricted by the slave's sensitivity and position is an unnecessary burden. Aiming the slave towards the trigger flash, without regard for the slave flashgun position, effectively increases its sensitivity. Nevertheless, some simple electronic flashguns with an integral slave, such as the Cobra 150S or the Wotan SC18, are useful for fill-in flash over relatively short distances.

A camera-mounted electronic flashgun provides the short-duration pulse of light which triggers the slave. Flashbulbs, with their slower flash, are

McFail's Cave, New York (E2, B5). Slave units are ideal for synchronising flashes where movement is restricted and photography must be completed quickly

unsuitable as triggers. Increasing the slave's sensitivity enables it to be triggered by a flashbulb, but an over-sensitive slave will also react to cavers' helmet lights and become a source of annoyance and wasted film. A slave unit is normally triggered by an electronic flash, but it should fire both electronic and bulb guns.

Thankfully, some slaves are caver-designed and can react to flashes at distances of up to 1km while remaining insensitive to helmet lights at close quarters. Such sensitivity – firing a flash at such a distance – is vast overkill, but it ensures flashes are consistently triggered at shorter ranges, even when there is no direct line of sight to the sensor. The ability to place a slave flash around a corner or in a shadow area, and trust it to fire, is invaluable. Testing and comparing slaves is easiest at night, away from street lamps: to be useful a slave might be expected to trigger at a line-of-sight distance of 100m or more.

Commercial slaves

Commercially, the choice of suitable ready-built slaves is limited. An American company, Wein, produces a range of extremely sensitive units, some of which can be triggered separately using a transmitter. This enables a photographer to gauge the effects of individual flashes, a potentially useful facility but far from essential. The Wein Ultra Slave is reliable underground, though expensive.

An infra-red slave unit combined with a capacitor flashbulb gun. The sensor is the protruding block on the left

The Firefly 2 from Firefly Electronics, built for caving use, is based on a design by David Gibson and is sensitive and reliable with a low current drain. The slave is connected to the flashgun's hot shoe (preferable to using a pc socket) via a cable, allowing the flash and slave to be aimed in different directions.

Slave unit design

Most caver-designed slaves are made with a trailing wire for the flash attachment. As well as allowing the slave to be precisely aimed, a side-effect of separating the units is a reduction in electrical interference between them.

Trailing leads must end in a flashgun connector, or the two must be permanently wired together. The latter option cuts out a weak point in the system, as any connection is prone to failure in humid conditions. However, carrying a range of separate flashguns and slaves means that when one component fails it can be replaced: there is greater versatility.

The flash–slave link in commercial units is commonly a pc connector, one of the worst possible options for cave photography. Change it for a flying lead of between 15cm and 30cm, ending with a hot shoe or a specially installed flashgun fixture such as a miniature bnc connector. A bnc connector provides a positive attachment point, but the flashgun has to be modified. When sharing flashguns between team members, or to allow a new flashgun to quickly be put into service, make a bnc connector (or other specialist fitting) to hot shoe adaptor to ensure compatibility.

When a flashgun is fired a current flows between the terminals of the hot shoe or pc connector. This triggers the main circuit and energises the xenon tube, which releases a flash of light. The trigger voltage also flows through anything connected to the flashgun, such as a camera or slave. The voltage is normally low in modern flashguns, sometimes less than 10V, while older guns might operate at 200V or more. The current

Slave unit design

- A hot shoe is preferable to a pc connector
- A 15cm to 30cm lead is better than a fixed slave position
- Small circuits can be housed in containers such as transparent film pots
- Infra-red sensors are less prone to misfiring than visible light sensors
- Slaves for underwater use should be fitted with visible light sensors
- Suggestions for waterproofing electronic flashguns apply equally to slave units
- A bridge rectifier of over 200V avoids polarity problems between slave and flash
- Use a simple, unambiguous switch

Ogof Ffynnon Ddu (E8, B5)

Ogof Rhaeadr Ddu (E8, B5)

Ogof Ffynnon Ddu (B6)

supplied by these flashguns could damage the semiconductors in automatic cameras; if in doubt, check with a meter.

The centre pin of a hot shoe or pc connector is the positive terminal in modern flashguns, but older designs are sometimes reversed. Slave unit components must withstand the surge of power from the flash, and match the polarity of its terminals. Damage can be avoided by using a bridge rectifier in the slave unit. This allows any polarity of flashgun to be attached and, if the rectifier is rated at over 200V, the slave should survive the trigger voltage from any electronic flashgun.

Most slaves require an on–off switch (others, such as David Gibson's, have such a low current drain that no switch is needed – the time taken for the voltage to drop to an unusable level due to continuous use exceeds the battery's shelf-life). The switch must be simple and obvious; there should be no confusion whether it is on or off. A reed switch, operated with a magnet, is sometimes used to avoid making a hole in the case and maintain waterproofing.

A multi-terminal plug, such as DIN plug normally used with audio equipment, also forms a practical connector. Mount a DIN socket in the slave, and short out two of the five pins in the plug to make a switch. Another two pins form the flashgun connection. It is also possible to recharge a nicad battery through the socket, without opening the slave. Phono-plugs and jack plugs are other options. Check the slave's operation with care; many will fire the flash when connections are made or broken.

Any short-duration pulse of infra-red light will fire a good slave unit. Although an ordinary electronic flash contains an infra-red component, a specially prepared flashgun trigger is more versatile. This is normally a small electronic gun with an infra-red filter either taped over the front or fitted inside the transparent cover.

Infra-red gelatine filters are available from Kodak, but are expensive. A cheap and completely successful alternative is to use a piece of black, unexposed but processed, transparency film. To cover a large area use a roll of 120 film, which yields enough infra-red filter material to keep most cave photographers supplied for years. Gelatine ('gel') filters, both home-made and Kodak, will succumb to water so a handy, cheap supply is useful for replacement and repair.

A slave and flash can be held in the best position with Velcro, for example to attach the slave to a caving oversuit. A slave can be attached to a wrist or battery pack with elastic, or hung round an assistant's neck with string, leaving the hands free for more natural poses.

A DIN plug can be used as a slave–flash connector; with a trailing lead, extension cables and adaptors to other fittings can be added. Whatever system you use, make all connections the same

The ideal slave unit

- Compact, light and waterproof
- High sensitivity to short-duration infra-red pulses
- Insensitive to ambient light
- Links to flashgun hot shoe or special connector via a cable
- Low current drain
- Will fire both electronic and bulb flashguns

Testing slaves

Slave unit reliability varies a great deal, partly due to the wide range of electronic flashguns which they are attached to. If misfiring occurs it may be the slave–flash combination causing the problem, rather than a

An infra-red slave circuit

This circuit, designed by David Gibson, is extremely reliable, sensitive and stable and can be housed inside a transparent 35mm film container. The two N-size alkaline cells need replacing approximately every three years (their shelf-life); the slave can be run continuously and the batteries will fire some 10,000 flashes.

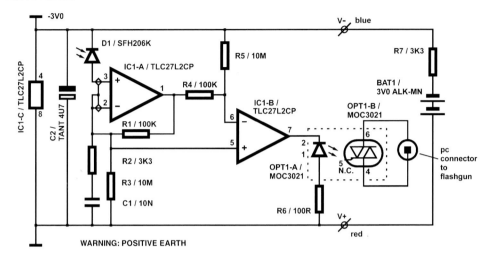

WARNING: POSITIVE EARTH

Component values should not be altered and, in particular, a higher voltage or different op-amp must not be used. Altering the value of C1 changes the sensitivity and enables the slave to be fired by a flashbulb. However, increasing sensitivity to bulbs increases misfires due to it detecting helmet lights.

The lower diagram shows two possible modifications to the circuit. On the left the flashgun connection is made via a DIN socket (shown from the soldered side) instead of a pc connector (the flashgun's connector must also be replaced with a DIN plug, or an adaptor is required). Pins 4 and 5 connect to the flashgun when the flashgun's plug is inserted into the slave's socket. The DIN plug also breaks the power to the slave across pins 1 and 2. These pins are shorted out in the socket, forming an on–off switch (the specific pins are not important, as long as all connections are consistent).

DIN plugs are available with a 180 degree or 240 degree spread of pins; the wider spread slightly diminishes the risk of shorting out when wet. If a switch is not required, and only the two slave–flash wires are needed, a miniature bnc connector is a better choice; both chassis-mounted and in-line connectors are available. Replacing a flashgun hot shoe with a bnc connector increases reliability.

The right-hand diagram shows a pc connector plus a capacitor and resistor. The components increase the slave's stability in flashgun–slave combinations which repeatedly misfire; some Vivitar guns are affected in this way.

If flashbulbs are fired using a series circuit, the battery short-circuits through the slave and can cause damage. To protect the slave when part of a series circuit, insert a 10 ohm resistor in one of the leads to the flashgun.

A pamphlet on the slave's operation and a set of components for DIY manufacture are available. Contact David Gibson, Cave Radio & Electronics Group, c/o BCM BCRA, London WC1N 3XX, UK. An enhanced circuit is available which can trigger a single gun several times or a number of automatic flashguns can be fired in sequence, without affecting each other's sensors (see p.31).

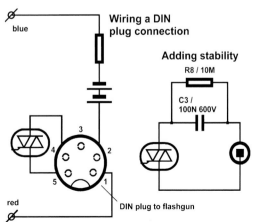

Wiring a DIN plug connection

Adding stability

DIN plug to flashgun

Ogof Draenen

Upstream Passage (left: E8, E5 from above, B4; below left: B7; below: B6) and Going Square (above: E2, E5). A 17mm lens was used to exaggerate the size of the crystals, which were 6cm from the camera

Although slaves have revolutionised cave photography, traditional techniques using a tripod (carried here in an ex-army bazooka tube) are still valuable (E8, B4)

specific fault with either. For example, the charging circuit of an electronic flashgun produces an alternating magnetic field around the flash which interferes with some slave units if they are placed too close together; Vivitar flashguns seem especially prone to this.

If problems arise, try separating the slave and flashgun by a few centimetres. If this fails, wrap the slave's circuit in thin, insulated copper foil wired to the common (normally negative) terminal of the battery to ground the signal. The sensitive part of the circuit is probably near the sensor; shortening the wires leading to the sensor may reduce the problem.

Vivitar guns, though often used in cave photography, have an unusual trigger circuit which permanently locks some slaves into an 'on' state after the first flash; subsequently, the flashgun will fire as soon as it has recharged. Breaking the flash–slave connection resets the slave. Experiment with a small resistor and/or capacitor in the connecting link between slave and flash to avoid misfires.

FILM

There is a wide choice of film available for slides or prints, and in colour or black and white. Prints are easier to show to friends, while slides are preferred for publication in colour. Printing your own dramatic, atmospheric photographs gives you a degree of control which is hard to obtain with a lab.

If you are serious about learning the craft of cave photography, even if your eventual aim is to produce prints, begin with slide film. It is less forgiving of mistakes and, as the projected slide is the original material used in the camera, faults can be seen and analysed with greater ease.

Colour prints rely on both the photographer's and the laboratory's skills. During printing, faults can be corrected or introduced, interfering with the assessment. If required, prints can be produced directly from slides.

Film characteristics

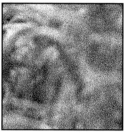

Grain affects the degree of fine detail which a picture can contain. These enlargements are from ISO 50 (upper) and 400 films

Film characteristics include colour balance, contrast, latitude (the ability to retain detail in over- or underexposed areas and cope with exposure errors), sensitivity and the amount of grain (clumps of chemical particles in the film's emulsion).

Finding a film with a pleasing colour balance is subjective: what one person likes, another will dislike. Some films record warm colours well, but turn bluish if underexposed. Others may be too vibrant in red areas, yet browns and greens are neutral and accurately represented. These factors are more evident in slide film, where there is no intermediate production of a print (see p.170).

Beware of budget-priced films which produce high-contrast, unnatural colours. As caves are intrinsically high-contrast subjects, this compounds the problem, as does the use of high-contrast black and white film. For projection, slide film has saturated, high-contrast colours compared with print film, as prints are viewed by reflected light.

Areas of over- and underexposure inevitably occur in cave photographs, in particular where a caver fires a flash within the picture. The film's exposure latitude, or tolerance to error, is generally worse in slides and better in negatives. Acceptable (though not ideal) prints from negative films can be produced after exposure errors of as much as two f-stops (the equivalent of two aperture settings, for example the exposure variation between f8 and f4) in parts of a photograph. This can be enough latitude to salvage an important, unrepeatable shot.

However, this description of latitude is somewhat simplistic. What is perceived as an acceptable exposure depends on the exact effect the photographer wishes to produce in the finished photograph. Take, for example, a dark figure against a black background, backlit so that only the outline appears as rimlit white. The picture contains no mid-tones or colour; errors of two f-stops will probably produce an acceptable image, even on slide film. The converse is true of an evenly illuminated, frontlit scene full of detail and colour and which includes both highlights and shadows: an error in exposure is less acceptable. This is why silhouettes are easier to take than photographs with a full tonal range. Nevertheless, for any given scene some films have a greater latitude than others. In general, high ISO films have good latitude, with fast black and white films giving the best latitude of all.

Film characteristics

Qualities of contrast, grain, latitude and sensitivity apply to all films. Colour films are also characterised by colour balance and saturation. Some attributes are in opposition and advantages must be balanced against disadvantages.

ISO 50	ISO 400
Lower sensitivity	Greater sensitivity
Higher contrast	Lower contrast
Less grain	More grain
Lower latitude	Greater latitude
Better colour saturation	Poorer colour saturation

Slide film	Negative film
Lower latitude	Greater latitude
Higher contrast	Lower contrast

NB: Latitude is dependent not only on film type, but also on the tonal range of the scene

pure black

highlight

mid-tone

Bridge Cave (E8, B5). Correctly exposed frontlit photographs normally contain a full range of tones from dense black, through mid-tones to pure white

A film's sensitivity – its 'speed' – is measured on a scale determined by the International Standards Organization (ISO; this unit of measurement incorporates the German DIN and American ASA systems, remaining the same number as the ASA). An ISO 100 film is half as sensitive as an ISO 200 film, which is in turn 'slower' and less sensitive than ISO 400. Each time an ISO speed halves or doubles, the film is rated at half or double the sensitivity; 'faster' (high-numbered) films are therefore more sensitive in dim light and require less light for a correct exposure.

It is tempting to choose a fast film for cave photography on the basis that less light is required, a logical deduction considering that fast film usually has greater latitude. However, as in most photographic decisions, there are trade-offs involved. As a film's sensitivity increases, so does its grain. Taken to extremes, the picture quality becomes unacceptable and, often, what should be pure, rich blacks record as dull grey or brown. A compromise is necessary: sensitivity against quality. Slower films yield better definition, but sometimes require inordinate amounts of light to expose them. Faster films require less light, but contrast and grain increase with a corresponding loss in saturation which produces weaker colours.

Film choice

For general slide work use films in the ISO 100 to ISO 200 range. Faster films can help when photographing large chambers, where problems in producing enough light may outweigh the need for ultimate picture quality. Equally, slower films of ISO 50 yield stunning results both in close-up and when the flash-to-subject distance is low. Avoid films colour balanced for artificial light; the blue component of an electronic flash matches daylight-balanced films rather than red-rich tungsten light.

For close-up subjects, such as these formations in Harrie Wood Cave at Yarrangobilly in Australia (E4), use a slow (low ISO) film to retain maximum detail

If you already have a favourite film, stay with it. For specific suggestions, Fuji's Velvia (ISO 50) and Sensia 100 slide films are excellent, as are Kodak's Ektachrome 100 Elite and Kodachrome 200. Once you gain experience, you should also consider the flash quality: electronic flash, for example, may produce a bluish tinge in the photograph. Often attributed to the colour characteristics of the flash, this is linked more to its short duration but can balance the warm colours of some films.

A colour shift and change in sensitivity caused by extremely short or long exposures is termed reciprocity failure. A film which has an inherent bluish tinge may become unacceptable for flash photography if it is accentuated by electronic flash. Some photographers find this situation occurs with Ektachrome film, while others consider that flashbulbs introduce an unacceptable reddish tint with Fuji film. The decision, once you understand the factors involved, rests with you.

Most slide film is developed using an E6 process. Results can be quickly seen and assessed before another roll is exposed. Kodachrome is an exception. In Europe, unlike the USA, Kodachrome is only available as process-paid film and has to be returned to Kodak for processing, which can take longer than E6 film sent to an independent lab.

While slide film is by far the best to learn with, the day may come when colour prints are required and the knowledge you have gleaned from your mistakes is applied to negative film. Most colour negative films from well-known manufacturers are suitable; again, ISO 100 or ISO 200 is a good choice.

If your results are disappointing, consider how the print is produced. The negative is developed, then either a machine or an operator decides how the final print should look. The machine assumes that all negatives correspond

---

Film choice

Films used for cave photography should possess as many of the following features as possible. These are interactive: fine grain, for example, implies a low ISO. Films should have:

- Saturated colours
- Low contrast and fine grain
- Good latitude to exposure errors
- ISO 50 to ISO 200 (ISO 400 for b&w)

Points to consider:
- Match the film speed and type to the subject (for example, ISO 50 for close-up work)
- Select slides or prints, black and white or colour
- Transparencies (slides) show mistakes clearly and are best for learning
- Chromogenic films offer a wide latitude
- Balance the flash to the film type: some combinations produce unacceptable casts

Ogof Ffynnon Ddu (E2, B4)

Easter Grotto, Ease Gill Caverns (E8, B4). Shot on FP4, this ISO 125 film has a good tonal range and fine grain.

A film's ISO can be raised (uprated, or 'pushed') or lowered (downrated, or 'pulled') by altering its development. Uprating increases sensitivity but also raises contrast and grain size; use a fast film rather than pushing a slow one.

Uprating colour film produces warmer results, while downrating can add a bluish tinge to highlights

to an 'average' density with an 'average' mixture of colour. Without a reference point for your 'unusual' subject, the machine is easily fooled. Distinguish between a poor print with degraded colours and one that is as good as can be expected from a poorly exposed negative. If blacks appear as very grainy, brown colours, the film is probably underexposed; do not blame the lab!

There are two tips. At the start of a film, take a properly exposed, evenly lit picture of a person, preferably outdoors using daylight (if you can, include a sign with your name and address in case the roll is lost). The operator (and, to a lesser extent, the machine) can use the picture to determine the best printing parameters for the rest of the roll. If you can talk to the machine operator, which is often possible in local labs, ask for a good black to be printed, even at the expense of detail. Any lab of worth will be prepared to listen, although you should expect to pay extra for individual hand printing.

There are no undue problems in extending the range of black and white films beyond ISO 200 to include ISO 400. Ilford's FP4-Plus (ISO 125), Pan-F (ISO 50) and HP5-Plus (ISO 400) as well as Kodak's T-Max 100 and Tri-X (ISO 400) are all suitable.

Chromogenic films, specifically XP2 from Ilford, also produce black and white photographs. The sensitive layer of film contains silver salts, just like 'normal' black and white film, but during processing these are replaced with dyes and can be printed alongside colour print film. They

are very forgiving of exposure errors; effectively, chromogenic films can be rated anywhere between ISO 125 and ISO 1600 (technically, they do not have an ISO but what is termed an exposure index – EI – which is numerically the same as an ISO). With this wide latitude range, detail is retained in areas of over- and underexposure: a major advantage. The disadvantage is that, for the ultimate in quality, prints from chromogenic films do not match those produced from conventional, correctly exposed and processed negatives.

BATTERIES

Electronic flashguns require a great deal of power. Avoid cheap carbon-zinc batteries as they will only produce a few flashes. Alkaline batteries are highly reliable and commonly available: they are a far better alternative. Rechargeable nickel-cadmium (nicad) batteries and a charger are more expensive, but soon repay their outlay.

Even so, do not expect nicad batteries to last forever. The number of recharge cycles stated by the manufacturer is not always reliable, and older batteries may not hold their charge. Cold batteries yield fewer flashes so always carry spares; a set of alkaline batteries to replace exhausted nicads is a useful addition to the pack.

TRANSPORT

Protective containers are essential for transporting photographic equipment within the cave. The requirements are basic: the container must be light, waterproof, large enough to contain the equipment, and rugged enough to withstand the cave environment. By implication, this means the container will be rigid, although a padded photographic bag may prove ideal for easy, dry caves.

Ammunition boxes, screw-top drums and specialist cases are all used to transport cameras underground

Containers

Rigid containers include the ubiquitous steel ex-army ammunition box, plastic screw-top drums and boxes, and commercially available photographic cases. Each has its advantages and disadvantages.

The three smallest sizes of ammunition box are suitable for cave photography. Cheap and waterproof, these boxes are heavy and unwieldy. Although ammunition boxes can withstand submersion to a depth of several metres, even when maintained with a smear of silicone grease or Vaseline the simple rubber seal can leak.

Plastic containers are light and convenient. Wide-necked, screw-top drums, sold through caving outlets or chemical suppliers (where they are used to protect laboratory bottles), are waterproof and available in a range of sizes. A large opening helps when inserting gear, but

Giant's Hole (B3, lit from below)

A drybag inside a tackle sack provides good, additional protection for cameras carried in drums and cases

the round design prevents neat packing. The seals are reasonable, but not totally reliable and should be supplemented with a seal around the outside. A wide band of car tyre inner tube stretched around the lid is suitable.

A drybag (such as made by Ortlieb) fits neatly inside a tackle sack and is useful in large caves, where there is space to carry the tackle sack on your back. For lightweight expeditions a drybag can protect locally purchased plastic boxes. While not ideal, food containers with snap-shut lids are readily available and the seal can be improved with PVC adhesive tape or a section of inner tube. Zip-lock bags are also highly useful.

A specially constructed case, such as made by Pelican, probably provides the best protection. The case is plastic, with an O-ring seal making it waterproof to a depth of 10m. Rigid photographic cases may require modifications to fit a shoulder strap.

The size of container is dictated by the equipment which must be carried. The Pelican range includes the 1200 and 1400 cases. The 1200 easily carries an SLR camera with a couple of flashes, while the 1400 takes two

This set of equipment is small and versatile, being based on a Rollei 35 LED, bulb and electronic flashguns, two slaves and a trigger flash. It will pack easily into a small drum or Pelican 1200 case, leaving plenty of room for bulbs, batteries and film

SLRs and three large flashguns, both with room for spare film and batteries. The 1300 case comfortably carries a medium format camera such as a Bronica ETRS without removing additonal items such as a speed grip.

Equipment is inevitably packed in two layers in a screw-top drum or ammunition box, a distinct disadvantage as repacking in muddy conditions is more difficult. Specialist cases are shaped to place the equipment in a single layer, and do not themselves require protection.

Internal protection

Containers must be padded to absorb shocks. Pelican and other cases are supplied with pre-cut open-cell foam, which should be removed. Open-cell foam acts like a sponge so that, even if no water enters the box while it is open, humid air soon makes it damp.

Neoprene does not absorb moisture and can be used as a lining. A cheaper option is 'bubble wrap' packing material glued to the lid and sides. By using the bubbles next to the box, any water which enters is trapped in the spaces and does not reach the cameras as easily. Camping mat, made from closed-cell foam, is the best choice. Cut the mat with scissors and glue it with contact adhesive to form a drop-in container with compartments for each item of equipment, aiding repacking.

PACKING

Closed-cell camping mat has been used to make dividers in this Pelican 1400 case, separating the pair of cameras, three flashguns and a range of accessories

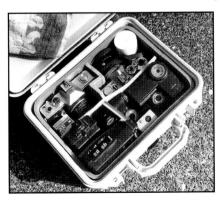

If camera containers are inaccessible, packed at the bottom of a tackle sack, the time taken to get equipment ready means that few photographs are taken; ensure that your camera is readily available. Additionally, consider the way that your techniques are evolving. If you frequently use a backlight, pack a separate, small container for equipment used away from the camera. The caver who normally fires this flash can set up the flashgun independently, immeasurably speeding things up.

Check that fresh or fully recharged batteries are fitted in the flashguns. Test all flashguns with a camera or slave unit; check flashbulbs with a meter. Inevitably, flashguns fail from time to time and carrying a spare is useful; give it the same checks. Load film in the camera and operate the wind-on; if the film is correctly inserted in an SLR camera the rewind knob will turn as the film is advanced.

Pack spare batteries for flashguns and camera, with a system to store used batteries separately from fresh ones. Place 'dead' flashbulbs in a separate bag inside the tackle sack rather than in the camera box, and ensure no bulbs are left behind to litter the cave. Do not forget extra rolls of film, a lens cloth and other miscellaneous items: each should have its place.

Do not pack equipment too tightly; it never repacks in the same way, causing frustration. Equally, do not leave empty spaces for cameras to move about. A few small pieces of camping mat placed between objects help to prevent movement. If equipment is packed in two layers, design compartments to keep the items used most often readily accessible. Pack a towel in the top of the box, covering the equipment. This is used to clean and dry hands before handling cameras or flashguns. Wear gloves while caving to keep your hands clean, taking them off just after releasing the catches on the camera box.

GENERAL MAINTENANCE

Clean and check photographic equipment after every trip; make repairs and recharge batteries. Do not neglect regular maintenance or leave things until you are in a rush to prepare for your next weekend's foray.

A pencil-mounted eraser is ideal for cleaning battery contacts. Corrosion can be removed using a mild acid such as vinegar

Flashguns

Keep battery contacts in electronic flashguns clean to prevent charging problems. If the contacts are difficult to reach, use an eraser on the end of a pencil.

If a flashgun has not been used for some time the capacitor will need to be 'formed' so that it can retain a full charge. Charge and fire the flash several times in quick succession using a spare set of batteries before packing the camera box, so that time and battery power are not wasted in the cave.

Cleaning

It is easy to neglect to clean equipment; to only wipe the dirt off a camera after a trip underground is not sufficient. Check the seals on the camera box are clean and maintained with a smear of petroleum jelly or, better, silicone grease; dirt or a hair across a seal or an O-ring is the difference between a dry or flooded container. Do not over-grease seals as this causes dirt to stick – no surface grease should remain after treatment. Grease an O-ring by removing it from its groove and rubbing it between two fingers with a small amount of silicone: the function is to keep seals supple, not to exclude water.

A cotton bud, moistened with lens cleaning fluid, is used to clean the lens and viewfinder

Open and thoroughly dry cameras. Clean mud from the viewfinder with a cotton bud dipped in lens cleaning fluid. Clean filters, inspect them for scratches, and use a replacement whenever necessary. Extend tripod legs to allow them to dry.

Pay special attention to the sensor on automatic flashguns. If this is blocked or dirty the sensor cannot accurately detect the reflected light and the flash emits too much light.

Never switch on a flashgun you suspect of being damp; it is dangerous and could ruin an otherwise salvageable gun. Drying an unmodified flashgun may take a long time as open-cell foam is sometimes used to hold internal components in place. Remove the batteries and any tape used to seal the gun before leaving it to dry.

Pollskeheenarinky, Co. Tipperary (E8, B5). Muddy and wet conditions demand careful maintenance

Batteries

At regular intervals run down nicad batteries and recharge them to maintain their condition and help hold a full charge. To run down a battery use a torch bulb until the light becomes dim. It is bad practice to totally flatten a nicad battery.

To check synchronisation set the aperture wide open, the shutter to its flash synchronisation speed and fire a flash through the lens

Checking synchronisation

Check the camera/flashgun synchronisation as a matter of routine. Without film in the camera select the flash synchronisation speed (usually 1/60 second, or 1/30 second with flashbulbs) and set the lens to its maximum

aperture. Open the camera back and aim the camera and flash at a white piece of card. When the flash is fired the card will be clearly visible through the open shutter if the flash is synchronised. Although this is a basic test, sticking or unsynchronised focal plane blinds or leaf shutters are obvious. The technique can also check that the lens iris is opening and closing, and what shutter speeds synchronise with electronic flash (at too high a speed only a portion of the shutter is open when the flash fires). When slave units are used, any delay in firing is apparent and a slower shutter speed can be used to compensate.

This quick check is useful when buying a second-hand camera. For greater accuracy expose a few frames of film or, if you have access to a darkroom, a piece of photo-graphic paper. Place the paper inside the camera as if it were a short length of film and close the back. Fire a flash through the lens, and process the paper. If it is only partly exposed the shutter is incorrectly closing the flash contacts and the camera requires servicing – but do not expect sympathy if the bill is high due to a mud-filled camera.

Insurance

There is always a risk of damage or loss to cameras and flashguns, even if every care is taken. Insurance companies have become wary of covering equipment while 'in use' and it is worth checking the small print to see if caving or 'high-risk sports' are excluded. Specialist policies exist, although an extension to a household policy is usually cheaper. Damage under the heading of maintenance, such as replacing a scratched filter, will not be insured. Bear in mind that, while some form of cover is useful, caves are high-risk areas for delicate cameras. In the long term damage is inevitable and minor losses should be absorbed by the photographer; too many small claims could result in a company raising its premium or refusing to offer a policy.

Many problems can be avoided with careful preparations. Learn to outguess difficulties before they arise and find a method of circumventing them, perhaps by using a different technique, training helpers before a difficult shot, or designing better equipment. Invention and innovation are the cave photographer's best weapons. Anything that increases reliability produces better pictures in a shorter time, which will help when enlisting assistants for another day's photography.

Top: Crystal Pool Traverse in Ogof Ffynnon Ddu (E2, B6)
Above: Strawberry Passage in Ogof Draenen (B6)
Left: Bridge Cave (B4)

Chapter four
CAMERA BASICS

There were so many people caving that it provided almost unlimited, unsuspecting models. As each unwary caver surfaced through the sump they were blinded by a flash as their picture was taken. Most spluttered and were amused. Others, the ones that swallowed silt in surprise, grumped. But everyone wanted a copy.

Swildon's Hole

KNOWING the fundamentals of exposure control in daylight is a prerequisite to cave photography; it is an essential foundation to build upon. The basic techniques are illustrated using a cave entrance as an example. Entrances (whether photographed from outside or within) present technical problems as the photographer cannot control the intensity of daylight and must apply knowledge of the relationship between shutter speed and aperture to take the picture. This understanding can later be applied to in-cave work.

Exposure difficulties

Taking a photograph of a cave entrance from the outside, using daylight alone, is straightforward. Most modern cameras have an exposure meter (also termed a lightmeter) which detects the level of light and suggests a 'correct' aperture and shutter speed. However, the meter must make assumptions about the scene – and these assumptions may not be valid. This is especially true in a large, dark cave entrance.

It is important to understand the principles of metering. The meter assumes that the scene is evenly lit with a range of colours that integrate to a mid-tone grey. A large dark or light area will 'fool' the meter into giving an incorrect exposure, and a black entrance appears grey in the photograph. A large area of shadow or highlight will always influence the exposure meter and produce false readings. The same situation arises with automatic flash sensors and flashmeters (see pp.22, 98, 104 & 115).

The calculated exposure can be adjusted on some automatic cameras, usually by setting a positive or negative, one or two f-stop correction to the aperture. On manual cameras the shutter speed or aperture is altered to give an 'incorrect' exposure, again by deliberately under- or over-exposing the scene with respect to the exposure meter reading. For example, a –1 setting represents a change from f5.6 to f8 (or from 1/125 second to 1/250 second): this one f-stop alteration halves the light reaching the film, and the final photograph appears darker.

Experience is needed to recognise when this exposure compensation is required, but an exposure meter can be used to accurately measure any

The compensation dial on automatic cameras adjusts the exposure by one or two f-stops to compensate for situations which produce inaccurate exposure readings

The entrance to Skull Cave, California, in bright sunlight. Large areas of black, often found in entrance photographs, affect the exposure meter, which attempts to integrate all the tones to produce grey. This overexposes the foreground (right), although more detail is recorded within the cave. To avoid this, base the exposure on a mid-tone. In the upper photograph the rocks near the figure were used for this purpose

correction which becomes necessary. Temporarily move towards the part of the subject which must be correctly exposed, such as a sunlit person standing in the entrance. With the subject filling the frame, take a meter reading from an area of mid-tones (an area which does not solely consist of highlights or shadows). Take the photograph from whatever position you choose, of course, but use this meter reading for the exposure. The objective is to accurately record the most important part of the scene on film, regardless of its surroundings.

In fact, any mid-tones receiving the same level of lighting can be used for the reading so, if moving to the subject is inconvenient, take the reading from some 'standard' object which you normally have with you. Technically, a meter operates correctly with a mid-tone grey which reflects 18 per cent of light. Fortunately for cavers, grey carboniferous limestone is close to this value and a measurement from this (avoiding limestone in deep shadow or bright sunlight) can be more precise than trusting the metered level of the overall scene. If in doubt, a good standby is to measure the light reflected from grass, other foliage or the ground. Obviously, none of these subjects will perfectly match an 18 per cent reflectance, but they should be close enough.

Ensure you understand the concept: a large, dark entrance fools the meter, which overexposes the scene and the cave mouth appears grey instead of black. A common mistake is to *overexpose* the picture in the belief that this compensates for the dark area, accentuating the problem (but introducing detail within the entrance at the expense of detail outside). With respect to the meter, *less* light, not more, is required to make large, dark areas record accurately – the exposure settings must reflect this.

Bracketing

Accurately estimating exposure variations, or deciding which part of the scene to measure, can be difficult. Bracketing overcomes this: take several photographs at slightly different exposure settings and choose the optimum one later. A good result is normally obtained, although film is wasted.

A single flash (E8) in the Ogof Ffynnon Ddu streamway illustrates the principle of bracketing: taking three or more photographs which span the estimated 'correct' exposure so that the chance of producing a viable result is increased

It is usual to bracket in one-third f-stop or full f-stop increments up to two or three f-stops either side of the calculated setting. When dealing with large, dark entrances from the outside the most useful bracketed exposures are probably –1 and –2 f-stops (f8 and f11 instead of a metered f5.6, for example). Bracketing is also common when using flash.

The film's latitude affects which exposure increments to use. Black and white film has more latitude to exposure variation than colour, so full f-stops might be used when bracketing. Transparency film tolerates underexposure better than overexposure (the reverse is true for negative film) but has less latitude, so finer increments are normal.

Develop a system for bracketing exposures: the first shot is your best estimate, then one f-stop overexposed and one f-stop underexposed. Using the same sequence each time reduces the chance of mistakes in the cave and exposures are easily and reliably linked to the results.

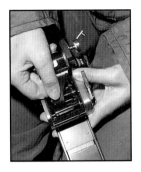

Changing films underground is risky. If you are forced to do so, take care not to lean over the camera: it is easy for water or grit to fall from your helmet

The 'correct' exposure

Pictures of an entrance, taken from the inside, can create enormous atmosphere, perhaps with light streaming through green foliage or a sparkling waterfall. Placing a diminutive caver in a large entrance gives a sense of scale and is highly effective.

There are two extremes in this situation. If the exterior, daylight-lit scene is correctly exposed the caver appears as a silhouette. The converse, exposing for dimly lit cave walls, produces detail in both the cave and the caver but overexposes the scene outside. Neither exposure is 'correct', but relates to the effect the photographer wishes to achieve.

Metering for detail

Two exposures at Hidden Forest Cave, Oregon. The left-hand photograph was based on the camera's exposure meter reading, which was affected by the very bright sky. Shadow detail within the cave has been lost and the trees are nearly silhouettes.

By taking a meter reading from the mid-tone area of rock near the entrance (requiring an adjustment of three f-stops), a more atmospheric picture is produced. Neither exposure is 'correct', but one is more pleasing than the other.

expose for shadows:
highlight detail lost

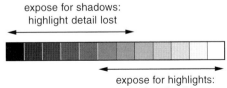

expose for highlights:
shadow detail lost

At best, a seven f-stop range of detail can be recorded on film

Dove Holes. The exposure was based on a meter reading from the ground outside the cave

Modern film, although excellent, cannot cope with the exposure range between the extremes of shadows and highlights: its latitude is not great enough. Negative film can record detail across a seven f-stop range. In other words, measured exposures which retain detail in black shadows and in bright highlights must lie within seven f-stops of each other – beyond this range, shadows become a dense, featureless black and highlights are a washed-out white. Slide film is even worse, with around a five f-stop range.

Imagine looking out of a cave into bright sunlight, with dark, shadowed recesses in the cave walls. This high-contrast situation may span some ten f-stops. You must decide what is required. For a correctly exposed exterior with dark cave walls take a meter reading outside the cave; shadow detail in the cave lies beyond the film's exposure range and the walls will be dense black in the photograph. For detail in the cave walls and sunlight streaming in through the entrance take a mid-tone reading from the wall, deliberately overexposing the scene outside. It is impossible to retain full detail in both highlights and shadows through a ten f-stop range, so one or both must be sacrificed.

It is usual to bracket photographs taken from a cave entrance, and an exposure somewhere between the two extremes – sacrificing some shadow and highlight detail – is often the best option.

Manipulating exposure settings

Camera settings can be manipulated while retaining a 'correct' exposure. There are direct links between shutter speed and aperture. Closing the aperture by one f-stop reduces light by half and, to maintain a correct exposure, the shutter speed must double. A constant amount of light must always reach the film.

Exposure is also linked with film speed: halving the ISO decreases the sensitivity by half (therefore requiring twice as much light for a correct exposure) and demands either double the shutter speed or one f-stop larger aperture; doubling the ISO demands the opposite effect. If ISO 100 film is correctly exposed at 1/15 second at f8, ISO 50 film requires either 1/15 second at f5.6 *or* 1/8 second at f8 (or another combination which retains the same relationship between time and aperture).

In this example with ISO 100 film a deliberate overexposure by one f-stop requires an exposure of 1/15 second at f5.6, while underexposure by one f-stop requires 1/15 second at f11.

Example exposure equivalents:
If a shutter speed of 1/60 second requires an aperture of f4, the same exposure is produced by 1/30 second at f5.6, and so on

Shutter speed	Aperture
1/60 s	f4
1/30 s	f5.6
1/15 s	f8
1/8 s	f11
1/4 s	f16

Flowing water

Photographs taken within a cave mouth often require a slow shutter speed. Because water in a river or streamway is moving during the exposure, in the picture it becomes fluid and evocative, flowing around and over black boulders. Slow speeds are sometimes deliberately used to create this striking effect.

The exposure should retain some detail: too long an exposure loses the water's texture, while if the shutter speed is too short the water is static, frozen and the picture appears poorly executed. Once again there is no 'correct' exposure, only an effect which the photographer requires.

The effect depends on a combination of shutter speed and aperture. These are linked in a direct relationship: closing the aperture by one f-stop halves the light it will admit and requires a longer shutter speed to compensate. A reading of f4 at 1/60 second can be converted to f5.6 at

A ten-second exposure at Porth yr Ogof gives time for the water to blur

1/30 second, or f8 at 1/15 second. To record flowing water the camera settings can therefore be adjusted to take both dim and brightly lit scenes into account and force a long exposure when necessary.

Predicting the exact result is not always easy and bracketing is useful. A tripod is essential to cope with the long exposures required.

Focusing

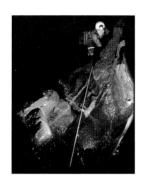

To focus on an off-centre subject most automatic cameras have a focus lock operated by a half-press on the shutter release. Check your camera's instruction manual and make use of the feature in situations like this one, in Ogof Ffynnon Ddu (E8)

Automatic cameras normally use an infra-red sensor to focus the lens. This works well underground, though a small subject in a large space will fool the system. Manually focused cameras are more reliable, but in the dark it can be difficult to use the focusing screen in an SLR so, to increase accuracy, focus on the subject's helmet light.

Estimates of the flash-to-subject distance are often required, even though foreshortening or an out-of-sight flash position causes problems. The caver controlling the flash, rather than the photographer, normally estimates the distance; the assistant must therefore be able to 'measure' a fixed distance if told to stand, say, 4m away from the subject. An aid to estimating length is to use your height as a yardstick, mentally judging how many times you could lie down in the space involved. Accuracy to the last centimetre is not required: realistically, an estimate to the nearest half-metre over short distances (and the nearest metre beyond 5m) is sufficient.

Calculating accurate exposures but placing the flash in the wrong position is pointless. Encourage regular helpers to practise distance estimation.

Depth of field

The depth of field is the distance between the furthest and nearest points in the picture that are acceptably sharp and in focus. The subject must lie within this range. When two or more subjects are in the photograph, such as a caver and a group of stalagmites, they must all lie within the depth of field. Apart from very near objects, the depth of field extends about one-third of the distance in front of a subject and two-thirds behind. For example, if the depth of field is 12m, 4m of this distance lies on the camera side of the subject and 8m lies further away. Outside this range the picture is increasingly blurred.

Just as there is a link between shutter speed and aperture, there is a direct relationship between aperture and depth of field: the smaller the aperture the greater the depth of field. In cave photography large apertures are common due to lighting limitations: a small aperture requires either a short flash-to-subject distance or extremely powerful flashguns. Depth of field is therefore normally shallow, and focusing (and judging distances) is critical.

An SLR lens normally has a depth of field preview button which allows the photographer

Depth of field

A caver stands between two stalagmites (S). At f4 the depth of field is too shallow to include all parts of the photograph and only the caver is in focus. By closing the aperture to f8 the depth of field is increased. All three subjects then fall within the depth of field and appear sharp in the photograph.

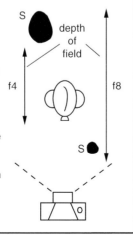

Limitations in the depth of field in this photograph means that this formation in a pool of water in Endless Caverns, Virginia (B7, E5), becomes increasingly out of focus as it nears the camera

to check how much of the scene is in focus. Unfortunately, when the button is pressed the viewfinder image darkens because, as the aperture closes, less light enters the lens. This creates difficulties in caves as, in the dark, poorly lit areas are no longer visible. There is, however, an alternative.

Distances which are in focus at a given aperture are indicated in a depth of field scale which is engraved on the lens. Pairs of f-stops are marked on the scale, representing the field's upper and lower limits: distances which lie between two identical f-stops will be sharply focused, although they may not appear so in the viewfinder. To make the best use of the available depth of field, focus separately on both the nearest and furthest subjects and note the distances. Manually refocus the lens, setting the furthest distance against the upper f-stop marking for the aperture in use. Check that the nearest subject is also within the depth of field. If it is not, increase the depth of field by using a smaller aperture. Alternatively, alter the composition to decrease the apparent separation between the subjects, or move one of the subjects (for example, a caver) closer to the other.

Depth of field is also affected by the focal length of the lens: wide-angle lenses apparently have a greater depth of field than a 'standard' 50mm lens. A 35mm lens gives a greater depth of field than a 50mm, is itself surpassed by a 28mm, and so on.

A qualification is needed (hence the word 'apparently' in the previous paragraph). The increase in the depth of field only applies if the pictures are taken from the same position. A wide-angle lens includes more of the

The depth of field scale

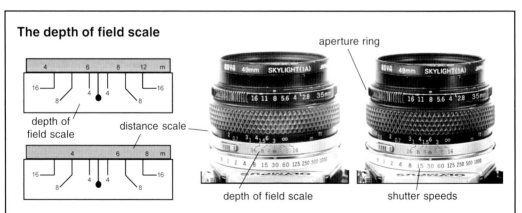

A depth of field scale is marked on most lenses. There are two sets of f-stops marked on the scale; distances between two identical f-stops are in focus. In the top diagram the lens is focused on an object about 6.5m away. At f4 the depth of field is very shallow, from 6m to about 7m: depth of field scales are never comprehensively marked and estimates are necessary. If the aperture was f16, everything from about 4.5m to 12m would be in focus.

If, as well as the main object at 6.5m, the foreground at 4m must appear sharp, an aperture of f8 is required. By placing the focus for 6.5m against the mark for f8 (lower diagram), both 4m and 6.5m fall within the depth of field. Although neither will appear sharp through the viewfinder, they will be in focus in the photograph.

The same principle is illustrated in the photographs. The lens is focused on the subject 3m away (left). At f8, resetting the focus brings objects as close as about 1.4m into focus.

subject's surroundings in the scene. If the photographer moves closer to the subject so that it fills the frame once more, the original depth of field is restored. It is therefore a myth that wide-angle lenses confer a greater depth of field: depth of field is dependent *only* upon aperture and magnification of the image.

The principle of depth of field applies to all photographs, whether they are taken by daylight or flash.

The Mini Columns, Ogof Ffynnon Ddu (E7, B5). The camera is focused on the caver, but the depth of field must be sufficient to include the stalagmites

Using a flashgun

Using a flashgun correctly is at the heart of cave photography. Where two sources of light are present, these may illuminate separate areas or work in combination as a fill-in flash technique. This balances the effects of one flashgun to the intensity of another flash or to daylight. Calculating the balance between lights requires information about the flashgun's power, which is indicated by its guide number.

As has already been noted, aperture and shutter speed are directly dependent on each other. A film requires a specific amount of light to ensure a correct exposure. A small aperture and long shutter speed equate to a large aperture and short speed, each combination allowing the same amount of light to reach the film. In daylight this relationship is easy to adjust, but in a cave the shutter speed is no longer part of the equation – it is replaced by the duration of the flash. In total darkness it makes no difference if the shutter speed is 1/30 second or 1 second: an electronic flash, fired while the shutter is open, has a much shorter duration and exposures are therefore controlled by the aperture and flash alone.

Small apertures provide a greater depth of field, but using a smaller f-stop is not always viable as flashguns are limited in power. There is therefore a trade-off: obtaining sufficient depth of field, without carrying more flashguns than required.

In practice, light is always at a premium. The cave photographer must determine the lighting angle, the exact position of the flash and, in turn, the aperture to use. While appearing a mysterious, arcane art and perhaps being the single most frequently asked question in cave photography (what aperture should I use?), the calculation is straightforward. It hinges on two factors: intensity and distance.

Guide numbers

Light radiates outwards as it travels from its source: the greater the distance, the lower its intensity. In other words, a caver 5m away from a

flash receives more light than one standing 10m away because at a greater distance the light is spread over a larger area. It is *always* the flash-to-subject distance that is important, *never* the distance between the camera and subject. The latter takes no part in determining the aperture.

A flashgun produces a maximum, fixed intensity of light; how much is lost with increasing distance can be calculated, but the first step in working out the aperture is to determine its maximum output. This is represented by a guide number: higher numbers indicate greater light production.

Abandoned barrels in Box Stone Mines (E8, B4)

The guide number is only valid if all factors in the flashgun are constant and the gun is fully charged. Electronic flashguns must be given time to develop a full charge. The ready light typically comes on at around 90 per cent charge; if the gun has a thyristor, a pulsing ready light indicates that full charge has been attained. Flashbulbs are normally given a guide number to indicate their relative power but, because they can be fired in a variety of reflectors (or no reflector at all), this is not necessarily accurate as the light may be spread over a different area. To be accurate, a bulb's guide number must be coupled to a specific reflector (as must an electronic flashgun, which normally has a fixed reflector).

The inverse square law

Light travels according to the laws of physics. The inverse square rule is particularly relevant to flash photography. When the flash-to-subject distance doubles, the light covers four times the area and its intensity is quartered, not halved. When altering flash positions this concept must be understood so that lighting effects can be balanced to the aperture.

Doubling or halving the flash-to-subject distance produces an aperture change of two f-stops, for example from f4 to f8 or f11 to f5.6.

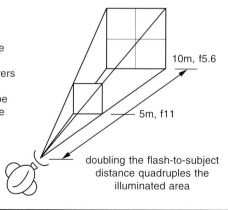

10m, f5.6

5m, f11

doubling the flash-to-subject distance quadruples the illuminated area

The effects of the inverse square law are visible in this photograph taken in Ghar Hassan, Malta. The single flash fired by the caver (B1) shows the shape of the passage but has overexposed nearby areas. A 'correct' exposure occurs a short distance away, while details in the distance and nearer to the camera are technically under-exposed

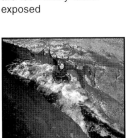

Calculate exposures using the front light and the flash-to-subject distance.

The front flash in each picture had a guide number of 32. The caver in West Kingsdale Master Cave (top: E8, B6) was 8m from the flash = f4. The caver in Ogof Rhaeadr Ddu (E8, B7 from below) was 4m from the flash = f8

Guide numbers are linked to both the film ISO and the units of measuring distance, feet or metres. In Europe the guide number is normally quoted for ISO 100 film and measurements in metres, but a guide number can be obtained for any film speed or for measurements in feet, as is more common in the USA. Guide numbers for flashbulbs, being older, were determined in feet but can be converted to metres to match your working methods.

Calculating a guide number is easy, even if the flashgun manufacturer does not provide one. An exposure table or chart which takes into account the film speed, aperture and flash-to-subject distance is usually provided. Select any combination of distance and aperture from the table, using ISO 100 film (or whatever speed film you prefer), to obtain the guide number:

Guide number = Distance × Aperture

Divide the guide number by the flash-to-subject distance to determine the aperture:

Aperture = Guide number / Distance

To complete the trio, to find the flash-to-subject distance for a specific aperture:

Distance = Guide number / Aperture

As an example, a flash with a guide number of 30 in metres placed 5m from the subject gives an aperture of 30/5 = 6. In fact, there is no setting on the lens for f6, but an intermediate setting between f5.6 and f8 can be used, or select the closest available f-stop: f5.6.

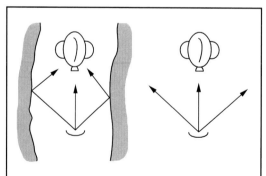

When faces – 'flesh tones' – appear in a picture (E8, E6, B5 below the water) the exposure must be extremely accurate; overexposed faces are unacceptable

Modifying guide numbers

Guide numbers can be modified to match different film speeds or to convert between metres and feet. To convert from a guide number in metres to feet, multiply by 3.3 (divide by 3.3 to convert from feet to metres). For example, a guide number of 30 in metres equates to 100 in feet (the answer is actually 99, but it is normal to round off small increments).

To alter a guide number to match a different film speed, multiply or divide the guide number by 1.4 each time the ISO doubles or halves. A guide number of 28 with ISO 100 film equates to 40 with ISO 200, and 56 with ISO 400 film. This rule of thumb makes use of the link between film speed and aperture: doubling the film speed requires a one f-stop smaller aperture, and so on. A more detailed formula appears on p.132, with multiple flash guide numbers covered on p.108. Matching the guide number to your working method reduces the risk of error underground.

Guide number accuracy

Guide numbers based on manufacturer's data only provide a theoretical aperture. This is accurate for an 'average' photographic situation, as defined by the manufacturer, and usually relates to a room with light-coloured walls and a flash fired from the camera position. However, a cave is very different with dark rock and mud. Exposure errors arise as light from the surroundings is not equally reflected onto the subject in the room and cave.

In confined spaces, where walls are nearby, the manufacturer's guide number may be accurate. However, in most caving situations, because there is less reflection from the surroundings, this guide number is too high: less light reaches the subject than the manufacturer anticipated and the film is underexposed. A new guide number, determined by experimentation, is required.

If a photograph is taken of rock at the 'wrong' aperture the error may be difficult to detect as, without a reference point, a wide variation of exposure can yield an acceptable image. Whether the exposure is incorrect is largely determined by your perception – it is only 'wrong' if it looks it. However, a photograph of a caver's face is easy to assess: flesh tones have to be exposed correctly, or the picture is unacceptable. A face therefore provides an ideal subject for checking a guide number under caving conditions.

In a large chamber underground, or outdoors at night, take a series of photographs of a person wearing typical caving gear. Use slide film as it is least tolerant of mistakes (making faults obvious) with the caver at the same distance but at different apertures. Write down details of the exposure; a waterproof surveyor's note-

Modifying guide numbers

Flashgun manufacturers assume that light will be reflected onto the subject from its surroundings, with ambient light present. In a cave this 'average' situation rarely holds true. On the left the caver is lit with both direct and reflected light, and a manufacturer's guide number may be accurate. However, away from reflective surfaces (right) less light strikes the subject and an accurate exposure relies on a modified guide number.

Indiana Highway, Ogof Draenen (E1, B5). In narrow rifts a flashgun's guide number differs from that in an open space because light is reflected from the walls onto the subject

book and pencil are ideal. Only with detailed information can you benefit from your experiments and learn from your mistakes.

Process the slides, choose the best exposure for the face and use the distance and aperture from your notes to work out the new guide number. For example, if an aperture of f5.6 gives a perfect exposure at 5m, the guide number is $5.6 \times 5 = 28$. If you are working in feet and always use ISO 200 film, an exposure of f8 at 15ft gives a guide number of 120.

Remember that the guide number is specific for those conditions and that film. Now your flashgun probably has two guide numbers: the manufacturer's, which assumes reflected light from surroundings, and the experimental one which does not. Write both on the side of the gun,

Ogof Draenen (B5)

making clear which is which – or extend your experiment to include a narrow cave passage or wet areas, and so on. Write the data from all your flashguns in the camera box lid; you will need the information even when an assistant is holding the flash. Typically, the modified guide number may represent one or two f-stops loss in light compared with the original.

Experience is needed to recognise which guide number should be used, but this is not difficult: match the situation to those you encountered when determining the guide numbers. As a cave photographer, you must keep thinking when underground.

The aperture can, obviously, be deliberately altered for a specific purpose. Some texts advise opening the aperture by one or two f-stops to obtain more detail in areas of dark rock. More detail *is* obtained, but it is a myth that *all* caving situations require a wider aperture than the manufacturer recommends; for example, a caver's face (which reflects light in a 'standard' manner) will be grossly overexposed if this is attempted. Beware of simplistic instructions: altering the theoretical exposure, determined using experimental cave photographs, can be dangerous. Find the guide number for a caver in an open space, and stick with it. If in doubt, bracket the exposure. The cost of film and time is slight yet ensures at least one correct photograph is obtained.

This chapter has introduced the relationships between film speed, aperture, shutter speed and flashgun guide number. Understanding these factors is part of your preparation for cave photography. Determine the correct guide number for your equipment and standardise on a film type. Only after the basic techniques have been mastered will true experimentation begin.

Chapter five
WORKING WITH FLASH

The flashgun stopped working. I changed the batteries, but the whistle as it charged faltered and failed. Ten minutes spent cleaning contacts amounted to nothing. In utter frustration, with all my might I hurled the offending gun into a wall. It fell to the ground, where it mockingly whined into life.

Goyden Pot

CAVERS have many interests – exploration, hydrology, surveying, biology and photography, to name a few – and, therefore, caving trips can encompass a huge variety of aims. Not everyone's interests coincide, and time is inevitably restricted. Limitations are imposed: equipment, the nature of the cave and the number of cavers willing to help. Underground photography takes time, though it should be the aim of every photographer to minimise this.

The route to the Mini Columns, Ogof Ffynnon Ddu (E8, B5)

Spending too long on a complex picture when other cavers have different objectives leads to failure and annoyance. Under these circumstances, carry a minimal, lightweight set of equipment and restrict the number of pictures you attempt. Organise a photography-only trip for intricate, multiple flash photography or when a large number of pictures are taken.

Teamwork, where everyone fully understands the nature of the trip before it begins, encourages efficient and more enjoyable photography.

This chapter concentrates on basic techniques with a single flashgun. These are suitable for sporting trips, and form the mainstay of more complex work. Planning and preparation – including checking all items of equipment – are highly important.

Flash on camera

Underground, a camera-mounted flash is simple and fast to use. Because humid or dust-laden cave air scatters and reflects light, a flash close to the lens often produces a white, washed-out and 'milky' photograph. The effect is akin to driving at night in fog with the car's headlights reflected from the moist air. Subjects near to the camera are least affected, as there

are shorter flash-to-subject and camera-to-subject distances involved and therefore less moisture.

Light from a camera-mounted flash can be reflected from the blood-rich retina at the back of the eye. If a person (or animal) is looking towards the camera, as the flash is firing from near the lens, this results in an effect known as red-eye.

To avoid misty photographs and red-eye the cardinal rule is to remove the flash from the camera: do not underestimate the worth of lighting the subject at an angle, even if the flash is only held at arm's length. Cave photographs *can* be taken with an automatic camera using its integral (and therefore close to the lens) flash but, due to other limitations as well as the difficulties introduced by the flash position, auto-only models are not as versatile as a manual camera. The remainder of this chapter assumes that, at minimum, the camera's shutter and

Removing the flash from the camera is vitally important, as is being demonstrated in this picture taken in Buckeye Creek Cave in West Virginia (above: E8, B5).

The photographs taken in Ogof Draenen (right) were lit with a single electronic flash. The left-hand picture (E1) suffers from light reflected from condensation in the humid air. Holding the flash at arm's length (far right: E8) is sufficient to avoid the problem

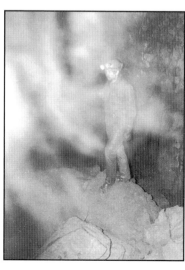

aperture are manually controlled and the flash can be removed from the body; automatic cameras are dealt with in chapter eight.

Open flash

With manual control of all camera functions the problems of cave photography are greatly simplified. In fact, one of the most effective and fastest means of taking a picture involves using B and a single flash.

A tripod, as here in Bridge Cave, is ideal for taking pictures using B, but requires more time than hand-held photographs (E8, B5).

A lightweight alternative is a vacuum cushion (right). Filled with polystyrene beads, when air is sucked out through a one-way valve by squeezing the bulb, the cushion solidifies and retains the shape of the rock and camera. When the valve is open the cushion can be used to pad the camera box

Cave photography traditionally requires a tripod-mounted camera. The method was evolved in the 1860s, removing and replacing a lens cap to control the exposure. Effectively, the modern B setting has the same function. In an 'open flash' technique the shutter is held open on B, either by hand or using a cable release. One or more flashes are manually fired by assistants, then the shutter is closed. As the flashes can easily be fired from any position at any time during the exposure, without needing further equipment or having to synchronise with the shutter, many cave photographers still use the open flash technique: it benefits a great deal from its simplicity.

With a tripod the photographer can take time to double check composition and carefully frame the picture. Against this, a tripod is bulky and adds to transport difficulties. Photography takes longer and, as a caver must sometimes stand still for an appreciable period, poses may appear static. Imaginative lighting can help remove this deficiency.

In total darkness there is no need to perfectly synchronise the flash with the shutter: the short flash duration of an electronic flash means that hand-holding the camera on B is viable if a single flash is involved (when two or more flashes are fired, the inevitable camera movement produces a double image). Hand-holding a camera for open flash is an ideal, fast technique to use during sporting trips.

Delays between opening the shutter and firing the flash must be minimised as, without a viewfinder image, it is easy for the camera to be moved: holding it precisely still is almost impossible. Bracing the camera or photographer's helmet against a rock, boulder, or some other immovable

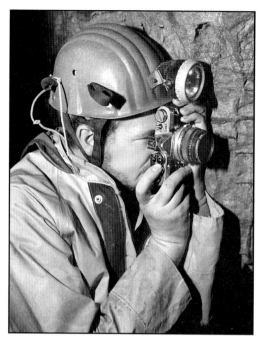 

Whenever possible, brace a hand-held camera to add stability, especially when using B. Press both your helmet and camera against the rock.

The caver on the right has fired a flash (B1) while the camera shutter was open on B, then turned and walked away before the shutter was closed. His helmet light has left a trail on the negative. Ensure the shutter is closed before any lights are moved within the photograph

object helps reduce this problem. The technique is crude, but highly effective and extremely fast.

Any moving light within the picture records as a streak across the photograph, as will stationary lights if the camera is moved. To avoid these 'light trails', extinguish all helmet lights before opening the shutter. This, unfortunately, introduces an unnatural appearance: a caver striding down a streamway without a helmet light looks somewhat unnatural. With care, if the shutter is not open for more than a second or so, the caver's light can be left on; it produces a pleasant glow which enhances any photograph. However, a light which shines in one place can create a bright spot in the photograph; using a dim, low-power helmet bulb or small carbide flame produces good results with less risk.

Using slaves

Slave units help to avoid light trails, provide the freedom to eliminate static poses, synchronise multiple flash arrangements, and speed up photography in general.

Slaves require a minimum of two flashguns: one on the camera to trigger the slave when the shutter is fired, the other to illuminate the subject. Slave units are sensitive to either visible or infra-red light (in fact, those which are sensitive to infra-red are usually also sensitive to visible light). When an infra-red slave is matched with an infra-red flash on the camera, no visible light is required to trigger the slave, and silhouettes and sidelit photographs can be taken with full shutter synchronisation. Taking the picture becomes similar to working in daylight: the photographer can use a hand-held camera without the disadvantages of open flash and B.

Because the flash and shutter are synchronised, moving helmet lights do not leave trails and action photography is made easier. Instead of posing while standing still, a caver can be asked to step into water and the picture taken when the splash looks photogenic. Cavers on rope can be photographed with two or more flashes in positions where it is impossible for them to stay still. Helmet lights make the picture more natural and provide reference points which help the photographer maintain the composition. Without a tripod the operation is faster and photography can be accomplished with greater ease in situations where a tripod cannot easily be erected.

The advantages are numerous. All in all, a slave unit is of incomparable value. Making or obtaining a good slave system should be a priority for all cave photographers.

Although slave units are invaluable for cave photography, it should never be forgotten that strong pictures can be produced in simple situations which require minimal equipment. This photograph in Little Neath River Cave (E8) was taken using a hand-held flashgun attached to the camera by a cable

Flash characteristics

Different types of flash possess vastly different characteristics, all of which will affect the appearance of the photograph. Three main factors are involved: intensity, angle of illumination and duration. Added to this are considerations of colour balance and how evenly the light is spread (which depends on the reflector design and flash-to-subject distance).

There are inherent differences between electronic flash and flashbulbs. Generally speaking, flashbulbs are more powerful than any portable electronic flashgun. However, the amount of *useful* light (and therefore

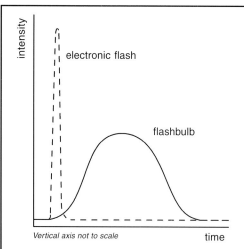

Vertical axis not to scale

Flash duration

An electronic flash produces a short-duration, high-intensity pulse of light. The flash from a bulb builds up slowly, peaks and tails away. A bulb peaks too slowly to consistently trigger most slave unit designs, while an electronic gun's shorter reaction time is ideal. Most slaves will *fire* both bulb and electronic flashguns, but only *be fired by* an electronic flash.

To make use of the total light output of a bulb use B or a shutter speed slower than 1/30 second

the guide number) from either source is also dependent on the reflector. The higher power of bulbs does not make them perfect for every situation, and there are many instances where an electronic flash is best and a bulb is a distinct liability.

Flashbulb guns are usually fitted with a shallow, wide reflector which casts light over nearly 180 degrees. Large reflectors equate, effectively, to a large light source which, in turn, gives a diffuse light that produces softer shadows. However, if the bulb is fired near the camera most of the light normally goes to waste because it falls on areas not being photographed.

An electronic flashgun reflector is normally smaller and gives more of a point source of light. Shadows are heavier and more defined, giving the appearance of a sharper, higher contrast photograph. When used as a front light an electronic flashgun's output covers the field of view of a 35mm lens, making the best use of the light. The opposite situation applies to flashes fired within the picture. The directional flash of an electronic gun only picks out a small area, while a bulb's wide angle of light is fully used and can easily be controlled by changing the shape of the reflector (or fired with no reflector at all).

The duration of the flash is extremely important. Flashbulbs build up light intensity slowly, peak and then tail off over a total of 1/30 second or more. The pulse of light from a flash tube is of much shorter duration, typically between 1/1,000 and 1/20,000 second.

These differences are valuable assets. As the photograph is characterised by the flash duration rather than the shutter speed, moving objects are 'frozen' by a short-duration electronic flash but can blur when lit with a bulb. Waterfalls and spray appear as static droplets with electronic flash. Flashbulbs record falling and flowing water as fluid, moving streaks. Both methods are valid: use the correct flash for the desired effect.

Flash characteristics

Electronic flash	Flashbulb
Typically lower output than bulb	High output of light
Reflector gives narrow beam	Reflector gives wide beam
Produces high-contrast pictures	Lower-contrast pictures
Sharp shadows	Shadows can appear 'soft'
Short duration	Long duration
Freezes motion	Permits blurring
Can appear bluish and cold	Can appear reddish and warm

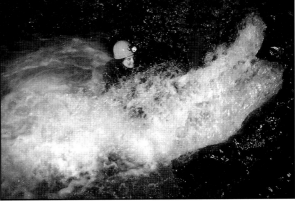

The different characteristics of electronic flash and flashbulbs can be used to advantage with moving water.

Both these photographs were lit using a single flash. Water splashing from the rocks in Ogof Ffynnon Ddu (left, B4) blurs due to the long duration flash from a bulb, while movement in flowing water in Dan yr Ogof (below, E8) is arrested. Use the type of flash to produce the results you require.

Further comparisons between electronic flash and flashbulb lighting appear on pp.31 and 92

Flashes appear white to the human eye; they are bright enough to mask any colour tinge, but appearances can be deceptive. Flashbulbs and electronic flash emit different spectra, even though both are theoretically matched to colour film. Bulbs invariably give warm colours in colour photographs (uncoated, clear bulbs sometimes unacceptably so), while electronic flash can look cold and bluish. These minor differences in colour balance are normally ignored unless there is a reason for exact colour rendering, when the choice of film is as important as the choice of lighting.

In an ideal world flashbulbs would always be available; in practice, supplies are limited as they are no longer manufactured, but are sometimes obtainable from warehouses and they remain in common use alongside their modern replacement, electronic flash. Both sources have advantages and disadvantages and, if bulbs are available, cave photographers should make use of the characteristics of each to suit the situation.

Placing lights

Whatever its characteristics and however flashes are fired, manually or by slaves, the flash's position has the most effect on the final photograph. Rules concerning flash placement are not inviolate and experimentation is important, but there are a number of basic ground rules.

As has been noted, the cardinal rule is to remove the flash from the camera. If not, the air's natural humidity (plus the photographer's breath) reflects light back to the lens to produce a low-contrast, uninspiring mist that occludes the subject.

A single-flash ring-round

This ring-round of photographs illustrates the effect that the angle of lighting has on the subject. In each case the camera position and aperture is unchanged, and an electronic flash has been fired at a constant flash-to-subject distance. Each picture is coded with a letter and number, indicating the use of an electronic flash and its relative position to the camera.

The most striking result is the clear advantage obtained from moving the flash away from the camera. Front-lit photographs (E1) are 'flat' and, although they contain detail, lack interest. Even holding the flash at arm's length (E2 and E8) is enough to improve contrast and add shadows.

The dramatic content of the photograph increases as the flash is moved towards a backlit position (E5). Flashes fired from E4 and E6 can easily induce flare in the photograph, so must be carefully shielded (see p.96).

E6

E7

Flash position codes

All photographs in this book are coded with the type of flash and its firing position relative to the camera and subject. An electronic flash is indicated with the letter E, and a flashbulb with a B.

Positions are numbered as portions of a circle (diagram, centre). E2, B5 would represent an electronic flash fired from position 2 together with a flashbulb from position 5

E8

E5

E4

E3

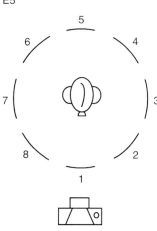

E2

E1

Two photographs of formations in Ease Gill Caverns illustrate the effects of changes in lighting. With an electronic flash at E7 (left) there is good modelling and contrast, and detail is retained. A low backlight on the same formations (E5) increases the drama of the picture, but details within the formations are lost

The effect is produced by reflection from *any* humid air along the lens axis. A caver within the picture firing a flash away from the camera, keeping his body between the flash and the camera, appears as a silhouette with a condensation-induced white halo. Here, the 'problem' has *helped* create the photograph. As is often the case in photography, once a problem is understood its causes can be avoided or used to advantage. A successful picture is often dependent on making use of what might be conceived as limitations.

The question remains: if the flash is not permitted next to the lens, where should it be placed?

The exact positioning depends on the effect that is required. To remove the worst effects of 'flashback' only a small camera-to-flash distance is required. Some flashguns, typically made by National, Sunpak and Vivitar, have a removable sensor which can be mounted on the camera's hot shoe. With the flash held at arm's length most unwanted effects are avoided. To totally remove red-eye from this essentially frontlit position, the caver should not look directly towards the lens.

Spider Cave, New Mexico (B6). Side lighting causes some loss of fine detail from the photograph, but introduces a dramatic effect

By moving the flash from the front of the subject to the side, highlights, shadows and texture are accentuated. When fired from directly behind the subject, a silhouette is produced. Spray glistens and condensation adds to rimlit effects. Side lighting and backlighting are used widely in cave photography as they add drama and atmosphere to the picture.

Flashguns fired within the picture are often held and controlled by a caver, producing an – albeit successful – cliché. A silhouetted caver, looking away from the camera, is a striking photograph and can be taken quickly and easily using a hand-held camera on B with a manually fired flash.

A wide spread of light is needed to show the passage shape. The directional beam of an electronic flash is often too narrow and, aimed

These photographs were each taken using a single flashbulb in a shallow reflector, making use of its wide spread of light to pick out the passage shape. This is particularly striking in Skeleton Cave, a lava tube in Oregon (right, B2), and Melidoni Cave on the island of Crete (below, B2)

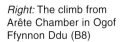

Right: The climb from Arête Chamber in Ogof Ffynnon Ddu (B8)

down the centre of a passage, does not light the walls: its output goes to waste. A bulb, with its greater power and wider spread, is ideal for this type of picture.

To be successful, the silhouetted caver must appear against an area which will reflect light, or else a black silhouette against a black background is produced. A wall, or sufficient moisture or dust in the air to reflect light back towards the camera, is suitable. Ensure the silhouette is complete (check by using the shadow cast by a helmet light from the camera position) otherwise a truncated silhouette is produced where, for example, parts of the shadow fall on rocks at different distances.

E1

B1

Firing a flash in the picture

A silhouette is produced when a caver fires a flash away from the camera. To be effective, light must be reflected from a cave wall or, alternatively, condensation in the air. If there is insufficient humidity, the later technique fails as the black silhouette then lies against a black background.

The diagram shows the differences between an electronic flash (E) and a flashbulb (B). Light from an electronic flash is more directional than that from a bulb and, in this case, only the flashbulb has lit the passage walls. The photographs, taken near a bend in a passage in Ogof Draenen, illustrate this point. The electronic flash (left) has picked out the rocks immediately in front of the caver extremely well, giving a good silhouette, but has totally failed to light the right-hand wall where the passage turns a corner. The wider spread of light from the bulb, using a 'normal' bulb flashgun's reflector, has lit the right-hand wall as well as considerably more of the roof and left wall.

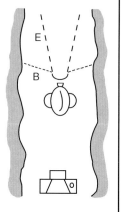

Choose your combination of flash and background with care: silhouettes may fail without prior thought, but with careful planning the results are predictable.

Backlighting

Backlighting is simple: aim the flash directly at the camera from behind the subject, so that no direct light reaches the lens. In the resulting photograph the silhouette is rimlit, and pure white highlights are added to the walls, ceiling and floor (mid-tones are controlled by side and front lighting, not backlighting). The technique works well in moisture-filled air, scattering light from the flashgun and picking out mist rising from damp clothing or condensing air from a caver's breath. Backlighting lifts an ordinary picture into the realm of the dramatic.

However, many rimlighting effects fail due to insufficient moisture in the air. A caver standing still or breathing heavily for a few minutes helps raise the humidity of nearby air, a worthwhile exercise when backlighting is involved. Some caves – and many disused mines – are very dry and this, coupled with a draught which prevents a build-up of condensation, is hard to overcome. Without sufficient moisture in the air, the effects of backlighting are reduced. Be aware of these circumstances and realise the limitations of the technique.

To produce a good silhouette the flash, subject and camera must be lined up accurately. To find the precise flash position, aim a helmet light

Backlighting

Firing a flash towards the camera, so that the subject casts a shadow on the lens, produces a silhouette.

As the diagram shows, a bulb flashgun, with its wider spread of light (B), helps to show the passage shape. This is demonstrated in the picture of Dan yr Ogof (right, B5). The narrower beam of an electronic gun (E) is more directional and would not have had the same effect, but is perfect for rimlighting subjects such as the caver admiring stalactites, also in Dan yr Ogof (E5). Backlit photographs are characterised by strong highlights and dense shadows.

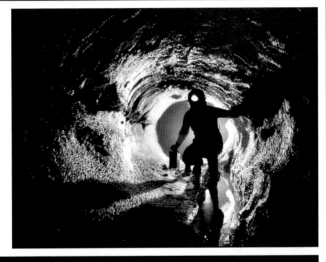

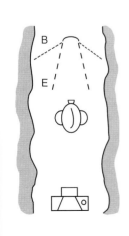

at the subject from the camera position; a flash fired from within the subject's shadow will be hidden from the camera. It is often easier to move the backlight than the camera to ensure a good line-up, although slave units allow fast adjustments by the photographer as the restrictions of setting up a tripod are not involved. An assistant's helmet light simulates the backlight effect, helping the photographer to compose the picture before pressing the shutter. This is particularly valuable when hand-holding the camera and shooting a silhouette.

The caver firing the backlight should not appear in the photograph. By holding the flash at arm's length there is less chance of stray light striking the person firing the flash, especially when using a bulb with its wide spread of light. If no light reaches the assistant's arms and legs, these blend into the background even if they are not totally hidden behind the subject. A caver who clearly understands what is required without constant instructions is a huge asset. Simulate the technique on the surface; communicating underground can be exceedingly difficult when surroundings are noisy. Accurately lining up the flash is the key to success.

By default, the subject's shadow will fall towards the camera. However, the size and shape of the shadow can be altered by varying the backlight-to-subject distance. Shadows increasingly diverge as the flash is moved closer. This is especially dramatic when lighting a cluster of straw stalactites. Firing from the base of a subject increases the length of the shadow, while aiming at an angle makes shadows shorter. When there is a lot of condensation and the flash is fired close to the subject, visible rays of light form in the air like fingers of a hand or the classic children's drawing of sunbeams spreading from a rising sun. Backlighting from a greater distance produces shadows that are more nearly parallel, with smaller highlight areas. All are valid positions, matched to the effect that is required.

Backlit waterfalls are particularly dramatic. Imagine a backlit picture of a caver standing in or near a waterfall. There are three basic positions for the caver: behind, within, or in front of the falling water. In the first position the shadow is cast onto the waterfall (see photograph, left) and a dark rim appears around the caver where the water has not been lit. Unless this is intentional, the result is intrusive; a pose within or on the camera side of the waterfall produces a more evenly lit photograph which shows more of the water.

The caver in Dan yr Ogof (below, B5) is standing behind the waterfall and is casting an unwanted shadow on the water. The lighting is more even when the caver is in front of or within the water, as in Ogof Ffynnon Ddu (opposite, B6)

Avoiding flare

Flare is caused by light striking the lens from a source either within or from outside the picture. Typically, flare appears in the picture as a series of regular, bright hexagons or other shapes arising from reflections of the iris within the lens, or else there is an overall reduction in contrast with degraded shadows. Modern lenses are coated to reduce flare, while older, uncoated lenses often flare badly.

Precisely lining up the backlight avoids most problems. For other flashes, use a shield: a strategic hand, a carefully positioned caver or rock – make good use of the cave's geometry to help control the lighting. As long as it protects the lens from direct lighting, the shield fulfils its function and can be placed at any position between the flash and camera. A lens hood reduces the chance of stray light from the side reaching the lens, and a piece of cardboard or plastic, fixed to the flash with an elastic band, is useful in directing its light only onto the subject while shading the camera. The shield's shadow must fall on the camera but not the scene. The shield, painted black one side and white the other, can double as a reflector in close-up photography (see chapter seven).

Sometimes flare is used deliberately as part of the photograph's composition, in which case experimentation with apertures, as well as a high-quality lens, is needed. The flash and flare within the picture appear on opposite sides of the photograph's centre: a flash in the top left causes a flare in the bottom right. A direct flash in the centre of the lens produces no flare; if an off-centre flash is required, flare is less noticeable if the composition is arranged so that the flare falls in an area of water or wet rock, as these will produce natural highlights which mask its effects.

Shielding a flash

These two flash positions lie outside the camera's view, and neither caver appears in the photograph. However, light from position (A) strikes the lens while light from (B) does not as there is a rock in the way. Use natural features to shield the lens or, if none are available, shield the flash with a hand or body between (A) and (C). Check that a shadow is not cast into the photograph.

The single electronic flash (E4), which was placed close to the edge of the picture to light these helictites in Breezeway Cave in Colorado, has been badly shielded. The result is flare: reflection within the camera lens, producing unwanted highlights

Determining the aperture

The 'correct' aperture is determined using the flashgun's guide number, but backlights allow a large variation in exposure.

An aperture error in frontlit or sidelit photographs produces an over- or underexposed subject, but with a backlit silhouette the highlights and rimlit areas merely change their size. In fact, highlights are localised areas which are overexposed: they are white and essentially without detail. Further overexposure increases the size of the highlight. There are obviously limits to this argument, and grossly overexposed areas are unacceptable. Nevertheless, theoretical errors in the intensity of the backlight equal to or in excess of one f-stop over- or underexposure (based on the guide number and subject-to-backflash distance) may prove acceptable.

The angle of lighting also affects exposure because the guide number was calculated using a frontlit picture. When a flash is moved progressively to the side of the subject, less light is reflected towards the camera. At an angle of 45 degrees or more, an increased aperture of up to one f-stop may be required: experiments will determine the best exposure and help

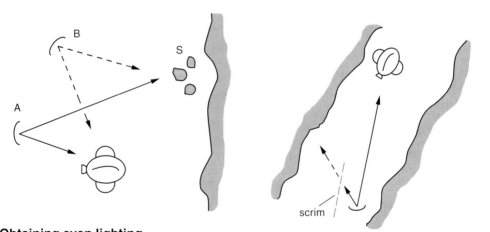

Obtaining even lighting

When two or more parts of a picture must be correctly exposed, as opposed to background detail which is allowed to blend into darkness, they must lie at an equal distance from the flash.

In the left-hand diagram the caver and stalagmites (S) are both lit by a single flashgun (A). However, either the caver will be overexposed or the formations underexposed because the flash-to-subject distances are different: only one of the subjects can be correctly lit. From position (B) each subject receives an identical level of light. When more than one subject is involved choose an intermediate lighting position, or light each part of the image with separate flashguns (for multiple flash see chapter six).

If the flash position cannot be altered and a second flash cannot be added to balance the lighting effects, position (A) is forced upon the photographer and the spread of light must be controlled using a partial shield called a scrim. This is normally a piece of gauze or thin cloth, essentially a shield with holes in it or made of translucent material. In the right-hand diagram the flashgun's output has been partially reduced on one side to balance the intensity on the passage wall with light reaching the caver. This technique is used in cine filming with continuous light sources. Bracket exposures and simulate the effect with a helmet light before taking the picture.

to adjust the guide number for different situations. As with all flash photographs, a guide number is only accurate for the conditions under which it was determined.

Auto-flash

Automatic 'computer' flash sensors detect reflected light and, by stopping the production of more light, theoretically ensure a correct exposure. The underlying principle is good, but the system is easily fooled as the sensors assume that reflection occurs evenly over the total area of the photograph.

If the subject is isolated, for example a stalagmite standing in a chamber where there are no nearby walls, most of the flashgun's light is lost into the distance. The only reflected light comes from the stalagmite, which is a small proportion of the overall scene. By the time the sensor has received the 'correct' amount of light reflected from this small area, the formation is grossly overexposed.

Automatic flash systems are easily fooled. In Lower Cradle Hole (top: E8, E5) light has been reflected from nearby walls, shutting down the auto sensor and underexposing the caver. Where the subject is near its background, as in Ogof Draenen (E8), the lighting is even and automatic systems can be used

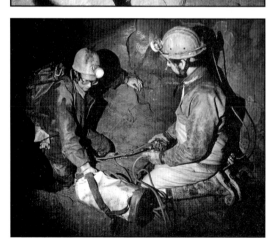

A similar argument applies with reflective surfaces, for example passage walls in a rift. Now, additional light is reflected to the sensor from nearby objects and the sensor shuts down light production too soon; the subject in the distance is underexposed.

Automatic flashguns can be used in cave photography, but their limitations must be recognised. If the subject reflects light evenly, for example a caver near a wall, the exposure may be accurate.

However, if the subject is surrounded by dark space and it is anticipated that an automatic flash exposure will be inaccurate, assess what area is filled by the subject. If it represents half the picture area, about half the light will be lost and it will be overexposed by one f-stop: close the aperture by one f-stop compared with the aperture indicated on the flash. If only a quarter of the scene is filled, close the aperture by two f-stops.

This assessment is approximate, but it gives a rule of thumb which works well in practice and helps ensure a good exposure – especially if these are bracketed.

Obtaining more power

More powerful, brighter flashguns permit the use of smaller apertures, thereby giving greater depth of field and making focusing less critical, and fewer flashguns are needed to light large chambers. Theoretically, there is nothing wrong with this argument. However, greater power normally equates to more cost and bulk and some of the apparent benefits are offset by disadvantages.

The caver has fired a single flashbulb (B2) in Cango Cave, South Africa. Inevitably, objects closer to the flash receive more light: the area at the caver's feet is overexposed, while formations in the distance (which should be white) are underexposed.

Using a more powerful flash would move the area of correct exposure further from the caver, making the foreground worse (but distant areas better). Better (more balanced) lighting is therefore produced by adding more, evenly distributed, flashguns, rather than increasing the power of the existing gun or opening the aperture to better expose subjects which are further away

Underexposed   Correct exposure   Overexposed

A caver, firing a flash within a picture, will always produce a correct exposure *somewhere*. For a particular aperture a weak gun giving its full output of light might produce a correct exposure at only 3m away, while a more powerful gun correctly exposes the scene 6m away. Higher power changes the useful flash-to-subject distance for any given aperture and film combination.

If the higher-powered gun is used to obtain a greater depth of field there are obvious benefits, but if the aim is to use fewer flashes to light a large area a problem arises. As the flash intensity rises, objects near to the flash – such as rocks at the caver's feet – become grossly overexposed. It is arguable, therefore, that an increased number of small flashes are more useful than fewer, more powerful guns as it is easier to produce consistent, even lighting.

Nevertheless, there are instances when larger flashes are required, typically in immense chambers. There are several options. One is to fire several flashes from the same position, simulating a powerful flashgun. A number of flashbulbs can be fired by taping them together so that the heat from one fires the others (removing the reflector from a Magicube or flashcube and pushing the four bulbs together is a convenient method). Triggering all the bulbs in a flipflash or flashbar is another alternative.

The light from two bulbs taped together does not double the guide number, but produces a one f-stop increase in output. Each time the aperture is closed by one f-stop the number of bulbs must be doubled: four bulbs are required for a two f-stop smaller aperture, eight bulbs for three f-stops. In fact, the theory does not hold true in practice as some of the light is absorbed as heat; experimental exposures and bracketing are required.

Photographing formations in Dan yr Ogof (E8, B4)

Communication

Communication between the photographer and assistants is essential so that flashes are fired correctly and problems are clearly described. This may be difficult if a chamber echoes, water creates background noise or distances are so great that shouting is unreliable. Even at close quarters, using a camera hand-held on B, a prearranged cue to fire the flash is needed. Codes using whistles or switching a light on and off are common.

At its most basic two signals are needed: one for assistants to indicate that they are *ready* to fire the flash, and one for the photographer to indicate *when* to manually fire the flash. Slave units do not entirely remove this requirement: assistants have to indicate when they are in the right position and ready, and the photographer needs to direct cavers to change their pose at a distance. Confirmation of the last message may be needed.

Instructions are easily garbled. Whatever code is used, it must avoid confusion: keep it simple. Shouting 'Are you ready to fire?' across a large chamber can result in a caver hearing 'Fire' and setting off a flash too early. When asked 'Are you ready?', 'No' is a better reply than 'Not ready' – if the photographer only hears the last word . . . Develop a set of unambiguous instructions which suit your operating techniques and are clearly understood by all.

The Punchbowl (B4, from below). Slave units not only aid photography in situations where setting up a tripod would be difficult or impossible, they also reduce the need for detailed communication with assistants (such as telling them when to fire the flash) and leave the photographer more in control

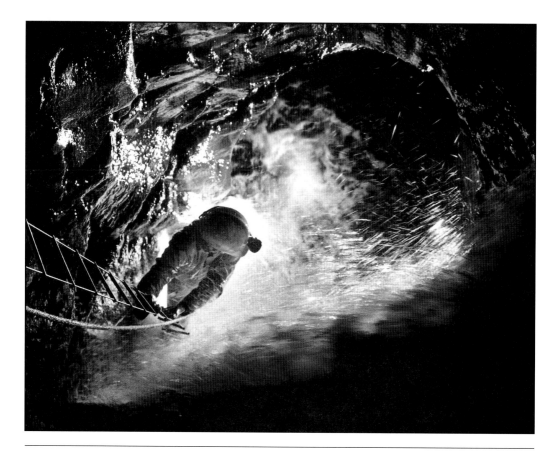

With open flash a sequence such as 'Three, two, one, fire', with the shutter opened on 'one', is useful. When shouting an instruction it is easy to inadvertently move a hand-held camera, so practise holding a camera to your eye while calling out. If camera movement is a problem, use a different system: have an assistant make the count, or open the shutter on 'one' without shouting 'fire'; cavers must pause before triggering their flashes. When multiple flashes are involved, use the closest flash to the camera as a signal to the other assistants to fire their guns; its operator will be the easiest for you to communicate with. Slave units avoid many of these problems as the flashes are fully synchronised with the shutter.

Standardising techniques

Standardising your technique reduces the number of decisions to be made; fewer errors arise and photography is faster. With less time spent working out exposures, more time can be applied to composition. Although experimentation is always valuable, standardising on a working method is a valuable goal for novices and experienced cave photographers alike.

For example, if your flashgun produces a perfect exposure at a flash-to-subject distance of 5m using f5.6 and ISO 200 film, leave the aperture set at f5.6 and always place the flashgun 5m from the subject. Write this 'ideal' situation on the flashgun alongside the guide number: f5.6/5m is now the 'standard' setting. Remember that some situations, such as when reflective walls are nearby, may require a modified guide number.

Carry out a 'dry run' with any new cavers on your team. Simulate taking a cave photograph on the surface so that helpers know what will be asked of them: where is the switch to turn the flashgun on, which button is pressed to fire it, how is a flashbulb inserted and ejected, how is the base of a broken bulb removed, where is the slave's sensor? Check accuracy in estimating distances; are your assistants more confident working in metres or feet? Accommodate them: convert measurements to suit your techniques rather than introduce confusion. All the instructions will be repeated underground, but going through the procedure beforehand cuts down wasted time within the cave.

The guide number of this flash has been modified from 32 to 20 for use under caving conditions. The guide number and an example of a distance and aperture combination have been marked on the gun

Goyden Pot (B5). The long duration flash provided by a bulb gives time for falling water to blur

Persevere and become thoroughly conversant with single flash techniques; it is well worthwhile spending the time to learn the basics and, with experience, what initially appear to be limitations will disappear or be turned to your advantage. Many fine, dramatic, atmospheric photographs are taken with simple equipment and a single flash. It is not necessarily the photographer with the most flashguns and slave units, or the most expensive camera, who produces the best pictures. Technique, imagination and originality have much more power and effect.

Chapter six
MULTIPLE FLASH

The waterfall was always best in winter, when plenty of water sinks in the river above. We spent several hours lying in the freezing stream and standing under the deluge before one person noticed slush flowing through the cave. Icicles had formed in her hair. The photographic trip ended, most unfairly, when everyone promptly mutinied and left.

Bridge Cave

T AKING pictures with a single flashgun is fast and effective; for many photographs no other equipment is required. In particular, the technique is suited to sporting trips, documenting digs or in confined spaces. However, large chambers and more versatile lighting combinations require multiple flash.

When multiple flash is involved good communication is required as, with more helpers involved, flashguns are fired at ever greater distances from the photographer and confusion soon increases. Photography is faster if clear, readily understandable instructions and prior training are given on the surface. Even more than when using single flash, the photographer and assistants must operate as a team.

Problems with movement

Multiple flash with open flash techniques using B carries an inherent problem: the possibility of cavers moving between flashes.

If a caver is lit with two flashes, perhaps to add effect or to build up the total intensity of light from a single, weak flashgun, any movement produces a double image. Shadows are cast in different directions and are half lit by the second flash; the background may show through semi-transparent parts of the caver. The effect is disturbing: avoid half-lit shadows and ghost images.

Assistants must understand the principles involved: they must not move between flashes, or until the shutter is closed. Without this being instilled, someone inevitably turns or walks off after the first flash, not realising that more are to come. A moving helmet light produces a light trail in an otherwise perfect picture. A successful photograph is never guaranteed so, in case of unseen mistakes, repeat the exposure as a safety net.

The difficulties of using B and multiple flash have been largely overcome with slave units. However, the tried and tested, traditional open flash technique still has a place in

Moving between two separate flashes (E8, E8) has produced a double image. Although the effect is exaggerated in this photograph, even small movements can be enough to ruin an otherwise perfect picture

cave photography – especially as there is little reliance on electronic technology. When all else fails, a photographer can keep working using open flash.

The limitations of automatic flash

Difficulties with automatic 'computer' flashguns have already been mentioned, in particular with overexposure of the subject if this is isolated from its surroundings and light is not reflected evenly from the whole scene. When using multiple flash there is also a problem of underexposure.

An automatic flashgun's sensor can detect light from any source, not just its own reflected light. If two flashes are fired at the same time each can detect the other's light and both flashes are quenched too early, underexposing the photograph. For this reason, manual flashguns are used for multiple flash photography.

There are, as always, exceptions to this rule. Using B, flashes can be fired at different times, or a delay built into the slave units might ensure that flashes do not trigger at precisely the same moment. Even so, the inherent difficulties of using automatic sensors means that multiple flash is more predictable with manual flashguns.

Flash interference

Exposure errors arise when the automatic sensor of one electronic flashgun detects the direct or reflected light of another flash.

In this example, flashgun (A) correctly detects light reflected from the subject but, in addition, receives direct light from flashgun (B), which is similarly affected. Both guns assume that all the light was reflected from the subject and, when a preset level has been received, quench their output too soon. The main subject of the photograph is therefore underexposed. When two or more electronic flashes are used, each flashgun must be set to manual.

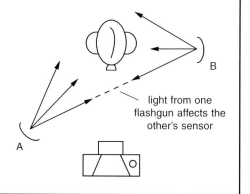

B

light from one flashgun affects the other's sensor

A

Obtaining even lighting

It is usual – though not a requirement – to light large areas of cave reasonably evenly; multiple flashes should not leave patchy pools of light surrounded by black rock.

A classic cave photograph depicts a large chamber with scattered flashes, or a line of cavers strung out down a long, straight passage. If the principles of using a single flash are understood, these multiple flash photographs are easy to produce.

Often, each flashgun in a multiple flash photograph is aimed at a different subject, whether this is another caver or area of wall. For even lighting, place each flashgun at the distance from its subject that is determined by its guide number: distance = guide number/aperture. With the shutter open on B (or using slave units), set off the guns at an agreed signal. The

Determining distance

Distances for individual flashes are determined using the formula:

$$\text{Distance} = \frac{\text{Guide number}}{\text{Aperture}}$$

For example, if a flashgun with a guide number of 30 lights the main subject 5m away, it requires an aperture of f5.6. A second flash with a guide number of 40 which is used to light the background must be placed at 40/5.6 = 7m away to give the same illumination. These distances are rounded off; the true answer would be 7.14m, but slight discrepancies will be masked by the film's exposure latitude.

first flash is often used as a signal to the other assistants; communication with the caver operating the nearest flash to the camera is normally easiest. Ensure the signal is clear and understandable. Multiple flash photographs take time to set up; wasting time and effort due to a lack of organisation is unwarranted.

Choose the aperture with care. Large chambers will probably require a wide aperture, perhaps f2.8 or f4. In passages the cavers and walls are often close together and, as each flash is relatively close to its subject, a smaller aperture is used. This is an advantage, as the increased depth of field keeps both distant and near objects in focus – a principle which applies to all multiple flash photographs.

As the flashes are lighting different areas the aperture is based on the most important flash: match the other flashgun distances to it. A change to the aperture is only required if two flashguns light the *same* area.

Given a choice, to produce even lighting a large number of 'normal' flashes are often preferable to one or two powerful flashguns, even though the combined light output of each option may be identical. One huge flash will overpower nearby areas while further parts of the scene remain underexposed. In fact, *any* flash will overexpose near objects and underexpose distant ones, but using too few high-intensity flashguns adds to the problem. Careful flashgun placement and a good choice of camera viewpoint are needed to control this effect. When trying to obtain even

Skeleton Cave, Oregon. By maintaining an equal distance between the cavers in the lava tube, each is correctly exposed. The relative power of the two main types of flash can be seen: the furthest caver has fired an electronic flash (E8), while the two nearer cavers have fired flashbulbs (B1, B1)

Multiple lighting positions

Place each flash at its correct distance from the next caver. Flashguns of similar power produce an even spacing between cavers. Take the distance to nearby walls or boulders into account to maintain consistent lighting. To help assign positions quickly and accurately, for commonly used apertures mark each flash with working distances.

The diagrams represent a passage and chamber. A hidden flash is fired at (A) and (B), helping to avoid a static, too-regular composition. Caver (C) is standing outside the picture area and is able to move during the exposure. Flashgun (D) backlights the caver (E) in the centre of the chamber. Some cavers are holding the flashgun to the side of the body to shield the camera from direct light.

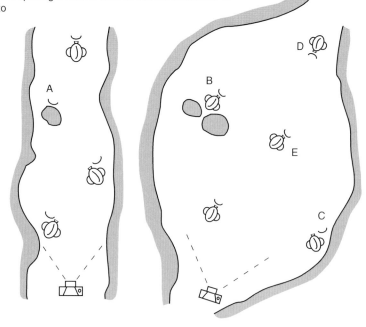

Below:
Buckeye Creek Cave in West Virginia (left: B1, B1, E8) and Old Illtydian's Chamber in Ogof Draenen (B2, B8, B1). Evenly spaced flashguns produce relatively even lighting; inevitably, areas nearest to the flashes are overexposed, but the main subjects (the cavers) are correctly exposed

Large scenes do not necessarily require flashes to be fired within the photograph. This picture, in Ogof Ffynnon Ddu, was lit with two bulbs (B8, B4)

lighting it is easier to avoid gross overexposure of the foreground by using an increased number of flashes of equivalent strength, rather than a few, more powerful guns.

This does not mean that every corner has to be lit, destroying the atmosphere of the cave. Patches of light are formed when too few flashguns are used, while too many produce an overlit scene without depth; strive for an effect which retains the mystery of the cave environment.

Even lighting depends, therefore, on placing flashguns to illuminate adjoining areas without their lights appreciably overlapping. If the distance between flashes is double the flash-to-subject distance any overlapping light will be negligible; closer flashes can be controlled with a judiciously placed hand as a shield.

In practical terms, there are no difficulties in determining the aperture. If earlier advice has been taken each gun is already marked with its guide number. Add a 'standard' distance and aperture to each gun, such as f5.6/5m. The aperture represents a common f-stop used with your flash/film combination, with a guide for the distance it must be placed at. The caver operating the flash knows exactly how far from the subject to stand. There is no limit to the number of flashguns which may be used, and organisational problems are minimised.

Cumulative flashes

Lighting the same area with a number of flashes, either fired at the same time or sequentially using B, increases the intensity of light. This can improve the depth of field or, when it is impossible to move the flash closer, balance the light in one area with a more powerful flash elsewhere in the picture.

For example, to balance lighting on a large stalagmite the lower portion might require one flash, with two more directed to the upper, more distant part. Fire an electronic flashgun, with its narrow beam of light, several times in different directions to simulate a wide spread of light, or change its position between flashes to cover a larger area and avoid a 'hot spot' forming in the centre.

In all these instances the lighting effects overlap. How do combined flashes affect aperture determination?

As might be expected, two identical flashes lighting the same area from the same position provide twice as much light. Each time the number of flashes is doubled in the sequence 1, 2, 4, 8 . . . the aperture is closed by one f-stop (the converse argument is also true: closing the aperture by one f-stop requires double the light – twice as many flashes). As an example, if one

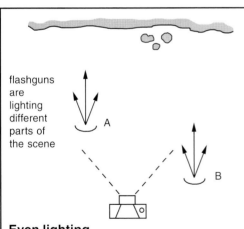

flashguns are lighting different parts of the scene

A

B

Even lighting

Consistent, even lighting with multiple flash requires care to balance the effects of one gun against another. This example shows two identically powered flashguns (A) and (B). The position of (A), as it lies within the picture, is fixed by the composition while (B) cannot be moved forward without intruding into the scene, but can be moved back to adjust its effective intensity; it can then be fired more than once to compensate for its greater distance from the subject and ensure even lighting.

Multiple flash

When several flashguns light the same area do one of the following:

- Change the aperture to match the number of flashes
- Change the number of flashes for a specific aperture
- Calculate a new guide number for a specified number of flashes

The last option is possible because multiple flashes lighting the same area are effectively the same as a single, more powerful flashgun. The table indicates the sequence: for two flashes multiply the guide number by 1.4, three flashes by 1.7, and double the original guide number for four flashes. Fired twice, a flashgun with a guide number of 30 has an effective guide number of $30 \times 1.4 = 42$

Changing aperture

Number of flashes	Close aperture by (f-stops)
1	0
2	1
4	2
8	3

Determining a new guide number for combined flashes

Number of flashes fired:	1	2	3	4	5
Multiply guide number by:	1	1.4	1.7	2	2.5

NB: This sequence assumes that identical flashes are fired from the same position

flash correctly exposes the scene at f4, an aperture of f5.6 requires two flashes and f8 requires four. The flashes are cumulative, and it makes no difference if they are fired together or at different times.

There is a proviso with this statement. Films can suffer from reciprocity, a reduction in sensitivity when exposures are extremely long or short (see p.162). Daylight in an entrance might introduce a long exposure, as does, theoretically, a series of flashes.

Exposure difficulties occur with flashguns of different power, when a variety of positions are involved, when light is reflected at an oblique angle towards the camera, and when flashes are not fully recharged before firing. When the lighting becomes complex, the simplest solution is to bracket the exposure. The practical chance of error (both in terms of exposure and possible movement within the picture) increases as more flashes are added: use the minimum required for the picture.

Working alone

Multiple flash techniques do not demand that several flashguns are used; a single gun can be repeatedly fired by one person. Using a tripod and B, it is possible to work alone.

The principle is simple: fire a flashgun once or several times, from one or several positions, then return to the camera and close the shutter. If the first flash produces a silhouette against a rock and the second flash, from a different position, lights the same rock, a ghost image will form. Lighting only part of the background introduces a truncated silhouette. However, with care the photographer can produce a series of silhouettes and appear several times in the same photograph.

The basic technique offers a number of possibilities. Hidden flash positions, or firing against a black background so that no light falls on

The left-hand caver's silhouette has been truncated because only part of it lies in front of a wall. Beware of this situation whether you are firing a flash several times while working alone, or cavers are firing a sequence of flashes, as here using three bulb flashes in Box Stone Mines

This lava tube in Skeleton Cave, Oregon, was lit using a single flashbulb fired by the caver in the foreground while the tripod-mounted camera shutter was locked open on B. The photographer then walked up the passage, firing an electronic flash approximately 30 times to build up a picture with foreground interest and a well-lit passage receding into the distance. The left-hand photograph illustrates the difficulties of this technique: it is easy to produce ghost images

Using one flashgun

Repeatedly firing a single flashgun, changing position between each flash, can produce an evenly lit photograph without showing a figure. Work away from the camera position, in this diagram from (A) to (E), so that a dim helmet light can be used. The technique is ideally suited to a solo photographer, using a tripod and open flash.

There are two possible objectives: to create a series of silhouettes, each outlined against its own background, or to produce an evenly lit passage with no figures appearing in the photograph; variations on this theme are possible, as illustrated above. In the second case, as in this diagram, flashes are directed to the opposite side of the passage (positions C and D) so that the photographer's silhouette falls on a black background and is not seen. The silhouette from (E) should fall against the black, continuing passage.

Careful planning is needed to avoid half-silhouettes or ghost figures, and in this diagram (and the top photograph) the photographer has made a mistake. Firing from (B), unsuccessfully trying to hide in an alcove, some light will spill onto the right-hand wall and leave a silhouette. This area has also been lit by the flash from (A), and a ghost image will form. To successfully hide figures the flashes must be completely shielded from nearby rocks.

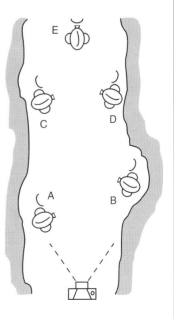

Working alone

When moving within the picture area:

- Use a tripod with the camera set on B
- Place a dim light behind the camera to help find the tripod in the dark
- Plan flash positions, equally spaced for even lighting, in advance
- To avoid ghosting do not allow light to spill onto the background
- Avoid part-silhouettes by firing from fully hidden positions
- Work away from the camera using a dimmed helmet light
- Show no light when returning to the camera
- Use a self-timer and slave units to increase versatility

the person, means that the photographer/model does not appear in the picture. Using the directional flash of an electronic gun and firing from alternate sides of a passage enables you to produce consistent, even lighting without leaving a silhouette. Hold the flash at arm's length (keeping the body between the flash and camera) to reduce the chance of light spilling from the flashgun back onto the body. Because each flash can be placed relatively close to its subject, the small aperture that can therefore be used increases the depth of field.

Moving while the shutter is open requires care. Working alone, move away from the camera using a weak helmet light. Do not shine it in one place for too long or a 'hot spot' or colour cast will appear in the picture and, to avoid light trails, never aim it towards the camera. Extinguish the light to return to the tripod. Leaving a weak light, such as a candle, behind the tripod helps find it again in the dark; kicking over a tripod-mounted camera is all too easy.

Working alone should not imply that all photographs have to be highly complex with multiple flash positions. It is equally valid to fire a single flash to create a silhouette, to side light a formation (perhaps with two flashes from different directions), or to use a self-timer to allow the photographer to appear in the picture with a flash on camera. Using a self-timer and a long shutter speed, it is viable to walk forward, listen for the shutter opening and fire the flash – without needing a slave unit to synchronise the shot. A helmet light presents no problems, and can be left on.

Even though these techniques can be carried out alone, an assistant is of great benefit, even if only to operate the cable release. If a thick cloth is draped over the lens between flashes the film cannot be affected by stray light and changing position is simplified as movement cannot leave a light trail: fire the flash, cover the lens, change position, uncover the lens, flash and repeat the sequence.

Working alone with a single flash to produce a silhouette, as here in West Kingsdale Master Cave (B1), is extremely easy

Shifting focus

Depth of field is often restricted in cave photography, preventing a nearby formation and a distant caver being in focus at the same time. The depth of field can be increased by shifting focus, even if there is no additional flash power available to allow the use of a smaller aperture.

Shifting focus is ideally suited to cave photography, where open flash is a standard technique. The principle is to focus and expose one part of the scene with a single flash, then refocus and light another subject; it is even possible to change the f-stop between flashes. Preplan the photograph; as the shutter will be open on B the focus must be reset manually using the scale marked on the lens. Focus on the first subject, fire the flash then,

Shifting focus

Two flashes were used to take this picture of Gnome Passage in Ogof Ffynnon Ddu. A 28mm lens was used to allow a close focus on the small stalagmites in the foreground, about 30cm away. These were lit with an electronic flash (E2). The distant figure of a caver (right) was lit with a flashbulb fired by a caver concealed within the photograph (B8), but even at a small aperture the figure was inevitably out of focus.

To keep both foreground and background sharp the focus was shifted between the two flashes. First, the focus was checked for both positions with the camera on a tripod. With the focus on the foreground and an aperture of f11 the shutter was opened on B in total darkness, and the first flash was fired. The lens was covered with cloth (so that light could not reach the film) before the lens was adjusted to f5.6 and focused on the background. The caver's light was turned on, the cloth removed and the final flash fired (below).

The enlarged area of the main photograph illustrates a defect in the technique. When the focus of a lens is altered

the size of objects is subtly changed; the distance from the lens and the amount of focal shift dictates how apparent the effect becomes. In this example, taken with the foreground lit before the background, the defect appears as a thin white band where the two areas meet. In colour photographs an unpleasant colour fringe can also form.

To eliminate or diminish the problem, avoid superimposing different parts of the scene and photograph the furthest subject before shifting focus to the nearest, producing a less obvious dark band.

covering the lens with a cloth, refocus the lens before removing the cloth and firing the second flash. The technique can produce stunning and, to the viewer, unexpected effects which are at their best when an 'impossible' depth of field (even greater than might be achieved with an ultra wide-angle lens) is attained.

Large chambers

Adequate photographs of large chambers can be lit using relatively few flashguns. The immense St David's Hall in Ogof Draenen has been lit with only three flashbulbs, each triggered by an infra-red slave unit.

The two foregound flashes were balanced with each other (B8, B2), and the right-hand caver was positioned so that no silhouette was produced. The distant caver (B2) was placed against a pile of boulders to produce a highlight area and avoid losing the figure against the background

Photographing a large chamber requires time and, sometimes, a faster film than normal plus enough flash power (for example, large bulbs) to handle the scene. Preplanning the shot is essential. Given the huge distances involved in some of the world's large chambers, slave units may not be sensitive or reliable enough, and it is common to resort to open flash. Communication is crucial: indicating precisely where a caver should stand and pose using whistled codes is difficult. Radios undoubtedly raise the success rate and speed up the operation.

It is easy to underestimate overhead distances so, if the roof is within the picture, bracket all exposures. To balance lighting it may be necessary to aim an additional flash upwards. This is normally better than opening the aperture to compensate for the flash-to-roof distance, as this would overexpose the foreground. Underexposure is more likely than over-exposure in large chambers, although overexposure of areas nearest the flash becomes more apparent.

Are you photographing the cave, or the cavers? Consider exactly what you are trying to portray: cavers in action, or cavers included purely for

scale. How will you arrange them? In regular rows, scattered evenly, or in concealment? A giant daylit entrance may push the exposure beyond the film's latitude, or prevent open flash. Take such pictures at dusk or night to combine flash with decreased amounts of available light: the velvet blue of dusk recorded on film or star trails over several hours' exposure are both spectacular sights.

Combining flash types

The different characteristics of bulb and electronic flash can be combined to produce striking, imaginative effects. With its greater power and spread of light a flashbulb is ideal as a backlight, and the long duration of the flash makes water appear to flow through the photograph. The narrow, directional beam of an electronic flash as a front or side light can pick out detail in the subject but retain dark edges to the picture, making the subject stand out amid dark rock. In cave photography the two effects can complement one another.

Because the electronic gun completes its short-duration flash before the flashbulb has begun to peak, the bulb is not detected by the electronic flashgun's sensor and its flash is unaffected. The combination of these flash types can add speed and accuracy to cave photography. In narrow passages or confined spaces, with plenty of nearby reflective surfaces, the front light's auto-sensor should give a correct exposure, while the backlight lifts the picture out of the ordinary. If two electronic flashguns are involved, the same effect can be achieved using slave units with an inbuilt delay which staggers the flashes.

A strong backlight from a flashbulb (left, B6) shows the scallops and flowing water in the Ogof Ffynnon Ddu streamway. Adding the directional light of an electronic flash (E1, B6), held at arm's length, has introduced detail to the figure and foreground without lighting the surrounding rock

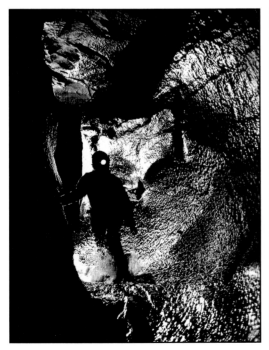
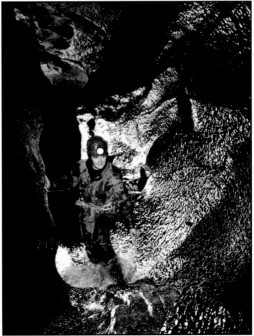

Building a picture by combining lights

Compare these photographs with the frontlit picture (top left: E1). A single flash can produce good detail, contrast and shadows by careful placing to the side of the subject (above: E2) or, for dramatic effects, as a backlight (top right: B5).

Combining a backlight and side light exploits the best features of each: an atmospheric photograph with detail in the subject is produced (right: E2, B5). Using a bulb retains the effect of flowing water.

Using a flashmeter

While guide numbers are perfectly adequate for calculating apertures, a flashmeter helps in complex or unusual situations where the exposure is critical. A flashmeter indicates extremely accurate f-stops and can measure separate flashes to adjust fill-in flash ratios. There is less need to bracket exposures and, therefore, less film is wasted.

The flashmeter's sensor is covered with a translucent dome which gathers light from a wide angle. Set the film speed, place the meter near the subject, point it at the camera (to read light from multiple sources; if there is a single flash involved, aim the meter at this), and fire the flashes to produce an *incident light* reading. The indicated aperture is extremely accurate as no account has to be taken of the subject's colour, tone, reflectance or how much of the picture's area it fills. A poorer alternative is to read *reflected light* by placing the meter at the camera position, aimed at the subject. This is far less accurate: stray light may strike the meter and, just as with exposure meters and automatic flashguns, the meter's assumptions about the scene may be incorrect.

Flashmeters measure the intensity of a flash and calculate the required aperture. Some designs link the meter to the flashgun with a cable intended for manually firing the flash in a studio; for caving use, choose a hand-held model without a cable. Nearly all meters are insensitive to the long-duration flash of a bulb, producing a reading which is too low. Others are oversensitive to infra-red light, which can confuse the meter if slave units are involved, or will not measure cumulative flashes fired at intervals during open flash techniques. All these factors should be considered before purchasing a meter.

A flashmeter can be helpful, but is not the answer to every problem. It is a useful tool, but is far from essential. Most cave photographers rely on their experience rather than adding a flashmeter to the equipment which must be carried, but in the right situation a meter is invaluable as an aid to determining exposure when multiple flashes are involved.

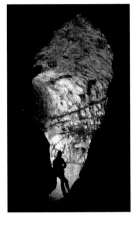

A flashmeter is of limited benefit when the picture is lit with a flashbulb, as here in Powell's Cave (E1, B6)

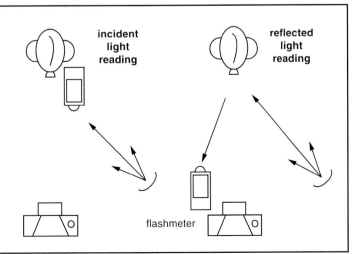

Using a flashmeter

Measure incident light with a flashmeter (left). Measuring reflected light is inaccurate because it is affected by the reflectance of the subject. Different readings can be produced by colour, tone and texture; shiny and wet surfaces reflect better than rough ones, which scatter and diffuse light in all directions. Reflected light readings commonly produce overexposed pictures.

incident light reading

reflected light reading

flashmeter

Flashmeters

- Help determine apertures in complex situations
- Separate flashes can be checked for fill-in flash ratios
- Measure incident light from the subject position
- Flashbulbs may give incorrect readings
- Metering with flashbulbs (if possible) is wasteful, but may reduce bracketing
- Backlighting effects are harder to assess than front or side lighting
- Some meter designs are unsuitable for open flash techniques
- Avoid meters with cable connections
- Meters may be sensitive to infra-red flashes and cause misreadings

translucent dome

film speed

Flashmeters do not need to be sophisticated. This simple model has detected a flash, indicating an aperture of between f8 and f11

Fill-in flash

Fill-in flash uses two or more sources of light which complement each other, reducing contrast by 'filling in' areas of deep shadow created by the main flash. For example, side lighting a caver's face or stalactite produces a harsh image, with a totally black shadow. By adding a second, less powerful flash on the opposite side the shadows are given detail without producing a 'flat' light.

In photographic jargon the main light is provided by the key flash, while the weaker light is the fill-in flash. At its simplest, each flash only lights a single area: the flashes do not appreciably overlap. The aperture is calculated using the key flash alone and the fill-in flash is controlled to complement it.

This is the crucial point of fill-in flash: the subsidiary flash is adjusted to match the aperture defined by the key flash. It is using a flash exposure guide in reverse: instead of the flash controlling the aperture, the aperture dictates the flashgun's intensity.

The balance of flash intensities introduces the concept of lighting ratios – the ratio between the effects of the two flashes. If two identical flashguns are placed at the same distance on either side of a subject, the lighting is extremely even: shadows are eliminated but the picture lacks depth and the effect is unexciting. The lighting ratio is 1:1.

A weaker secondary flash produces a better effect. If the fill-in flash is placed further away, or is of lower power, its effects are diminished. When the fill-in flash has half the intensity of the key flash, the lighting ratio is 1:2; with a quarter intensity the ratio is 1:4, and so on. In practical terms this means that the aperture is calculated for the key flash and, to produce a ratio of 1:2 or 1:4, the fill-in flash is positioned to provide one or two f-stops lower illumination respectively. Technically, the shadow areas are underexposed, but the fill-in flash adds enough light to dispel dense shadows and remove the harsh effects of directional lighting.

The key light for this caver in Old Ham Iron Mine came from the right (B3), and was balanced by two weaker fill-in flashes (E8, E6)

E8

E3

Fill-in flash

Fill-in flash helps to dispel heavy shadows and add detail to an otherwise harshly lit subject. Two flashes (E8, E3) were used in this series of photographs, taken at f8.

Individually, these flashes produced the effects in the upper photographs. When both flashes are fired at an equal distance the lighting ratio is 1:1 – they have an equal effect and produce balanced lighting but a picture which lacks interest (far left). The flash from E8 was then fired from a greater distance, corresponding to one f-stop less light;

this gives a ratio of 1:2 (centre). Finally, the flash intensity was decreased again to produce a ratio of 1:4 (bottom right).

There is no 'correct' fill-in flash ratio but some ratios are considered to appear more pleasing than others. Compared with the upper right-hand photograph, where there is no detail in the shadows, ratios of 1:2 or 1:4 are likely to be the most acceptable. If a backlight is added this should lie between a quarter and twice the power of the key flash (a ratio in the range of 1:4 to 2:1).

The streamway in Salubrious Passage in Ogof Ffynnon Ddu presented this photographic opportunity. Two flashes were balanced to give a ratio of 2:1. The backlight (B5) is brighter than the frontlight (E8), which was held at arm's length below the level of the camera. The relative effects of the flashes can be best seen on the caver's right shoulder

Fill-in flash distances

Produce a table of fill-in flash distances which matches your flashgun, film and working techniques. This example (with distances rounded off to one decimal place) gives the fill-in flash distance in metres for a gun with a guide number of 30 with ISO 100 film.

Similar tables can easily be constructed. For a ratio of 1:1 (the top row) use the distance = guide number/aperture formula. Follow the pattern to insert the other distances, or calculate each row using one f-stop smaller aperture for each successive ratio.

To use the table:
1. Determine the aperture, dictated by the key flash
2. Choose a fill-in flash lighting ratio
3. Read the fill-in flash-to-subject distance in metres

Aperture		f2.8	f4	f5.6	f8	f11	f16
Ratio	**1:1**	10.7	7.5	5.4	3.7	2.7	1.9
	1:2	15.0	10.7	7.5	5.4	3.7	2.7
	1:4	21.5	15.0	10.7	7.5	5.4	3.7

Controlling fill-in flash

There are several ways of controlling the intensity of the fill-in flash so that it matches the required aperture and lighting ratio.

As the light from the key flash would interfere with the auto-sensor of the fill-in flash, automatic systems are not appropriate. However, some electronic flashguns have a variable power control: half power gives half the light and a ratio of 1:2, a quarter power gives 1:4, and so on.

By increasing the fill-in flash-to-subject distance the flashgun's effect decreases and a precise lighting ratio can be obtained. How far away should the flash be placed to obtain the chosen lighting ratio? While there cannot be a definitive answer (the distance depends on the required lighting ratio and the aperture fixed and controlled by the key flash), there is an excellent rule of thumb.

Remember the sequence: a ratio of 1:1 produces even, flat lighting; half the fill-in light is needed for a ratio of 1:2, a quarter for 1:4. It is the same sequence used for aperture settings: each time the aperture is closed by one f-stop, half the light reaches the film. With a starting point of f4 and given a fixed intensity of light from the flash, half the light passes through the aperture at f5.6, a quarter at f8, an eighth at f11; the sequence continues down the f-stop scale. In effect, this scale – marked on every SLR camera – can be used to determine the fill-in flash distance by translating the f-stops into distances.

The scallops on these walls in Ogof Ffynnon Ddu (E8, B5) show up particularly well because the lighting ratio of 2:1, with the backlight brighter than the front light, adds relief

As an example, suppose the key flash requires an aperture of f5.6 and the fill-in flash would correctly expose the film (and give a ratio of 1:1) at this aperture at a distance of 4m. Moving the fill-in flash to 5.6m gives a ratio of 1:2 and 8m gives 1:4. The units are not important: centimetres, feet, inches or any other system is valid. If a flash at 8ft gives a correct

---

A distance/aperture tip

The aperture (f-stop) scale on a lens runs, typically: f2.8, 4, 5.6, 8, 11, 16 (with further apertures at each end of the scale). This scale can be converted to flash-to-subject distances for placing a flash.

Each ascending number represents half the amount of light admitted to the lens. Converting the apertures to flash-to-subject distances means that each distance (in feet, metres or any other unit of measurement) gives half the illumination. A flash moved from 2.8m to 4m has half the intensity, and at 5.6m has a quarter of the original intensity. A flash moved from 11ft to 8ft has double the intensity.

In this example, changes in the flash-to-subject distance require corresponding alterations to the aperture. If a distance of 4m produces a correct exposure at f8, 5.6m requires a one f-stop wider aperture of f5.6 (or, with the aperture left at f8, produces a fill-in flash lighting ratio of 1:2).

Use this sequence to quickly match the flash-to-subject distance (for either a fill-in flash or main flash) with a fixed aperture. If a main flash determines the aperture, other flashes must be placed at the correct distance to provide light at a corresponding intensity.

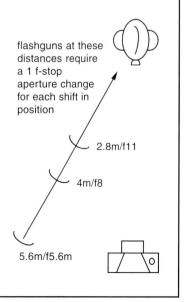

flashguns at these distances require a 1 f-stop aperture change for each shift in position

2.8m/f11

4m/f8

5.6m/f5.6

Fill-in flash ratios

A meter reading was taken from the vegetation outside this disused silica mine and used for the initial exposure, without fill-in flash (1). The result is a 'correct' exposure with dense shadows within the mine and little depth.

By deliberately overexposing the vegetation, in photograph (2) more of the rocks and walls in the entrance are brought within the film's exposure range and the exterior appears brighter: the picture takes on more mood and atmosphere.

Adding a fill-in flash provides detail in shadow areas. The flash was fired from the same position (E2) in each picture. Because it was a fixed-intensity flashgun and as, obviously, the intensity of daylight could not be altered, the aperture and shutter speed had to be adjusted to produce the different lighting ratios. By using a slower shutter speed the brightness of the exterior and the reflections on the rocks could be changed, as in photograph (2), but, to make the fill-in flash effects more obvious in these examples, the daylight was kept at a constant and only the fill-in flash effects were adjusted in photographs (3) to (5).

In picture (3) a ratio of 1:1 was achieved using a shutter speed of 1/60 second at f4. However, the same daylight exposure could have been produced using a shutter speed of 1/30 second at f5.6 (see p.72). This also reduces the fill-in flash by half to give a lighting ratio of 1:2; the result is seen in picture (4). The final example, (5), was made using a shutter speed of 1/15 second at f8, producing a lighting ratio of 1:4.

None of these exposures is more 'correct' than any other; each produces a different effect and, additionally, many other combinations of ambient and fill-in flash are possible. A good balance between daylight and fill-in flash is normally considered to be a ratio of about 1:2.

exposure and a ratio of 1:1, 11ft gives 1:2 and 16ft gives 1:4. It is a highly useful technique and an easy sequence to remember.

For fill-in flash set all flashguns to manual, determine the aperture according to the key flash, and adjust the fill-in light's distance to suit the chosen lighting ratio.

Fill-in flash in entrances

When fill-in flash is balanced with daylight, rather than a second flashgun, the technique is sometimes referred to as synchro-sunlight. This is essentially the same as using two flashes.

The intensity of daylight streaming through an entrance cannot be controlled. However, exposures for this key light (taking the place of the key flash) depend on both the aperture and shutter speed: by changing the shutter speed a suitable aperture can be selected which allows the fill-in flash to be effective. The only requirement is that the shutter speed

An abandoned crane in the Cliftworks, Box Stone Mines (E8, B6). The effect of distance on lighting ratios is clear: while the caver is lit with a ratio of about 1:2, the roof near the flashbulb has been overlit in comparison with the shadow of the crane. It is important to consider relative distances to different parts of the scene if precise lighting ratios are required, and compromises may be necessary

Ogof Dan-y-Lleuad Wen (E8, B6). In this photograph the main lighting is from the front, while the stronger backlight (at a 2:1 ratio) has produced highlights and picked out edge details. Its effects can be seen on the roof above the caver's head and along his arm

must synchronise with the flashgun. This normally means using a speed of 1/60 second or slower for electronic flash or 1/30 second or slower for flashbulbs. With intense daylight this creates a problem, in that a faster shutter speed cannot be used and thus a small aperture is required. This may be so small that the fill-in flash cannot be positioned without intruding into the photograph, or it may be beyond the scope of the lens.

For example, the intensity of daylight dictates an exposure of f11 at 1/60 second, the minimum normally used to obtain flash synchronisation. For a flashgun with a guide number of 30, the fill-in flash-to-subject distance is only 3.7m for a lighting ratio of 1:2, or 5.4m away for a ratio of 1:4. Depending on the circumstances, this may require a change in composition to accommodate the flash position, or the photographer will have to wait for clouds to cover the sky or dusk to fall.

Fill-in flash techniques, of whatever nature, are not as complicated as they may, at first, appear. Remember that, to retain atmosphere, shadow details should be revealed with care rather than allowing additional flashes to overpower the picture with light.

Both in entrances and underground it is possible to take good cave photographs without using fill-in flash but, when the situation demands it, fill-in flash is a useful technique to have mastered. It is, in effect, a form of contrast control, bringing the ratio between highlights and shadows within a recordable range. Poorly used, fill-in flash can produce truly awful results. Used well, with discretion, the effect is superb.

Conclusion

Although multiple flash techniques give a wide range of freedom in placing and combining lights, it is wise to restrict the number of flashes. It is sometimes enough to know what the pitfalls are; by being aware of these, most of the difficulties in using multiple flash can be avoided.

Use flashguns with subtlety; it is surprising how many successful pictures are made using only one or two flashes. Because a number of guns are available this does not mean that all of them must be used in every photograph. As is often the case, the photographer must find a balance between what is viable in the time and under the conditions which are encountered, against the perceived ideal. A simple composition and arrangement of light is invariably the easiest to predict and control.

Chapter seven
CLOSE-UP AND MACRO PHOTOGRAPHY

'There,' the archaeologist said. 'Photograph that for me.'

I could only see a jumble of stone-filled mud. 'Photograph what?' I asked.

A finger poked downwards. Partly obscured, a tiny, curved bone smaller than a fingernail clipping lay at the side of the path. 'It's a shrew's rib,' he said.

I looked at my wide-angle lens, then back at the mud. I hadn't expected remains the size of shrew's ribs when agreeing to photograph 'some old bones' for the museum.

Charterhouse Warren Farm Swallet

C AVES are filled with a stunning array of formations and patterns. Straw stalactites end in miniature crystal worlds enclosed in a droplet of water, rocks and sediments carry intricate patterns and, if the time is taken to search it out, many caves are found to support a rich variety of fauna. Most cave photographers concentrate only upon large subjects – cave passages and huge stalagmites – yet an excursion into close-up and macro photography is well worthwhile. Added to this, because it is so predictable, close-up photography is arguably the easiest branch of cave photography to tackle.

This chapter focuses on close-up techniques which can be applied to cave photography, together with two related subjects which include close-up photography: archaeology and cave life.

Definitions

By definition, close-up photography begins with subjects too close to the camera to allow a 'normal' lens to focus, and spans from approximately one-tenth life-size (×0.1) to life-size (×1, also expressed as 1:1) images. Beyond this point a larger than life image is produced; macro photography records images between life-size and ten-times life-size (×10). Photomicrography overlaps with but extends beyond this range, and is beyond the scope of this manual.

Close-up photography is therefore concerned with images on film which are smaller than reality, and macro photography when the image is larger than life. In each case it is the image size *on film* which is important; a print can be made any size, but it cannot

This picture of cave pearls in Ogof Draenen (E8) is defined as close-up as the image on film is less than life-size

Determining magnification

There are two forms of magnification: magnification on film and after production of a print, for example a photograph taken from a negative. Ensure all records note *which* form of magnification is quoted, a common failing. It is usual to quote the magnification on film, as the data can be used to calculate different reproduction sizes. The formula is:

$$\text{magnification} = \frac{\underline{\text{image length}}}{\text{actual length}}$$

Magnification on film
Measure the length of the scene and the long axis of the film (36mm for 35mm format, 55mm for 120 roll film), *or* the specimen's actual length (which may not fill the frame) and the length of the specimen on film.

For example, if a 35mm camera can focus on 70mm of a ruler's scale, this produces a magnification of 36/70 = ×0.5 (results can be rounded off).

Magnification in print
Measure the image length on the negative (actual length) and in the finished print (image length). This magnification represents the enlargement from the film's image. Multiply by the magnification on film to find the total magnification compared with the specimen.

For example, the image on film at a magnification of ×0.5 is 30mm long, but is 180mm long in a printed photograph. The final magnification compared with the specimen is:
$$180/30 \times 0.5 = \times 3$$

reveal detail which is not present in the negative. If the size of the subject is known this can be compared to the image to determine its magnification. It is therefore important to note the specimen size (or to read the magnification directly from a macro lens). Make the record clear: does it refer to magnification on film or in print? Ensure the former is *always* recorded.

As the photographic techniques are often identical, the term 'close-up photography' is commonly used to describe *any* photography of small objects, whatever the subject; that generalisation is used in this chapter to cover all magnifications.

EQUIPMENT

Lenses are restricted to a limited range of magnifications by their design. To enter the realm of close-up and macro photography, specialist cameras, lenses or supplementary equipment is needed. These include close-up lens attachments, a lens reverser, extension tubes and bellows. Some are more suitable than others for specific magnifications, although the photographic techniques remain substantially the same.

Cameras

Different approaches are required with compact (rangefinder) and SLR cameras. As the viewfinder is physically separated from the lens in a compact camera, the photographer sees a slightly different view from the image which reaches the film; the effect is termed parallax. This makes little difference when photographing distant objects, but nearby subjects may cause suffer gross errors in composition. The only solution is a tripod

Not all photographs of formations and cave features have to be taken using special equipment. This picture, of mud splashes in Ogof Draenen (E8), was taken using a 35mm lens at close focus. Close-up lenses are also ideal for subjects which do not demand high magnifications

and careful measurements using a tape measure – a cumbersome and unnecessary technique.

On the other hand, images on the film and in an SLR viewfinder are identical as the scene is viewed through the lens using a prism and mirror. Problems with close-up photography are substantially reduced, and this chapter concentrates on the use of an SLR camera.

Many SLR cameras have interchangeable focusing screens. A 'standard' screen is usually patterned to aid focusing on distant objects but, at high magnifications, this is intrusive. Change to a specialist close-up screen if this will be a major part of your work. How necessary this is depends on the screen's availability for your camera, your commitment to close-up photography, and how difficult you find focusing with a standard screen.

Close-up lenses

Close-up lens attachments are fitted like filters. They increase magnification without requiring a change in exposure

Close-up lenses (often referred to as close-up filters) are screwed onto the front of a normal lens and magnify the image. They are cheap, easy to fit and small enough to carry in case they are required. In addition, no exposure adjustment is involved and adding a close-up attachment does not involve removing the camera lens, which avoids the possibility of dirt and water entering the camera. These are all advantages over other methods of close-focusing (extension tubes, bellows or specialist macro lenses).

However, the quality of the resulting image is often low. Manufacturers make camera lenses to give the best definition possible; adding a piece of shaped glass to the front can introduce

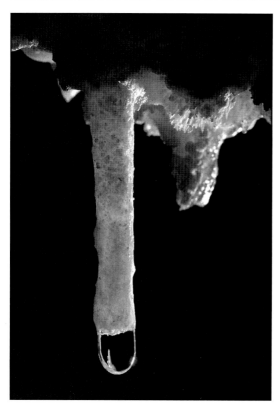

Straw stalactite, Ogof
Pasg (E3, with reflector)

serious distortions. Only use good grade close-up lenses; crude engineering will inevitably cause a loss in photographic quality.

Close-up lens attachments are usually available in three strengths of +1, +2 and +3 diopters. Uncommonly, some makes are measured in focal lengths; a +1 diopter lens has a focal length of 1m, and so on. A +3 diopter lens is strongest (has the greatest degree of enlargement), the exact magnification relating to the focal length of the lens it is attached to. This is not normally more than about one-third life-size (×0.3), which means that subjects smaller than about 10cm long cannot fill the frame.

Stacking close-up lenses on top of each other increases the magnification but, while this technique works, it is not recommended as the quality of the photograph inevitably suffers, particularly towards the edges of the picture. If you are forced to follow this path, place the strongest diopter lens closest to the camera lens and use a small aperture so that, effectively, the image is formed by the centre of the lens. The quality of magnifications greater than ×0.4 is unlikely to be acceptable. Close-up lenses are ideal for occasional or unexpected use, but are not recommended for serious close-up photography.

Lens reversers

Set at infinity, a lens focuses light from distant objects onto the film, which is close to the rear element of the lens. By using an adaptor to reverse the lens – literally, so that the rear element is aimed at the subject – light is focused from a near distance onto the film to produce a life-size magnification. The disadvantages are that the lens element is unprotected, the aperture control is no longer linked to the camera body unless additional equipment (a Z-ring) is used, and magnification is restricted to around life-size. Although a lens reverser is cheap, it is not suitable for cave photography.

Extension tubes and bellows

When a lens is moved away from the film, the image is magnified; this is why a lens moves outwards as it is focused on a nearby object. Anything increasing the distance between the lens and camera will, therefore, increase magnification without involving an additional lens: greater distances produce higher magnifications.

There is a direct relationship between the length of the extension and the focal length of the lens: magnification = extension/focal length.

Increasing magnification

Increasing the distance between the lens and film has the effect of increasing the magnification of the image. Extension tubes (above) offer a low cost, reliable solution; here, two tubes of the set are fitted to the camera with the third lying down on the left.

Bellows (above) allow greater magnification than extension tubes, but are less robust. Lens reversers (left) leave the main lens element unprotected.

A 50mm lens mounted on a 50mm extension produces a life-size reproduction on film; a 50mm lens with a 25mm extension produces a half-life-size magnification. This means that a 35mm lens only requires an extension of 35mm for life-size reproduction. With an extension of 50mm it is well into the range of macro photography; whenever the extension is longer than the focal length of the lens, the magnification is greater than life-size. As always, there is a trade-off. As magnification increases, more light is required for a correct exposure and compensations are necessary.

Extension tubes form, effectively, a hollow pipe which fits between the lens and camera. Like supplementary close-up lenses, tubes are normally made in sets of three (for example, 10mm, 18mm and 28mm long; other sets vary considerably). However, unlike close-up lenses there is no loss of photographic quality if tubes are stacked to obtain a greater magnification. They may be manual or automatic, depending on whether the camera can still operate the lens aperture; auto tubes are obviously preferable.

Bellows perform the same function as extension tubes, with a greater possible magnification (the bellows 'tube' is longer than a stacked set of extension tubes). They also permit mid-points of magnification, as the concertina-like

Close-up photography equipment

- An SLR is preferable to a compact camera
- By preference, use a macro lens or extension tubes
- Use electronic flash

Points to consider:

- Supplementary close-up lenses are useful for some situations
- Dedicated flash automatically adjusts for exposure variations
- A macro lens with a focal length greater than 50mm increases the lens-to-subject distance
- A specialist close-up focusing screen aids focusing at high magnification

bellows are infinitely variable in length between the maximum and minimum limits. Mounted on a tripod, a racking system moves the camera and lens into a perfect position with respect to the subject. Against this, bellows are less robust, more expensive, and physically larger than tubes.

Extension tubes or a macro lens are considered the most suitable for cave photography.

Macro lenses

Although many lenses are advertised for macro use, few attain a true life-size magnification; most focus to half life-size at best, and need an extension tube or supplementary lens to extend the range. The majority of macro lenses are 50mm focal length, although 90mm and longer lenses are available (shorter focal length macro lenses give greater magnification but are even more specialist).

Assuming the same magnification, longer focal length lenses focus further away from the subject. This is highly useful as there is less risk to fragile speleothems, living specimens are not disturbed, and there is less chance of the flash casting a shadow of the lens into the picture. A long focal length macro lens therefore gives more room for manoeuvring, but is larger and weighs more than short focal length lenses or extension tubes; it should not be considered essential.

Macro lenses carry a scale indicating the magnification in use

Flashguns

Setting up a tripod for an accurately aligned photograph is slow and cumbersome, and it is customary to hand-hold the camera. Some camera shake is inevitable, but a short-duration electronic flash freezes movement and produces a sharp picture. Slave units are unnecessary, as the flash-to-camera distance is short enough to allow a cable connection with the flash firing at an angle to the subject.

Normally, manual flashguns are used. As only short flash-to-subject distances are involved a small electronic gun is powerful enough and gives a small aperture with a good depth of field. Automatic flashguns can introduce errors into close-up exposures, just as they do when shooting 'normal' pictures. However, a dedicated flash system (where the flash sensor measures light entering the lens, rather than light reflected to the flashgun) confers extremely accurate exposures at any magnification and, when the subject fills the picture, removes guesswork and additional exposure calculations.

BASIC TECHNIQUES

Many of the principles of 'normal' cave photography apply to close-up work. However, at close range some difficulties diminish (such as the problem of humidity; there is less air between the camera and subject to interfere with clarity of the image), while others increase. This section considers those difficulties peculiar to close-up photography, together with specific underground techniques.

Beaded helictites in Silent
Splendor, Cave of the
Winds, Colorado (E4)

Straw stalactite with
secondary crystal growth,
Ogof Craig a Ffynnon (E8,
with reflectors)

Depth of field

The depth of field is the zone of focus in front of and behind the subject; these zones are roughly equal in close-up photography. The actual distance depends on the aperture and magnification of the image. The following examples assume the use of 35mm film, but the same arguments (though not the specific measurements) also apply to other formats.

Depth of field for 35mm format film

Magnification	f5.6	f8	f11	f16	f22
×0.1	36	52	72	106	148
×0.25	7	10	13	19	26
×0.5	2	3	4	6	8
×0.75	1	1.5	2	3	4
×1 0.7	1	1.3	2	2.7	3
×2 0.25	0.36	0.5	0.7	1	1.3

- Measurements are given in mm. To convert to inches, divide by 25
- The depth of field extends roughly half in front of and half behind the area of sharpest focus

Modifying the aperture

To obtain a smaller aperture, and therefore increase the depth of field, strip down an old lens and shorten the pin controlling the diaphragm stop. At high enlargements, for example ×10, the resolution of the photograph (the ability to record two distinct points in the image, rather than merging them into one) will become increasingly unacceptable. Further theory on the subject will be found in standard photographic texts. If you choose to experiment, determine the new f-stop using the formula:

$$f\text{-stop} = \frac{\text{film-to-diaphragm distance}}{\text{diameter of aperture}}$$

High magnifications and wide apertures produce a shallow depth of field; decreasing magnification or closing the aperture to a smaller f-stop increases the depth. Even so, there is less than 2mm depth of field in a life-size photograph taken at f16.

It is often said that wide-angle lenses produce a greater depth of field than standard or telephoto lenses. This is supposedly one reason why a 35mm lens is more popular than a 50mm lens for cave photography, where wide apertures and a shallow depth of field are common. However, a greater depth of field is only gained by including more of the scene in the photograph; if the camera is moved closer to the subject to obtain the same magnification, the depth of field remains constant.

The same situation is true for close-up photography: as magnification increases, the depth of field decreases, whatever the lens. In fact, there are some theoretical errors in this statement, but in practical terms these can be ignored. A 50mm lens, either a true macro lens or one on extension tubes, gives no advantage in depth of field compared with a 90mm lens (it is a common misconception that wider macro lenses produce a greater depth of field). The depth of field depends *only* upon aperture and magnification.

Determining exposure

Exposures are always based on the film's speed. For close-up work there is no difficulty in providing a high-intensity flash (as the flash will always be close to the subject), and hence the greater definition and colour saturation of slow (ISO 50) films are prefered.

The exposure with a supplementary close-up lens is determined by the flash-to-subject distance alone; no exposure compensation is needed. However, the increased magnification obtained with extension tubes, bellows or a macro lens results in a loss of light reaching the film and this

Determining the flash-to-subject distance

A theoretical determination of the flash-to-subject distance uses the image magnification and flash guide number for the film speed involved.

Example

A 50mm lens is fitted to a full set of extension tubes (50mm), enabling 36mm of ruler to be seen in the viewfinder – a life-size image with a magnification of ×1. The flashgun has a guide number of 28; always use the smallest aperture, in this case f22. The guide number is in metres; the answer is given in centimetres.

flash-to-subject distance =

$$\frac{\text{guide number} \times 100}{\text{f-stop} \times (\text{magnification} + 1)}$$

$$= \frac{28 \times 100}{22 \times (1 + 1)} = 64$$

Thus, the flash-to-subject distance = 64cm

must be balanced by an increase in exposure; at a magnification of 1:1 up to two f-stops of light are lost.

There are four ways of controlling the exposure: changing the aperture, adjusting the power of the flashgun, using dedicated flash (which makes automatic adjustments of light output based on light received through the lens or reflected from the film), and altering the flash-to-subject distance. Even at f16 the depth of field is slight and therefore the smallest aperture should always be used, so the first option is unacceptable.

Some flashguns have a variable power control which allow half, quarter or lower intensity settings. To find the right setting fix the flash relative to the camera and take a series of test pictures, altering the power for each, and choose the best exposure for future use.

Dedicated flash systems are matched to a specific camera because the auto-sensor is built into the camera body and measures light entering the lens, rather than what is reflected to the flashgun. The system is extremely accurate as exposure variations due to changes in magnification are automatically taken into account. When the subject fills the frame this is an ideal, fast solution, but in other cases – for example, a stalactite tip surrounded by space – an alteration to the exposure is needed; base initial experiments on a –1 or –2 f-stop exposure compensation on the camera.

Using a manual flashgun with an experimentally predetermined flash-to-subject distance is a cheap and reliable method of beginning close-up photography. The principle is simple: when higher magnifications require more light, the flash is moved closer to the subject. Effectively, with a fixed aperture and flashgun power, magnification is directly related to the flash-to-subject distance.

Although flash-to-subject distance tables can be constructed, there is a wide range of equipment in use. Lenses of various focal lengths may be matched with differing combinations of extension tubes, and it is more useful to understand the parameters involved and produce your own, accurate exposure table for your own equipment.

The correct flash-to-subject distance can be found using the image magnification or by making an experimental series of exposures.

Macro lenses are engraved with their magnification, but extension tubes require a different approach. The magnification can be related to the extension and focal length of the lens (see pp.126–7). As a practical exercise, use each separate extension tube (or variations in a bellows' extension) and focus the lens on a ruler placed parallel to the film's longest edge. Note the number of millimetres seen in the viewfinder. Although

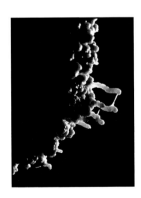

Rimlit helictites in Whisker Cave (E4)

the viewfinder does not show the complete picture (there is always some cut-off around the edges), this is accurate enough for the calculation. The long axis of 35mm film measures 36mm, so when a distance of 36mm is seen on the ruler the magnification is life-size (×1). If the viewfinder covers 72mm, the image is half life-size (×0.5). The formula is:

$$\text{magnification} = \frac{36}{\text{length of ruler in mm}}$$

Using the smallest f-stop and a guide number in metres, giving an answer in centimetres, magnification is related to the flash-to-subject distance using the formula:

$$\text{flash-to-subject distance} = \frac{\text{guide number} \times 100}{\text{f-stop} \times (\text{magnification} + 1)}$$

Each combination of extension tube and lens produces a different result; mark the flash-to-subject distance on the tube. Tie a piece of string to the flashgun, with knots at the relevant distances for each magnification, to quickly measure the flash-to-subject distance in the cave.

A practical approach can be more accurate as it takes into account all factors of equipment and technique. The system is calibrated by running a test series of exposures.

The experiment can be completed in the cave or at home, using a suitable subject such as an upright, light-coloured pencil (to represent a straw stalactite) or pieces of limestone (to represent a cave wall). Standardise the flash set-up, such as a single hand-held flash or twin flashes fixed either side of the lens. It should be possible to change the flash-to-subject distance and angle of any bracket-mounted flash to suit different apertures and whether the camera is held upright or horizontal.

Using a life-size magnification and the smallest aperture, probably f16 or f22, take a series of photographs with the flash distance altered in increments of one or two centimetres either side of the theoretical starting point. Use slide film, rather than negative film, as it is easier to assess the exposure errors.

Note the flash-to-subject distance for each photograph, and after processing select the best slide: this gives the distance for life-size photography. If all the slides are overexposed the flashgun is too close, and if underexposed it is too far away. If both over- and underexposed pictures are produced the incremental distances are too widely spaced; in each case, repeat the series. If the slides are overexposed move the flashgun further away, or reduce its output by covering the gun with white,

Film speed and guide number

To determine the flash-to-subject distance in close-up photography the guide number *must* be for the correct film speed. A convenient rule of thumb is to multiply the guide number by 1.4 each time the ISO is doubled (see p.78). To convert a guide number to a different film speed precisely, for example ISO 50 instead of ISO 100, the formula is:

$$\text{new guide number} =$$

$$\text{old guide number} \times \sqrt{\frac{\text{new film speed}}{\text{old film speed}}}$$

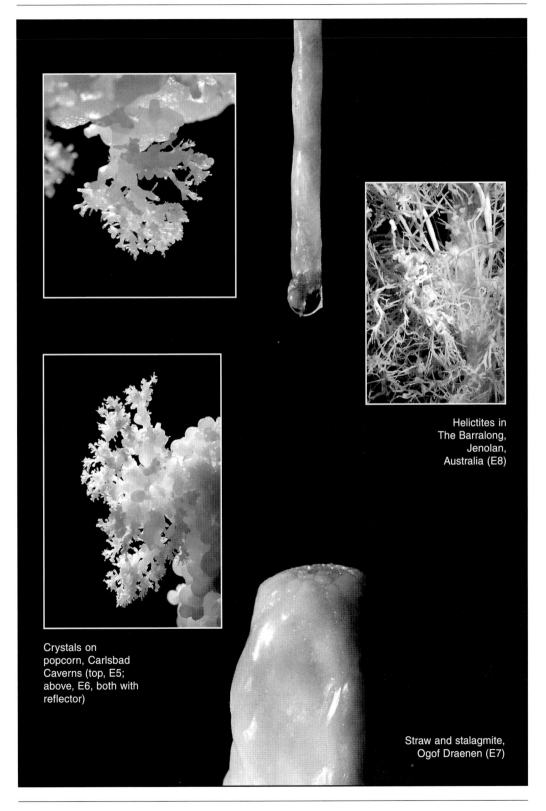

Crystals on
popcorn, Carlsbad
Caverns (top, E5;
above, E6, both with
reflector)

Helictites in
The Barralong,
Jenolan,
Australia (E8)

Straw and stalagmite,
Ogof Draenen (E7)

Exposure determination

Exposure for close-up photography can be controlled by: changing the flash intensity, using a dedicated flashgun, or altering the flash-to-subject distance. Always use the smallest aperture to maintain the greatest depth of field.

1. Changing the flash intensity

- Fix the position of the flashgun relative to the camera
- Make a test series of pictures, varying the flashgun power
- Select the best exposure and use this power setting

Advantage: flashgun is conveniently placed and set-up is accurate for most magnifications
Disadvantage: flashgun may not have a variable power control

2. Using dedicated flash

- Subjects filling the frame are accurately exposed
- Viewfinder warnings of incorrect exposures are given

Advantage: exposures are automatically calculated at any magnification
Disadvantage: an exposure correction may be required

3. Changing flash-to-subject distance

- Select equipment for life-size reproduction
- Take a series of pictures, varying the flash-to-subject distance
- Select the best exposure and note the distance
- Fix the angle of flash relative to the camera and subject, ensuring the direction, angle and distance are correct

Advantage: set-up is accurate for most magnifications
Disadvantage: flash position may not be ideal for hand-holding; a bracket or assistant may be required. New magnifications may require recalculation and altering the 'fixed' flash position

translucent material such as plastic tracing paper or thin cloth. Light can also be reduced with a neutral density filter on the lens, but this is not recommended as it darkens the viewfinder image and makes composition and focusing harder.

The exposure test series carries an unseen benefit. Technically, the test should be repeated for any lens, flash and magnification: each new magnification requires a separate exposure correction. However, a wide range of magnifications can be photographed without difficulty if the flash is kept at approximately the same position relative to the camera.

A life-size magnification was used for the test series as this also represents the closest camera-to-subject distance (and therefore, if the flash position is fixed relative to the camera, the closest flash-to-subject). Lower magnifications require less exposure correction, but also move the camera further from the subject and this increases the flash-to-subject distance. For all practical purposes, over the range of magnifications involved in close-up photography, the factors of camera-to-subject distance and magnification balance out. Less light is required for the lower magnification, and the more distant flash conveniently delivers less light. Once the camera and flash set-up is standardised, exposures for close-up photography are straightforward.

Exposure compensation in close-up

Decreasing the magnification from life-size to half life-size is achieved by moving the camera further from the subject, as shown in the diagram, and then refocusing. If the flash position relative to the camera remains the same, the flash-to-subject distance is also increased. In practical terms, over the range of magnifications commonly used in close-up photography, these factors balance out and no alteration to exposure is required with a manual flashgun.

The straw stalactites in Ogof Draenen were photographed at half life-size using a macro lens and an electronic flash fired behind and below the subject (E5). If the magnification remains the same the camera can be moved to a different viewpoint without altering the aperture because the flash-to-subject distance remains constant.

However, if the magnification is changed an exposure compensation must be applied: taking a close-up photograph of one of the straws at life-size would require moving the flashgun closer or opening the aperture to a wider f-stop; either option would compensate for light lost due to inceased magnification. In fact, a dedicated flash was used to take this picture. Because the subject was backlit and also does not fill the frame an exposure compensation was required. A compensation of −1 f-stop was applied, after which the system automatically controlled the flash output for an aperture of f16, chosen to obtain the maximum depth of field for that lens.

Focusing

As magnification increases, the depth of field decreases. This makes accurate focusing crucial. Unfortunately, depth of field is normally estimated using a preview control on the lens. The simulation closes the aperture without taking a picture, but as less light passes through the lens the viewfinder image is darkened – a distinct problem in a cave. There is little to be done, other than remembering how shallow the depth of field is and photographing suitable subjects.

Using a tripod and measuring distances carefully can help focusing, but hand-holding the camera is faster and perfectly viable. Select a magnification, sway gently back and fore moving the camera slowly through the point of focus and release the shutter at the right moment, relying on the electronic flash to freeze all movement in the photograph. Practise your timing at home without a film in the camera; it is not as difficult as it sounds.

Placing the flash

As with 'normal' photographs, a camera-mounted flash gives good detail but a flat, uninteresting result. Some cave photographers use a flash bracket to place the flash to one side, but it is easy to hand-hold the flash and therefore cut down on the amount of equipment that has to be carried.

Texture is accentuated by placing the flash to the side of or (if it is translucent) behind the subject; crystals take on form, and otherwise invisible ridges become lined with shadows. Standardise on a flash-to-subject angle of roughly 45 degrees to, and slightly above, the subject to add relief and to approximate overhead lighting. This may not suit some situations, but for others it may help a non-caver to appreciate the picture as the lighting angle simulates sunlight, which is a familiar angle to the viewer. Even so, do not hesitate to experiment: backlighting a translucent speleothem is dramatic. Unless a dedicated flash or flashmeter is used (with careful interpretation of data), you will need to guestimate how much light is transmitted through the calcite; bracket your shots.

Working in close-up a number of things must be accomplished at the same time: light the subject, aim the flash, focus the camera, protect nearby formations . . . An assistant is valuable in removing some of these difficulties by holding the flash and giving a warning if the camera sways too close to the subject. A helmet light held alongside the flashgun (or a small, pencil-beam torch attached with an elastic band) helps ensure it is correctly aimed. If the light is too intense it may introduce a hot spot or colour cast, but given the small aperture in use there should be no appreciable effect on the photograph.

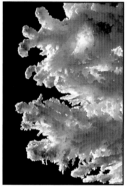

Front lighting leaves these crystals in Carlsbad Caverns dull and uninteresting (top, E8) but backlighting brings out their translucent nature (E6)

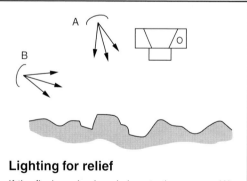

Lighting for relief

If the flashgun is placed close to the camera (A) the resulting photograph is detailed but very 'flat' and lacks interest. Light textured surfaces obliquely (B), so that ridges and shadows are clearly shown. Match the lighting position to the subject's characteristics.

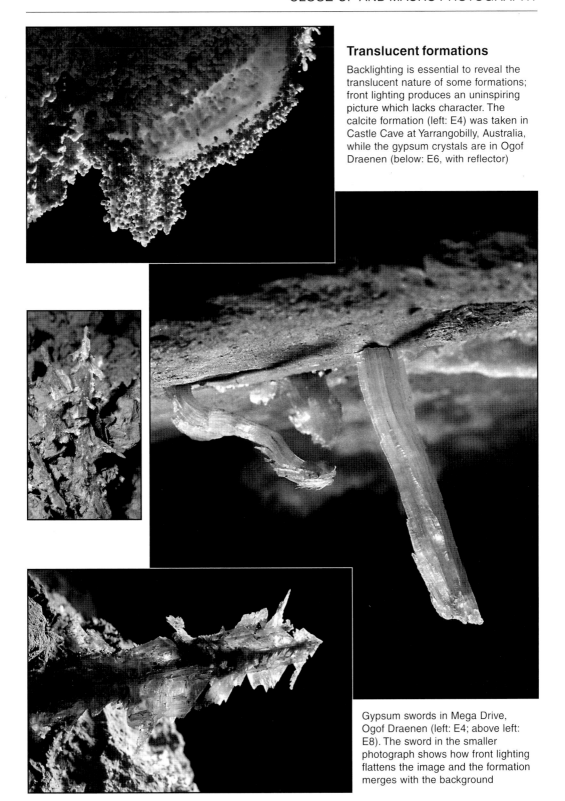

Translucent formations

Backlighting is essential to reveal the translucent nature of some formations; front lighting produces an uninspiring picture which lacks character. The calcite formation (left: E4) was taken in Castle Cave at Yarrangobilly, Australia, while the gypsum crystals are in Ogof Draenen (below: E6, with reflector)

Gypsum swords in Mega Drive, Ogof Draenen (left: E4; above left: E8). The sword in the smaller photograph shows how front lighting flattens the image and the formation merges with the background

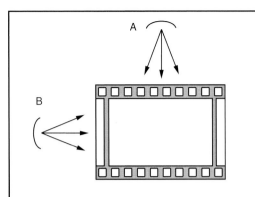

Flash orientation

The orientation of the flash, with respect to the format of the picture, is important in close-up photography. When the subject is illuminated along the long axis of the photograph there is a greater variation in lighting than when it is lit from the side. Position (A) is better than position (B).

Keep both the flash and camera square to the subject to make best use of the limited depth of field and maintain even lighting. At close quarters the flash, if not positioned with care, can cause huge problems of over- or underexposure. Nearby parts of the scene may receive appreciably more light than others: a few centimetres difference in the flash-to-subject distance may be enough to ruin a photograph by introducing a variation in lighting. Although the area may be small, tackling the problem is crucial.

To minimise the problem, aim the flash across the short axis of the photograph. That is, the shortest dimension – flashing across the width of a 35mm format picture – has less chance of exposure variation than the long dimension. Likewise, flashgun reflectors are normally rectangular; their orientation should match the shape of the photograph to produce lighting that is as even as possible: hold the flash so that it casts light evenly, upright for an upright photograph and vice versa.

Using two flashguns

If a single flash results in uneven lighting, a logical solution is to use two flashes with one each side of the subject. As with 'normal' photography one is the key flash, while the other is a weaker fill-in flash. If the second flashgun is the same power cover its reflector with a sheet of plastic tracing paper to reduce its output; altering the flash-to-subject distance would be inconvenient at the distances involved.

Twin flashes are normally mounted on either side of the camera using a bracket. Most commercially manufactured 'arms' permit independently

Using two flashguns

- Place one flashgun each side of the subject, usually on a bracket. This home-made system is based on two electronic flashguns. The components have been removed and housed in a separate container which is attached by a cable; this reduces the weight on the front of the lens. The flashguns are fixed to a lenshood which attaches to the lens by its filter ring
- The bracket must allow the camera to turn through 90 degrees, so that upright pictures can be taken without altering flash positions
- Designate one gun as a key flash, the other as a weaker fill-in flash. In this example, one gun will be partly covered with tissue paper to reduce its output
- Run tests to determine the exposure

aimed flashes, realignment after changing magnification, and turning the camera through 90 degrees to take an upright picture without altering the flash position. The camera and flashes are normally linked using a dual pc cable; either 'cave proof' this connector or permanently attach the cables to decrease the chance of misfires.

While a two-flash set-up is fast, predictable and easy to use, the two shadows it produces can appear disconcerting and texture is less distinct without a lighting ratio of 1:4 or more. For many cavers a single flash, combined with a reflector, is sufficient and produces excellent results.

The Anemone in Silent Splendor, Cave of the Winds, Colorado (E3)

Reflectors and shields

A reflector offers an alternative to using twin flashguns by reflecting light into dark, featureless shadows. Reflectors are specially suited to close-up work as the distances involved are short and the reflector itself is manageable; for 'normal' cave work large, unwieldy reflectors would be required.

Using a reflector can have an astounding effect in softening harsh lighting, especially when the key flash is from an acute lighting angle and produces hard shadows. Use a helmet light alongside the flash to assess the reflector's effect, allowing it to be precisely positioned. Any reflective, lightweight material is suitable for making a reflector; a white polythene bag (which doubles up as protection for the close-up equipment) is one option. Aluminium cooking foil can be folded into a shaped reflector, although it can cast a somewhat 'cold' colour cast.

Using reflectors

A reflector is used to lighten shadows (left) or provide a soft, diffuse light by bouncing all the light produced by a flashgun (right). Exposures are normally based on the total flash-to-subject distance (in the second case by adding the flash-to-reflector and reflector-to-subject distances), but a lot of light is absorbed by the reflector, which makes the guide number inaccurate. Dedicated flash measures the light entering the lens and automatically calculates the correct aperture.

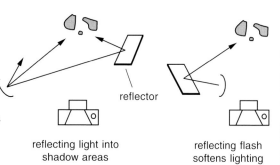

reflector

reflecting light into shadow areas

reflecting flash softens lighting

A 'bounce' flash is one where the flashgun is fired directly into the reflector so that there is no direct light. Crumpled plastic or foil produces a very soft, diffuse light over a wide area, while a normal reflector gives some directional light. The effect is pleasant, though not often used for large magnifications as precious light is lost. Nevertheless, with a dedicated flash system it is easy to produce accurate, well-lit results.

Shields, placed between a flash and camera to prevent stray light reaching the lens and causing flare, were discussed in chapter four. They are equally invaluable for close-up photography, as the direction of light can be precisely controlled.

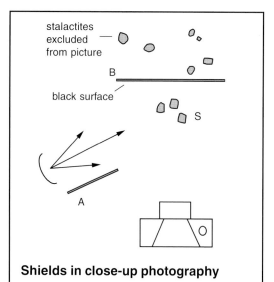

stalactites excluded from picture

B

black surface

A

S

Shields in close-up photography

The shield at (A) avoids stray, non-image-forming light (which causes flare) from reaching the lens. The shield at (B) prevents out-of-focus objects appearing in the picture, for example isolating the stalactites (S) against a plain background.

A rigid sheet of white plastic, used for modelling or stiffening envelopes or cut from discarded packaging, is perfect for making a combined reflector/shield. Paint one side matt black to absorb light; this is also useful as a background, where it can block out confusing shapes or intrusive, reflective surfaces. Carefully held behind a white straw stalactite, for example, the straw glows against a black background instead of a myriad of bright water droplets and other straws.

A shield need not be solid; gauze or thin cloth partially covering a flash both directs and diffuses light. A half-covered flash has a reduced emission on that side, the cloth acting as a convenient scrim (see p.97). Covering the whole flash with tissue paper or thin white plastic also reduces the flash intensity; firing through the base of a white, plastic food container or milk carton reduces harsh shadows to a minimum, although a powerful gun is needed to maintain a small aperture.

Photographing water

Photographing through a water surface, for example to take a picture of crystals in a pool, can be difficult as reflections may destroy the picture's clarity. Hold the camera at right angles to the surface to avoid distortion, and aim the flash at 45 degrees to the surface to ensure that reflections do not appear in the photograph.

Curved water surfaces, because they reflect light in many directions, are harder to cope with. The drip at the end of a straw stalactite is a classic example. Problems are reduced (but not eliminated) by avoiding large droplets. When the drip is about to fall, extra curves form which are so complex that reflections are bound to occur; a smaller drip is more predictable, and reflections can be assessed using a pencil-beam torch attached to the flash.

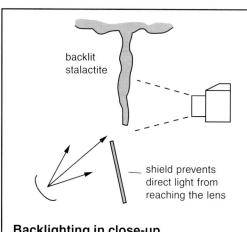

backlit stalactite

shield prevents direct light from reaching the lens

Backlighting in close-up

Backlighting small subjects is difficult as the flash cannot be hidden behind them. If necessary, light the subject from an angle, either to the side or below. A shield can then be used and specific areas lit by the flash.

A second solution is to backlight the straw, using a diffuse reflector to provide fill-in light from the front. Backlighting helps retain the complete edge of the water drip, which is often only partly present using a side light, but concealing the flash is difficult. Fortunately, aiming the flash from behind but to one side or below the subject works well, with a shield to prevent flare. Although this means that the flash is not

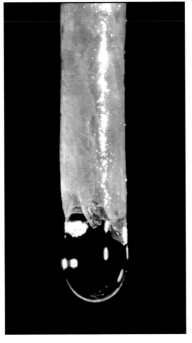
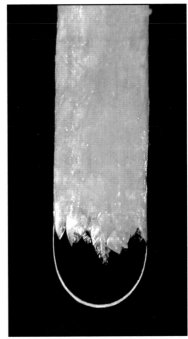

Large drops, about to fall, are difficult to light without causing reflections (left, E2). By moving the flash behind the stalactite and firing from slightly below the formation (in this case, E6), while shielding the lens from direct flash, many or all the reflections can be eliminated

parallel to the subject and lighting is technically uneven, the translucent nature of the straw masks the effect and crystals in the calcite show up superbly. Indeed, it is magical to discover a clear reflection of the roof in the droplet, unmarred by intrusive flare from the flash.

HISTORY AND ARCHAEOLOGY

A photographic record is needed at an archaeological site both to show its potential and to document ongoing work. Photographs should show the disposition of artefacts and the nature of the site, but much cave-based archaeological work will probably entail close-up record photography. The function of these pictures is to record information in a standard fashion that will aid workers at a later stage.

Archaeological finds are easily destroyed by thoughtless actions. If bones or other materials are found during exploration of a cave, do not disturb them: photograph the site and ask advice. Do not remove loose rocks or clean around a specimen as this can disturb mud layers which, potentially, can reveal additional information of use to the archaeologist. Leave everything *in situ* until it has been properly examined; exploration will wait until another day. Removing specimens before a full examination has been completed is an emergency measure to be taken only after consultation, and could be illegal without the landowner's permission.

Cave art in Inanke Cave, Zimbabwe (E8)

141

Bones are calcited into the talus (left, E7) in Charterhouse Warren Farm Swallet, including a cattle sacrum (below, E8). Part of a human mandible lay nearby (below left, E8). The general view helps to record the area where the finds were made, before it is disturbed

Making records

Recording archaeological material on film presents two problems: how information is documented, and what lighting is required. While there are no formally agreed archaeological rules to work with, important conventions and standards exist which, if followed, add immensely to the value of the resulting photograph.

These calcited bones, also from Charterhouse Warren Farm Swallet, are identified with a paper notation coding the cave, location and group (bottom right). A similar note can be seen to the left of the cattle sacrum, and a scale appears at the bottom of the photograph of the talus

Recording information about the subject is essential. When possible, so that this cannot be confused with other photographic records or otherwise separated from the picture, include the information within the photograph itself. Photograph something for scale (an object recognisable to a non-caver or, preferably, a metric ruler) in a consistent position, normally along the base of the photograph or alongside the specimen. The size of the scale must be in keeping with the specimen – a coin or pencil beside a large skeleton will be 'lost' within the general scene.

Even better, prepare a ruler with alternate black and white wide bands of consistent width, say 1cm each along the length of a 30cm ruler. These bands will be easily visible in both colour and black and white photographs, without needing a magnifying glass.

Include a paper or plastic label bearing a unique, pencilled number. This might be a simple ascending series (specimen 1, 2, 3, etc.) or a code which details cave, location and specimen group. For example, CC3/5 might indicate Chartist Cave, location 3, specimen 5 at that location.

Keep number codes short; they must be simple, consistent, unambiguous and expandable to include further finds. In particular, avoid codes that can be misinterpreted. In the example, two letters denote the cave while two numbers indicate a location and specimen within the cave. Avoid using a number for the cave itself; does 3/5/2 indicate cave 3, location 5, specimen 2 – or could it be location 3, specimen group 5, specimen 2? Make slashes obvious: they must not be confused with the number 1.

Carefully document all codes and photographs, marking the exact location in a notebook or on a survey – especially if there are several specimens from different areas in the cave. By implication, ongoing work means that specialist help will be on hand to record numbers and sequences, but it is up to the photographer to ensure that this work is completed. Make it easy for any person, perhaps years in the future, to identify the specimen's original location and which photograph applies to it. Take a general shot to indicate the proximity of bones to each other and, to aid in finding the area again, any nearby passage feature.

Building a mosaic

Photographing a specimen or scale at an angle introduces distortions and, while an oblique viewing angle might yield a better composition, an archaeological photograph has a different purpose: to produce a scientifically useful record. If an 'artistic' photograph is taken, ensure it is in addition to and not in replacement of this function.

This often requires a plan view, looking vertically down on the specimen or area. If time is limited, perhaps during an expedition when the area cannot be revisited, it may not be possible to prepare the site for specialised photography. A controlled, long-term dig is a different matter, but the area's dimensions, holes in the floor, boulders occluding the view or a low roof which limits working space, may all dictate different approaches.

A set of pictures taken at right angles to the site can be overlapped and assembled into a single, large picture. Constructing a mosaic in this way, whether it is of an archaeological site, passage wall or panoramic view of

A scale in documentary photographs is important as an aid for their later analysis. A ruler was used for this picture of a decomposing mouse in Ogof Draenen (E8). If all else fails, use a finger for scale, as with these calcited cat vertebrae in Ogof Ffynnon Taf (E8)

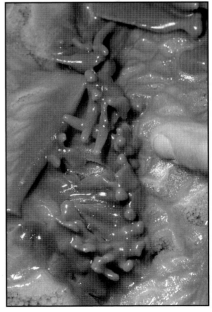

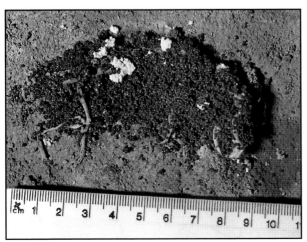

Photographing cave art, historic graffiti and ancient pictographs is part of a recording discipline. The signatures were taken in Mammoth Cave at Jenolan in Australia (below) and in Spider Cave, New Mexico. The prehistoric artwork is from Inanke Cave, Zimbabwe, and the depiction of a man in Wemyss Caves, Fife. The grooves were made by elephants in Kitum Cave, Kenya, as they gouged the rock in search of salt. All pictures (E8)

a larger chamber, requires inconspicuous joins. Variations in lighting angles and focusing, as well as lens distortion, lead to inconsistencies. If there are changes in the camera-to-subject distance the size of the image alters between frames, and accurate joins cannot be made. If the lighting angle changes, shadows may be truncated or lie in opposite directions. A wide-angle lens, an attraction when space is limited, introduces edge distortions which become obvious across successive sections of a mosaic.

To minimise problems use a 50mm or 35mm lens: wider angles introduce excessive distortion. Overlap photographs by at least 50 per cent and only use the centre of each; this removes the part with the most distortion.

Building a mosaic

Build a photographic mosaic if space is limited or a high-quality record of a large area is required. To obtain consistency in individual frames:

- Avoid wide-angle lenses
- Overlap all frames by at least 50 per cent
- Lay a grid pattern over the area
- Use a small aperture and constant camera-to-grid distance
- Use a tripod (with a boom arm when necessary)
- Do not refocus
- Use a consistent lighting angle

Fire the flash from the same, high angle with respect to the subject to even out exposure variations, using a reflector to lighten shadows if necessary.

Ideally, lay a grid of regularly spaced string or wire over the area to provide a scale and to help when assembling the mosaic. Keep the grid-to-camera distance consistent and prefocus the lens. Use a small aperture to obtain a good depth of field, thereby avoiding the need to refocus if the floor dips and rises. For vertical work a tripod with an offset arm keeps the legs outside the working area, preventing damage by either the tripod or photographer. A tracking system which moves the camera along a wall or floor at measured intervals offers the ultimate in control; such techniques have been used to record historic signatures as well as archaeological material in caves.

Because the exposures, camera angle and lighting are consistent the print quality (both colour and contrast) should match. Roughly assemble the mosaic by laying prints over each other, then cut through overlying prints with a scalpel. Glue the portions to a base using a suitable photographic adhesive which permits repositioning, then photograph the mosaic. Joins can be retouched on the resulting copy print.

Lighting angles

The lighting angle controls the degree of texture and detail. To an extent these are antagonistic factors: increasing the texture in a photograph may lose some fine detail. There are no immutable lighting rules as each situation is different: only one flash position might exist in a confined location, for example.

Because close-up photographs are taken at short distances, it is easy to hold or mount the flash to one side of the camera and introduce some side lighting while retaining good detail in the specimen. This compromise – coupled with a reflector when necessary – is a useful technique. Side lighting shows subjects such as animal scratches on a bone to advantage, while backlighting brings out any translucent qualities. Match the lighting angle to the specimen's characteristics and, if in doubt, take alternative views with different lighting.

Archaeological recording

- Report all finds to the appropriate authority
- Record the specimen *in situ* without disturbance; do not 'clean up' a specimen
- Avoid distortions caused by photographing at an angle; take a plan view if possible
- Where space is limited, or for added detail, build a mosaic
- Use a reflector to lighten shadows
- Include a scale, such as a ruler, and assign a unique record number
- List photographs separately giving the subject, location and record number
- Use appropriate lighting angles: side light for texture, front light for detail

Documentary photography

Archaeological photography is not the only documentation that is required in a cave; transitory techniques and activities, club meetings or ceremonial occasions which will become historically important in the future, geological details such as wall scallops or mud sediments, or a breakthrough into a new section of cave are all important. Add to this historical artefacts and graffiti, and documentary photography is seen to encompass a vast range of subject matter.

Documenting passages soon after they are explored, often before taped paths are laid, is a useful part of conservation. 'Then and now' comparisons can be made years later and show what damage – or otherwise – may have arisen. If time is limited, concentrate on areas which are perceived to be fragile or most at risk; an active streamway is unlikely to change quickly, while mud or speleothems in a narrow passage undoubtedly will.

CAVE LIFE

Most life underground goes unnoticed by cavers and mine explorers as, although it is far commoner than most people believe, much of it is small and fragile. The ecosystem is easily damaged by carelessly dropped food, unwarranted disturbance and unrestricted collecting, and is far from being fully understood. With careful observation and study, using their photographic recording and artistic skills to the full, cave photographers have much to offer this relatively young discipline.

Fungal fruiting bodies erupting from the remains of a Herald Moth (*Scoliopteryx libatrix*) in Ogof Capel. Partly backlighting the subject (right, E6 with reflector at position 2) accentuates its texture while front lighting retains good detail in the picture (E1, aimed from slightly above the camera)

Photographers should be aware of their responsibilities in this specialised field, as they will be working closely with frail and possibly unique organisms. Whether it is a mammal such as a bat or a small, seemingly insignificant isopod in a stream, the specimen's welfare must be treated as would a delicate speleothem: with incredible care.

Photographing bats

Bats deserve a special mention and warning. In many countries, including the United Kingdom, disturbing bats is prohibited. As protected species since 1981, under UK law approaching a bat without a licence is illegal and, even with a licence, photography near bats is only permissible as an incidental part of conservation or scientific work. Extension licences are required for specialist photography.

It is therefore assumed that photography of bats – whether at roost or using specialised electronic detectors and 'broken beam' triggers for bats in flight – will only be attempted under supervision as part of an organised project, and as such specific details lie outside the scope of this manual. Any photography which is undertaken, for example in countries where there is no relevant legislation, should be performed with care. Avoid using flash near hibernating bats as the light and associated noise (the whine of a charging electronic flashgun is quiet to human ears, but may not be to bats) can cause disturbance. A person can, within only a few minutes, warm the air sufficiently to disturb and wake a hibernating bat, which may not have the fat reserves to survive until spring.

A colony of Schreiber's Long-fingered bats (*Miniopterus schreibersii*) roosting in Wynberg Cave, South Africa (E8)

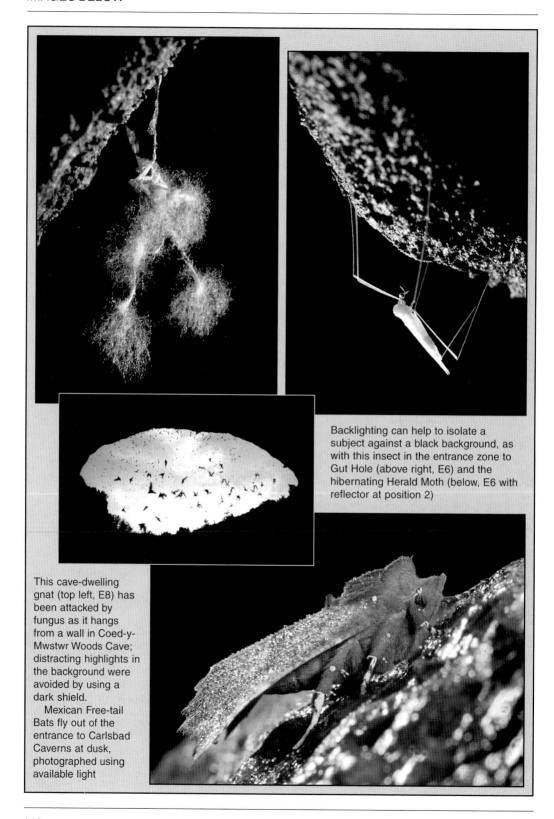

Backlighting can help to isolate a subject against a black background, as with this insect in the entrance zone to Gut Hole (above right, E6) and the hibernating Herald Moth (below, E6 with reflector at position 2)

This cave-dwelling gnat (top left, E8) has been attacked by fungus as it hangs from a wall in Coed-y-Mwstwr Woods Cave; distracting highlights in the background were avoided by using a dark shield.

Mexican Free-tail Bats fly out of the entrance to Carlsbad Caverns at dusk, photographed using available light

Recording data

Classifying cave life is often difficult and, as with archaeology, it is assumed that a specialist will help with identification. To do so the diagnostic features of the organism must appear in the photograph, which implies some knowledge of cave biology. Always record the species (if known), the place, date and the specific environment – open stream passage or mud-filled tube, draughting or still air, in threshold illumination or the dark zone? What was the time of year? Is there a nearby inlet which could have washed the organism into the cave? Was any behavioural activity observed, such as feeding or mating? Such factors add valuable information to the picture.

In particular, include a scale in the photograph for this type of picture. This may not be possible with 'wild', free-moving organisms. Altern-atively, you may be taking an 'artistic' photograph where the inclusion of a scale would be intrusive. As with archaeological artefacts, it is up to the photographer to assess the function of the finished picture and select an appropriate camera and lighting angle accordingly. Nevertheless, record the photographic equipment used so that the image magnification can be calculated.

A cave cricket (*Speleiacriz tabulae*) in Snedegar's Cave, West Virginia (E6), recorded at half life-size on film

Care of organisms

The nature, size and location of the organism determine the best photo-graphic method and present different problems. For example, some species change their behaviour under continuous lighting, so the photographer is

A male cave-dwelling spider, *Meta menardi*, in Coed-y-Mwstwr Woods Cave (E2)

forced to focus in the dark. An electronic flash has such a short duration that specimens are unlikely to react during the exposure, although they may do so afterwards. Estimating distance, prefocusing with a good depth of field, minimises disturbance of bat colonies. An assistant controlling a dim light during setting up, removing it at every opportunity, is invaluable.

Some form of restraint or capture may be required with small or fast-moving organisms. This may mean that the specimen is removed, temporarily, from its niche. Avoid this whenever possible and replace the organism in precisely the same place; if it was found under a stone, replace the stone the same way up. This might not be a legal stipulation, but there is certainly a moral requirement. Conserving the cave environment is obviously important; to care for its denizens is vital and, whenever possible, photography should be done *in situ*.

Techniques

Cave life includes fungi, slime moulds, bacteria and other sessile subjects. Bacteria are best cultured and photographed under a microscope outside the cave. Fungi, slime moulds and other slow-moving or static specimens (for example, a hibernating moth in an entrance), including associated substances such as guano or moonmilk, can be photographed using normal close-up techniques. However, aquatic and fast-moving organisms require a different approach.

Aquatic organisms

Aquatic organisms include crustaceans (for example, isopods), turbellarians (flatworms) and annelids (segmented worms). These groups differ a great deal in their external structure: flatworms are best photographed from above, while the feeding behaviour of a worm emerging from a layer of mud requires a side view. For all but the slowest-moving aquatic

Proasellus cavaticus is Britain's only troglobitic isopod, living on rocky substrates in streams and on flowstone. This specimen, from Lesser Garth Cave, was photographed in a specially constructed miniature aquarium using two shielded electronic flashguns (E4, E6) with foreground reflectors

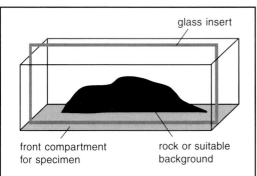

glass insert

front compartment for specimen

rock or suitable background

A small aquarium

Small aquariums can easily be constructed at home or on expedition. Glue glass with silicone. A smaller section, inserted as required, confines the organism towards the front. Add a suitable substrate and a background in the rear portion to produce a natural setting.

The larva of a fungus gnat on its web, Ogof Rhyd Sych (E3)

organisms, they must be captured or restrained with the minimum of disturbance.

Containers, particularly for flattened organisms which are photographed from above, may be as simple as a dish containing mud or gravel covered with shallow water. Allow time for fine, silty mud to settle before and after introducing the specimen. A ring cut from a plastic bottle, pushed into the *in situ* substrate around the organism, also prevents it from escaping. The photograph's background is genuine, water clarity is maintained and there is less risk of altering the animal's behaviour. Use a tripod to help maintain the focus, taking the picture when the animal moves into the required position.

A side view of an aquatic organism requires a miniature aquarium. This can be easily constructed at home or during an expedition using thin glass and silicone sealant. Polish the glass before assembly to remove any residues of grease or oil and allow twenty-four hours for the silicone to cure. A robust mini-aquarium can be made using slide mount glass for the front and microscope slides for the rest of the structure. Slide mounts for 120 format film are ideal; use plain glass mounts, not those with anti-Newton textured glass. Photography through this incredibly thin material does not distort the subject.

Include enough substrate to make the photograph appear natural, with the rear of the aquarium far enough away to be out of focus. Photography of a moving subject is easier with an additional glass insert to confine the specimen to the front of the aquarium; with water on both sides, the insert does not show up in the photograph. Prefocus on the front zone and allow the animal to settle down in the dark, then use a dim light to view the scene before taking the picture. Check the front glass and internal divider for air bubbles, dislodging them with a toothpick-shaped piece of plastic or wood.

As with photographing through water surfaces, keep the camera at right angles to the glass and the flash at an angle or fired through the side or top of the mini-aquarium to avoid reflections. Reflectors and shields are useful: a black card with a hole for the lens will reduce the risk of reflections of the camera itself. Using a polarising filter to reduce reflections is unnecessary if lights are correctly placed.

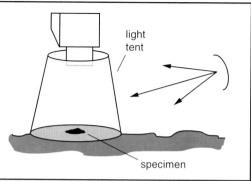

Making a light tent

Use a light tent to confine moving specimens and diffuse harsh lighting. Make a plastic cone which folds flat for transport but with edges which clip together. The upper edge of the cone should support the camera so that the substrate lies at the furthest limit of the depth of field; the specimen should then fall in the zone of sharpest focus. Flashes are fired from the side, through the translucent material.

light tent

specimen

Confining organisms in air

Fast-moving animals in air are best confined using a small aquarium or a ring restricting the distance they can travel. However, such organisms have an uncanny tendency to jump, climb or move into a corner, well away from any suitable photographic position.

One solution is to confine the animal using a 'light tent'. This is a simple cone or box with a hole for the camera lens. If designed with care, the tent can be carried flat and assembled in the cave. Placed over a specimen, either pushed into mud (even through water) or on a flat rock, the camera is supported at roughly the correct distance from the specimen. The flash is fired from close range through the translucent plastic, giving an excellent, diffuse light. Reflections are totally eliminated and, with a dedicated flash system, exposure calculations are not required.

Removing specimens

The practical difficulties of working within the cave should not be glossed over, as dirt in the wrong place and failure of delicate equipment is all too common. It is therefore tempting to remove the specimen to a situation where photography can be completely controlled. This is a last resort for essential, extended study or when, by the nature of the photograph, more specialised close-up equipment or techniques are required; return the animal immediately after photography is completed.

Minimise fluctuations in temperature and light in the studio. Do not use strong lights; even if specimens are blind and apparently do not react, there will be an unacceptable, detrimental temperature rise. For example, some species of flattened amphipod typically lie on their side to feed and swim, but in bright light abnormally crawl upright. Trout, observed to be 'white' in a cave, change colour within hours in a lighted aquarium. Interfering with the natural life cycle of a cave-dwelling species can cause a behaviour change resulting in unrealistic photographs; removing specimens adds to the likelihood of this occurring.

The cavernicolous woodlouse, *Androniscus dentiger*, in Ogof Rhyd Sych (E1)

Photographing cave life

- Care of organisms is paramount
- Remove specimens only as a last resort
- Confine specimens with a ring or light tent
- If necessary, construct an aquarium
- Allow time for the substrate to settle and specimens to behave normally
- Aim the camera at right angles to water or glass surfaces to avoid distortion
- Aim the flash at an angle to water or glass surfaces to avoid reflections

Chapter eight
AUTOMATIC CAMERAS

It was amusing to watch. Two sets of cave photographers, out of sight of each other around a passage corner, each frustrated by slave units that refused to stabilise. Automation! No sooner was a picture set up and the capacitors charged than all the flashes fired. Check and recheck flashguns, curse, swear . . . It took a long time for them to realise that each group's slaves were being triggered by the other group's tests.

Ogof Draenen

Fully automatic cameras are not ideal for serious cave photography as they do not permit precise control of the aperture or shutter speed. However, point-and-shoot cameras can be used with success as part of a small and light package of photographic gear. Some are waterproof, a great advantage (although see the warning on pp.42–3), and the built-in flash will enable reasonable record photography over short distances, albeit without any side lighting or finesse. To make better use of an automatic camera its limitations must be understood and counteracted.

Camera types

Automatic cameras fall into two categories, depending on whether the photographer can manually control the aperture and shutter speed (by overriding the auto exposure setting) or not.

Automatic exposures are adjusted by using a fixed aperture and altering the shutter speed to accommodate changes in light intensity, or by using a fixed shutter speed and a changeable aperture. Sophisticated cameras may also alter the 'fixed' component if the exposure falls outside an acceptable range. For example, with a fixed aperture of f4 and shutter speeds restricted to between 1/60 second and 1/500 second, very bright light might overexpose the photograph. Either a faster shutter speed or smaller aperture is required. When the limits of the range have been exceeded some 'fixed aperture' cameras select a second, smaller aperture and benefit from the leeway this allows the speed setting.

Most automatic cameras are fitted with an inbuilt flash. The first tenet of cave photography is to avoid 'flat', misty photographs and a red-eye effect by removing the flash from the camera, so having the flash next to the lens is a serious design fault. Some cameras have a shutter lock which prevents a photograph from being taken unless the flash is used; the machine is unable to determine that the tiny flash is insufficient for lighting a large

The Olympus Mju camera (left) is fully automatic with an integral flash just above the lens. The aperture on the older Olympus XA can be overridden, but the ISO setting has to be manually adjusted to 'fool' the system's exposure readings

chamber, or that the photographer is using separate flashguns and simply does not require a flash from the camera position. All these factors present difficulties.

Controlling exposure

An obvious solution is to cover the flash with an infra-red filter and use it to fire slave units. As the aperture and shutter speed on a fully auto camera cannot be manually controlled, the photographer must alter the slave flash intensity to match the camera's settings. The shutter speed and aperture range are rarely stated in the camera's manual so, although a direct question to the manufacturer may help, the settings must first be deduced.

In total darkness the camera selects its widest aperture. This is normally marked on the lens: an f2.8 lens indicates a maximum aperture of f2.8. Finding the slowest shutter speed is more difficult, though of less importance. Usually 1/60 second (sometimes slower but less commonly faster), it will certainly synchronise with electronic flash; a slower speed is required to

Although it produces low contrast results, an automatic inbuilt flash is useful when recording digs (here, in Ogof Draenen) and other activities underground which do not require sophisticated lighting

make full use of flashbulbs, but this may not be available and the full range of a bulb's characteristics often cannot be used in cave photographs taken with fully auto cameras.

Check that the camera synchronises with the slave flashes as some slaves have a slight delay in firing which only becomes evident with faster shutter speeds. Synchronisation is easy to check by firing a slaved flash while looking through the open camera back: if the flash is seen through the lens, it is synchronised with the shutter. If the camera will not operate with its back open, expose a frame and process the film (or manually depress the 'back closed' pin which is normally located in the groove which the camera back fits into, fooling the system).

Once the aperture is known, use fill-in flash techniques to modify the flash intensity: alter the flash-to-subject distance or adjust the power setting to suit the fixed aperture (see p.116).

Using TTL

Opposite: Ogof Draenen (B5). Using a slave unit in conjunction with an automatic camera is perfectly possible but, if bulbs are involved, ensure the shutter speed is long enough to accommodate their slow production of light

Some automatic cameras, in particular good quality SLR models, use TTL (Through The Lens) flash metering to control the exposure. The camera's flash sensors measure light reflected from the film itself *during* the exposure and adjust the flash output accordingly. This is more accurate than relying on a reading taken just *before* the shutter is released, and far more accurate than detecting light reflected to the flashgun itself.

Typically, in total darkness, fully automatic TTL cameras select the widest aperture possible and alter the flash output to match. Semi-auto cameras (where there is a degree of manual override) allow the aperture to be selected, forcing the flash to produce more light.

Automatic cameras are ideal for taking action photographs, as here in P8. The integral flash has acted as fill-in as well as triggering a main or key flash (E1, B3)

In dim light or darkness some automatic cameras, having selected their widest aperture with no flash attached, leave the shutter open until enough light for a 'correct' exposure has reached the film. To prevent unnecessary battery wastage, after some predetermined period the system 'times out', often after several minutes. In the dark this system effectively provides an 'automatic B setting'.

To photograph a large chamber place the camera on a tripod and release the shutter. Fire a series of flashes from one or more positions; when the camera detects that the exposure is complete the shutter is closed. The technique is doubly useful when complex lighting arrangements are involved, as calculations are automatic and it also enables a photographer to work alone.

It is a mistake to place too much reliance on automation. Apart from the obvious problem of using complex and expensive electronic equipment in a cave, a single flash can overexpose a photograph if the camera is at its maximum aperture. When successive flashes light different areas, the shutter can close before all the flashes have fired. It is safer to determine the correct flash-to-subject distance for that aperture and work manually. Nevertheless, using an automatically operated shutter can open up new areas of experimentation which can be helpful in some situations.

The DX code

If there is no manual control of shutter speed or aperture on a fully automatic camera, it is possible to fool the system by changing the film speed. The effect this has depends on whether the camera maintains a constant shutter speed or aperture; a lower ISO forces the camera to use a

ISO	25	50	100	200	400	800	1600	3200
Square 1								
Square 2	■		■		■		■	
Square 3			■		■	■		
Square 4	■	■	■	■	■			

Reading a DX code

Stand the cassette upright with the spool at the top and read the right-hand column of squares from top (square 1) to bottom (square 6). Squares 2, 3 and 4 control full f-stop increments, while squares 5 and 6 control increments of 1/3 f-stop.

For example, a film is coded silver–black–silver–black–silver–black. Square 1 is always silver. Squares 2, 3 and 4 indicate an ISO 100 film. Squares 5 and 6, silver–black, show that there is no modification to this, but if these squares had read silver–silver a 2/3 f-stop increase would be indicated, from ISO 100 to ISO 160. To change ISO 100 film to ISO 200, square 2 must be changed from black to silver.

Increment	+0	+1/3	+2/3
Square 5		■	
Square 6	■		

NB: With the spool at the top, read the grid from top to bottom

DX coding

The DX code identifies the film speed. The left-hand cassette is FP4 black and white film. Its ISO column indicates a speed of ISO 100 plus a 1/3 f-stop increase in speed, making ISO 125. The right-hand cassette is rated at ISO 400.

The DX code (top to bottom): silver–black–silver–black–black–silver represents ISO 125

slower shutter speed (normally, the aperture is already at maximum), while a higher ISO closes the aperture (the shutter is already fixed at its slowest, or only, speed).

Many modern cameras detect and set the film's speed, type and length using a pattern of conductive squares – the DX code – on the film cassette. Without an override feature on the camera, exposures cannot be individually controlled: the camera is in charge! However, the DX code (and therefore the exposures) can be changed for an entire film. This is a useful emergency technique for adjusting a camera which always under- or overexposes the film and for exposing the film at a different ISO from the manufacturer's recommendation, something particularly applicable to caves and black and white photography. When used at a higher ISO the film is underexposed, but this is balanced by an increase in processing time. This technique, known as uprating, forces the inbuilt flash to emit less light and helps to avoid overexposing a subject which is isolated against a black background.

To read a DX code stand the cassette upright with the spool protruding from the top, leaving the film extending to the right. The code is arranged in two columns, with a bar code to the right of the squares. The left-hand column indicates the film length and type, while the bar code contains data used by the manufacturer. The right-hand column, next to the bar code, is the one of interest as it controls the film speed.

In this orientation, read the pattern of six silver (conductive) and black (non-conductive) squares from top to bottom. The top square, square 1, is always silver. Squares 2, 3 and 4 govern full f-stop increments (25, 50,

Using automatic cameras

Advantages:
- Small and light for fast photography
- Inbuilt flash is ideal for short distances when sophisticated lighting is not required
- Slave units can be fired using an integral flash
- Multiple flash exposures are automatically calculated if the shutter is left open
- SLR cameras with both auto and manual modes are available
- Waterproof models suit adverse situations

Disadvantages:
- Incomplete control of aperture and shutter speed
- Possible overexposure of part or all of the scene when additional flashes are used
- Underexposure with the inbuilt flash is common over medium and long distances
- Slave flashes must match the fixed aperture
- Depth of field is often shallow
- DX code may need altering for exposure compensation
- Many traditional techniques are impossible

Automatic exposure systems are easily fooled by large areas of darkness (E1, E4). In Llygad Llwchwr the inbuilt flash has exposed for the whole scene, resulting in an overexposed face. Exposures of skin are crucial and *must* be correct. One solution is to alter the ISO setting on the camera to force it to 'underexpose' the scene

100, 200, 400, 800, 1600, 3200), while squares 5 and 6 set intermediate 1/3 f-stop increments.

Some cameras detect only a limited range of f-stops, for example ISO 100 and 400 (other films, no matter what their speed, are set to ISO 100 by default). If the manual does not include the information, these can be identified by inspecting the number of contact pins in the cassette-loading area. Four contact pins are needed to detect all the full-f-stops. It is obviously pointless to modify a cassette to provide a film speed which cannot be detected by the camera. To change the speed, cover a silver square with electrician's PVC tape to make it non-conductive. Cover a black square with silver foil to make it conductive. Taping over the complete DX code forces most cameras to revert to ISO 100.

Putting your knowledge to use

From the foregoing discussions it might seem that using an automatic camera is more trouble than it is worth and that, rather than easing the pain of exposure calculations, the difficulties are added to. While this is often true and methods of fooling the automatic system have to be used, for many photographs an auto-system is not only viable, it encourages photography and can yield excellent results.

An automatic camera equipped with manual override can give the best of both worlds: cumulative flashes with an automatic shut-down, or conventionally with manual control. How useful this is depends on your preferences. At best, automatic functions are a useful addition to the cave photographer's arsenal, but will not replace traditional techniques. It is, however, great fun to work without pausing to consider apertures, power and distances. At worst, automation demands the use of delicate, sophisticated electronic equipment in an environment it was not designed for and requires thought and care to avoid problems which do not exist in 'normal' cave photography.

Auto-flash tips
- Use colour print film as it is the most forgiving of exposure errors
- Slow speed film produces less grain in the photograph
- Adjusting the film speed to a faster ISO underexposes pictures and helps offset overexposure from auto-flash systems. An ISO 50 film with the DX code completely taped over sets the camera to ISO 100 and underexposes the film by one f-stop
- Do not use an inbuilt 'flicker-flash', available on some models, to reduce red-eye (and certainly not if slave units are used as the pre-photographic flash will trigger the slave)
- Cover the inbuilt flash with an infra-red filter to trigger slave units. If fixing the filter is difficult, cover the flash with black pvc tape, which transmits infra-red light
- Determine the camera's widest aperture and set a slave-operated automatic flash for the same aperture. The flash can be fired from any position within its marked range
- For manual flash, use a gun at its correct distance for the camera's aperture
- Using an automatic camera means you must accept some limitations, but you gain by avoiding exposure calculations and excessive setting-up. In short, it is a way to make pictures while having a bit of fun

Chapter nine
ALTERNATIVE LIGHTING

It was confusing, talking caving and photography across the Atlantic. An electronic flashgun in Britain (aren't all flashguns electronic?) is called a strobe in the US, while in Britain a strobe is a light in a discotheque. Then there's a flashlight which, depending where you live, is what comes out of a flashgun or is a hand-held light. The US flashlight is a torch in British-English, which translates back as a flaming brand or arsonist. Never mind, at least we share a common language.

NSS caving convention

ELECTRONIC flash and flashbulbs are convenient and predictable. However, before these were invented cavers and cave photographers relied on light sources such as magnesium powder and ribbon, flashpowder, paraffin and acetylene lamps, arc lights, petrol burners, limelight and even candles. All these, and more, are good for special effects.

Some of these 'alternative' sources are not considered safe in all circumstances; as one example, flashpowder is an explosive with roughly twice the power of gunpowder. Experimentation is rich and rewarding, but safety and cave conservation come first.

COLOUR CONTROL

Colour films are balanced to a specific light source, the commonest being noon-time daylight; other films might be specified for a tungsten or infra-red spectrum. To render colours accurately, the film must be matched to the light source.

Colour temperature

The exact colour that a film is balanced for, or that a flash emits, is termed its colour temperature. This is a comparison with the colour emitted by a heated iron bar: at different temperatures the iron glows with different colours. Thus, the temperature is linked to the light it emits and is measured in kelvins; daylight film, for example, is rated at 5,500K.

In effect, 'correct' colours are produced if daylight film is exposed with daylight, tungsten film with tungsten. Electronic flash emits light at close to daylight's colour temperature, but mismatching light source and film results in a colour cast. Artificial light sources with a cooler colour temperature, such as magnesium, produce a reddish colour with daylight-balanced film. Likewise, using an artificial light film (designated Type A or B, or marked as Tungsten film) with daylight-balanced flash will introduce a blue cast.

Although these results may look false and 'wrong', there is no such thing as a 'correct' colour as even daylight varies in its quality depending on the time of day and weather conditions: light at sunrise and sunset is redder than at midday. Different films – even though they are all daylight balanced – are sensitive to slightly different spectra and may produce slightly warm or cold results when compared with each other. For this reason photographers often develop a preference for the colours of one film over another; such factors are purely subjective. Personal choice plays a huge part in the decision whether to deliberately mismatch film and light source for a special effect.

Filtration

An exact match between the light source and the film's colour temperature is not always possible. Colour correction filters correct unwanted imbal-

Colour temperature and colour casts

Light source	Colour temperature K	Effect with daylight film (no filter)	Effect with tungsten film (no filter)	Correction filter for daylight film
Electronic flash	6,000	Slightly blue	Strongly blue	81A
Daylight (noon)	5,500	–	Strongly blue	–
Blue flashbulb	5,400	Slightly yellow	Strongly blue	–
Carbon arc light	5,000	Slightly yellow	Blue	82A
Flashpowder	4,300	Yellow	Blue	80D
Clear flashbulb	3,800	Yellow/orange	Slightly blue	80C
Magnesium ribbon	3,600	Yellow/orange	Slightly blue	80C + 82A
Photoflood bulb (500W)	3,400	Orange	Slightly blue	80B
Tungsten floodlight	3,200	Orange/red	–	80A
Tungsten bulb (60W)	2,700	Yellow/red	Slightly yellow	80A + 80D
Carbide (acetylene)	2,400	Strong yellow/red	Yellow	80A + 80B or 78A
Candle	1,900	Strong red/golden	Strong yellow	80A + 80A

- Colour temperatures and filter numbers for some light sources are not exact as there is a wide variation in manufacture, for example in the density of the blue coating on flashbulbs
- Data is intended for guidance only, as colour assessment – including that of daylight – is very subjective
- Theoretically, an 80C filter is required for converting clear flashbulbs for daylight film use. In practice, a weaker blue 80D filter usually gives a more pleasing result. A blue polythene bag over the flash or dying the bulb blue is an alternative
- Correction filters require an exposure adjustment, typically up to 2 f-stops. Refer to the manufacturer's guide for specific values
- Colours vary from their theoretical values according to the duration of the exposure: dim sources of light require a longer exposure than bright ones. Longer times cause reciprocity failure and a greater colour shift
- Avoid using more than two filters as this causes cut-off with wide-angle lenses
- Filtration is not accurate at the extremes of the scale, such as candlelight
- Flashpowder produces a wide range of colour temperatures (between 3,000K and 4,500K) depending on its formula
- For colours created by showcave lights see pp.166 and 176

ances by altering the colour of light to match the film's sensitivity, and are placed over the flash, whatever light source is in use or, more commonly, screwed onto the front of the lens. A red cast is corrected with a blue filter, and so on.

In practice, in cave photography an exact correction is rarely needed; there is little point in experimenting with alternative light sources if a major effort is then made to attain a perfect daylight correction. Additionally, cavers use artificial light in the form of an electric or acetylene helmet light, and are therefore not viewing the cave in 'correct' colours in the first place. Despite this, filters can remove an extreme effect and are used to produce an accurate rendition on film for scientific recording or with showcave lights.

Filters are numbered in the Kodak Wratten series, which is divided into two groups: strong colours for coarse correction, and weak colours for fine-tuning. Wratten numbers 80 and 82 are blue, 85 and 81 are reddish-yellow. The first number in each pair is the strongest colour. As a generalisation, the colour cast on film becomes redder when the colour temperature drops and an increasingly dense blue filter is needed to compensate.

Calibrated gel filters are available from Kodak and other companies. Theatres are a cheaper source of large gels for filtering light sources, rather than the light entering the lens

Filter factors

Filters remove one or more of the component colours of light, resulting in less light reaching the film. To compensate for this, heavy filtration requires an exposure correction: the decrease in light demands a wider aperture, a longer exposure or a more intense light source.

Automatic cameras which measure light reaching the film take this loss of intensity into account and increase the exposure. However, the camera's exposure meter (or flashmeter if, rather than filtering light entering the lens, the light source itself is filtered) assumes that the spectrum of light conforms to 'average' daylight. A strong colour such as red may be misread and cause underexposure. Filters are therefore given a 'filter factor' which indicates an increase in exposure by opening the aperture by a stated amount. This filter factor is ideal for underground use.

Filter factors

Blue filters		Filter factor	Open the aperture by (f-stops)		Filter factor	'Warm' filters	
Dense blue	80A	4.0	2	2/3	1.7	85B	Reddish
	80B	3.4	1 2/3	2/3	1.7	85	
↑	80C	2.0	1	1/3	1.3	85C	↑
	80D	1.3	1/3	2/3	1.7	81E	
	82C	1.7	2/3	2/3	1.7	81D	
↓	82B	1.7	2/3	1/3	1.3	81C	↓
	82A	1.3	1/3	1/3	1.3	81B	Pale
Pale blue	82	1.3	1/3	1/3	1.3	81A	yellow

Filter factors are approximate: check the manufacturer's data for the specific filter

EXPOSURE

Long exposures from weak light sources suffer from reciprocity, but do not overcompensate what appears to be dim lighting or the mood of the picture will be ruined. Here, a sitting (and therefore static) caver is maintaining his helmet light using a chemical lightstick, the sole illumination for this 20s exposure

In the dark, the aperture and flash intensity control the exposure. Given a fixed aperture a bright light for a short duration equates to a dim light for a longer period; both theoretically produce the same exposure as the total light emitted is identical. However, when a long-burning source is involved, such as the continuous light from an acetylene flame, magnesium ribbon or showcave lights, some additional exposure calculations are needed.

While the short burst of light from flashpowder is almost as predictable as that from a flashbulb, a long exposure using candlelight or a carbide headset presents difficulties. There is a temptation to deliberately over-expose the photograph to account for what is perceived as a weak light source, but beware of taking this reasoning too far. Overexposure will certainly reveal more of the surrounding area, but then the source itself

becomes unacceptably bright in the picture. If the exposure and composition are handled carefully, light from an acetylene flame on a caver's helmet will spill or reflect onto a caver's face and body from the surroundings but leave the background to trail into darkness. Longer exposures force a static pose: sitting positions are easier to maintain than standing ones. Reflective surfaces such as calcite, wet walls or a pool of water all help to ensure a successful picture when using atmospheric lighting effects.

The difficulty lies in assessing what aperture to use and how long to make the exposure with an unfamiliar, and often dim, light source. Potentially, it can be measured at close quarters with an exposure meter. The indicated aperture and shutter speed are then extrapolated for a greater distance. In practice, it is more usual to make a test series of pictures and bracket the experimentally determined exposure.

Reciprocity

Normally, shutter speed and aperture have a direct link: closing the aperture by one f-stop requires double the shutter speed or flash intensity. However, this relationship breaks down at extremely short and long exposures and, outside the range of about 1/1000 second and 1 second, film becomes increasingly insensitive to light. The effect is termed reciprocity.

Reciprocity is not normally noticeable when using an electronic flashgun because its short-duration burst of light is taken into account when the guide number is calculated. Long exposures are another matter, when underexposure with a continuous light source has much to do with a film's reciprocity failure. As well as an alteration in sensitivity, reciprocity also causes a change in colour towards blue and may require a corresponding correction filter in the 81 range to maintain a 'correct' colour balance.

Reciprocity

Indicated exposure	1s	10s	30s	1 min	10 min
Open aperture by (f-stops)	+1	+1.5	+2	+2.5	+3
or					
Increase time to	2s	30s	2 min	6 min	80 min

- These corrections are practical values, to be used in conjunction with bracketing. Effects with longer exposures are more difficult to assess. An exposure of 1 minute (translating to a 6 minute duration) is a practical limit
- Black and white negatives are theoretically affected less. Reducing development time by between 10 per cent (for 1s exposures) and 30 per cent (10 minute exposures) helps control a contrast rise

The table above is pragmatic and forms the basis for further investigation. The interrelated effects of using an unusual light source, reciprocity and the inherent difficulties of cave photography combine to make this area ripe for experimentation.

LIGHTING

Colour balance, filtration and reciprocity failure affect most or all photographs taken with alternative light sources. Take each into account, even if only in order to make a calculated decision to ignore their effects.

Some light sources are inconvenient or unacceptable for underground use as they produce pollutants: take extreme care and carry a first aid kit. This section considers the sources which are commonly considered appropriate for underground use, in each case suggesting experimental starting points for exposure determination.

Acetylene flame

Any continuous light source can be used to 'paint' a scene while the camera shutter is locked open on B. 'Painting' a photograph builds up a picture just as an artist might decide which parts of a canvas to cover. Keeping the light source moving prevents hard-edged shadows from forming, a trick employed by early photographers using magnesium ribbon.

In particular, an acetylene flame on a caver's helmet, produced by a expedition-style carbide generator, produces a pleasing, warm golden glow within a photograph. Here is an opportunity to create feeling and depth in a moody, atmospheric photograph with minimal lighting, for example a caver beside a pool of water or wet, light-coloured rock; lighting every corner of the photograph destroys this effect. Relatively short-duration exposures are possible and, with fast film and an open aperture, 1s might be enough for a reasonably close-up subject. Timed exposures of several seconds or minutes are more suitable for general scenes.

It is impossible to give an exact guide number for an acetylene flame as its size, light output and reflector can vary a great deal. An exposure of 30s at f4 with ISO 100 film and a flame-to-subject distance of 2m is a

This square-cut section of a mine was lit solely using the caver's helmet-mounted acetylene light. Although a pure silhouette might be expected, there is often considerable reflection from the surrounding walls and water during a long exposure (in this case 30s at f4) which adds detail to shadow areas

basis for experiment, but what is perceived as acceptable results from a test series will vary extensively from one person to another; the same flame might require only a few seconds' exposure if it is prominently within the picture. When painting a scene, remember that doubling the light-to-subject distance quarters the illumination; this quadruples the exposure time. Doubling a painted area requires twice the total exposure time. Take both factors into account when planning a shot, and make further allowances for reciprocity failure.

Magnesium ribbon

The first cave photograph was taken in 1865 using a taper made from strips of magnesium. Being rich in the blue actinic component of light that photographic plates were sensitive to, magnesium soon helped establish the basic tenets of cave photography.

Large magnesium flares will burn underwater and the metal is still used

The clouds of magnesium fumes are all too obvious in this photograph taken by Charles Waldack in 1866 in Mammoth Cave, Kentucky. These fumes must be taken into account when planning any magnesium-lit photograph

in a few showcaves for lighting. However, in the form of ribbon, pure powder or flashpowder, this traditional light source produces copious clouds of pungent smoke and fumes. In the past, cave photographers notoriously had one, and only one, opportunity to take a photograph before having to move on or waiting for the air to clear – modern cave photographers take note.

For reasons of conservation, using magnesium is extremely questionable in all but limited circumstances. Both the cave environment and, in particular, the cave life will be affected. Experiments with magnesium should be restricted to areas where damage will not occur, perhaps in large cave or mine entrances which have a good outward draught. The term 'large'

Acetylene

ONLY the caver's helmet-mounted acetylene light was used to take this picture, which relies on reflection from the water to add detail to shadow areas. The exposure was 20s at f4 on ISO 200 film

ALTERNATIVE LIGHTING

Magnesium

MAGNESIUM ribbon and powder record as a warm, golden light on colour film. Igniting two or more ribbons at precisely the same time can be difficult. Here, the caver in the picture lit one strand then another caver, concealed in an alcove (right) and behind the subject to provide a backlight (inset), lit the second ribbon. The ribbons were gripped in a clothes peg and lit with a cigarette lighter

Each picture was taken in a disused silica mine in South Wales using two 15cm lengths of ribbon

SHOWCAVE LIGHTING

SHOWCAVES may use a mixture of light sources which appear white to the eye but record with different colours on film. These include sodium (yellow), metal halide (blue-white), mercury vapour (blue), tungsten (orange-red) and fluorescent (green). These pictures were taken in Cueva del Nerja in Spain (left), Ghar Dalam in Malta (below) and Carlsbad Caverns in New Mexico (both bottom pictures). See p.176

Underwater lighting

DIFFERENT effects can be produced using 'standard' lighting if it is used in 'non-standard' ways. In Youd's Level the caver is firing a blue (AG3B) flashbulb, without a reflector, about 30cm below the water surface. The water in this case is a vibrant green colour, but peaty water will produce rich browns.

There are distinct differences in light quality between the underwater light and the backlight, an electronic flash which has produced a cold, bluish tint to that part of the picture as well as freezing the movement of the water drips above the caver's head. Electronic flash is normally colder in colour than blue bulbs, with clear bulbs producing an orange or yellow glow

Candles and flashpowder

THIS scene in Gough's Cave (above) was lit by candles during an underground wedding.

Flashpowder was used in the picture of Browgill Cave (right). The powder was fired, then the resulting smoke was backlit with a flashbulb (see also p.175)

FLUORESCENCE AND PHOSPHORESCENCE

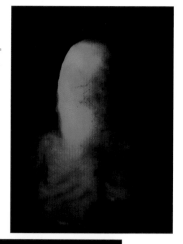

THESE calcite formations in Ogof Ffynnon Ddu were photographed to show phosphorescence and fluorescence. The phosphorescing stalagmite (right) was lit with 20 flashes at f4 (guide number 30 flashgun at 25cm distance), covering the lens during each flash.

Compare the record photographs (below left, E8) with pictures taken using a small, hand-held ultra-violet security light while the camera shutter was locked open on B (ISO 400 film, f4). The photograph at bottom centre illustrates the shortcomings of this technique: some non-calcite areas appear blue instead of black, indicating that the light was impure and exposed the film directly. Removing the blue wavelengths on a computer revealed the fluorescing calcite (middle and bottom right). These examples were taken using ISO 400 film at f4 for four minutes at 1m distance. (See also p.178)

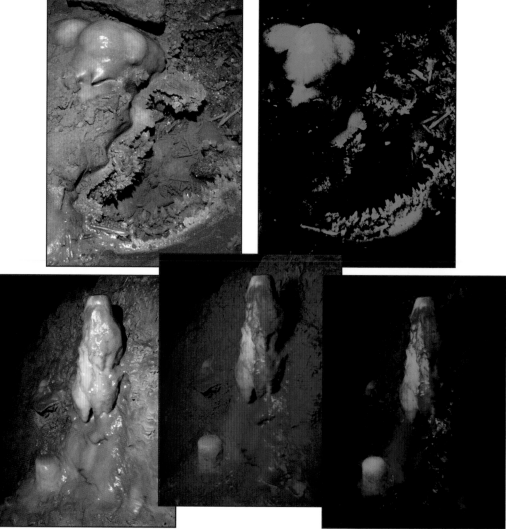

PRESERVING SPELEAN HISTORY

Printing-out paper

PRESERVING historical cave photographs begins with identifying the nature of the print. A common type is printing-out paper (otherwise known as 'pop'), typified – as in this example – by a rich sepia or reddish-brown colour. Introduced in the mid-1880s, printing-out paper was common through the 1920s but not totally abandoned until the late 1940s. Prints were normally made by contacting the negative with the paper and exposing it to sunlight; 'pop' prints are therefore normally the same size as the negative they were made from.

This photograph was taken by Ben Hains in 1892 and depicts a group of tourists (a guide is on the far right) enjoying a meal in Mammoth Cave, Kentucky

Silver image degradation

NOT all photographic images are based on silver; many modern colour processes replace the film's silver content with photographic dyes during processing. However, while these dyes fade in light, most older negatives and prints – at least those found within the caving sphere – are silver based and subject to silver degradation.

When sensitised material (film or print) is exposed to light, a reaction occurs and a latent image is formed. During development the silver-based chemicals darken and become visible, with any 'unused' silver salts removed when the image is fixed so that the rest of the image does not darken when placed in the light. Unfortunately, the remaining silver reacts readily with sulphur to form silver sulphide (sulphur may be present in low-quality mounting boards, as an atmospheric pollutant or, most commonly, as a residue from the fixing process) which causes blackening or staining.

The most important cause of deterioration comes from a cyclic oxidation and reduction of silver, producing faded prints and a typical 'silvered' image, most obvious when light is reflected from its surface.

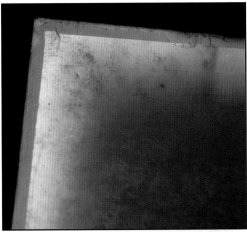

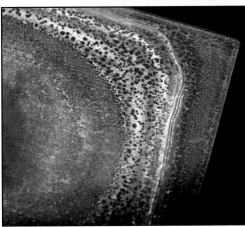

The two illustrations show corners of glass plate negatives which have reacted with airborne contaminants and suffered degradation. The cause of oxidation is likely to be pollutant gases such as fumes from paint, glue (including those present in plywood), low grade cardboard and many organic chemicals. To protect and preserve such images it is essential to keep them at a constant relative humidity of between 25% and 35% (total dessication causes the photographic emulsion to become too brittle), cool and dark; of these, moisture contributes more to silvering than any other factor (see p.251)

USING COLOUR AND BLACK & WHITE

Black and white photographs contain a range of tones representing the colours in the original scene. However, due to differences in sensitivity, some colours may translate to a darker or lighter tone than anticipated. This can cause problems with some subjects, for example red against a black background, which darkens in black and white to give black-on-black (see p.212).

Compare the colours in the pair of photographs above, taken on Fuji Velvia slide film and FP4 black and white film (E8, B6). Reds are considerably darker in the black and white version, where there is little tonal difference between the black boots and the oversuit. Conversely, the yellow sack and light green helmet show up well. Take colour into account when working in black and white and, if possible, decrease potential problems by using models wearing appropriate colours.

The formations in Gilwern Passage, Ogof Draenen (E8, B4) were taken on Fuji Velvia (right) and Kodachrome 200 films and show marked differences in colour saturation. Using a strong colour is important: one caver is wearing a muddy oversuit while the other has changed into a clean oversuit carried in for the purpose

FORMATIONS are ideal subjects for colour photography. In Ogof Ffynnon Taf the curtain (left, E4) has been backlit from below the level of the camera to add texture as well as show its translucent nature. The small detail is from an area of flowstone in Ogof Draenen (E8)

THESE photographs in Dan yr Ogof (above, B6) and Little Neath River Cave (B5) were lit with a single, 'clear' bulb intended for use with black and white film, giving a red cast to the picture

MAKING A
SANDWICH

SANDWICHED photographs are produced when two slides are placed in the same mount; the combination of images can be extremely strong.

These examples, from Bacon Hole, were created in the darkroom by making a lith positive silhouette of the entrance (above) from a colour transparency. Lith film yields only black and transparent tones (there are no greys). It was sandwiched with the background, the helmet light added, then rephotographed on a slide duplicator.

Making a lith is not difficult; the equipment required is simple and full darkroom facilities are not needed. The use of lith film is described in standard photographic textbooks. Sandwiches can obviously be constructed on a computer (see p.239), but these pictures demonstrate that hi-tech equipment is not always needed in order to experiment

Exposures with magnesium ribbon

Length (cm)	15	30	60	120	240
Weight (g)	0.15	0.3	0.6	1.2	2.4
Burning time (s)	20	40	80	160	320
Guide number	16	22	32	44	64

Theoretical figures are based on:
* A film speed of ISO 100
* Ribbon 2.5mm wide in a single length
* No reflector

Note also:
* Tapers decrease the total burning time, but not necessarily in direct proportion to the number of lengths of ribbon
* The weight of magnesium ribbon can be transferred to powder as a starting point for experimentation
* No account has been taken of reciprocity failure when constructing these figures

is operative. Given the problems of fumes and highly sensitive film emulsions, other forms of lighting are more suitable in confined spaces. However, for working in immense chambers magnesium provides a very cheap, high-intensity light for its size and weight.

Magnesium ribbon is available from chemical suppliers, normally in 25g rolls approximately 2.5mm wide. Clean the oxidised surface of old ribbon by gently scraping it with fine sandpaper. Several strands can be twisted together to form a taper, so that if one strand goes out the others relight it and the total burning time is reduced. Grip the ribbon or taper in tongs or pliers, or clip it to the rim of a large reflector (for example made from a car headlight or metal dish) so that it hangs downwards in front of the reflector. Light the magnesium using the continuous flame of a cigarette lighter rather than a match.

Take the clouds of fumes which will occlude the scene into account when planning the composition. A caver holding a taper will soon be enveloped by the white smoke it produces, although burning short lengths to produce a silhouette can be effective. Place the magnesium well away from the camera, down-draught if possible. Shadows can be softened by moving the ribbon while it burns, although undue vibration may cause the burning tip to fall off and extinguish the light.

Exposure guides are necessarily approximate as they are affected by the size and type of reflector. With ISO 100 film and an aperture of f4, experiment with a 15cm length of ribbon at 4m from the subject:

Two 15cm lengths of magnesium ribbon, one held by the caver and another as a backlight, were burned in this mine adit

effectively, this gives a guide number of 16. Theoretically, 30cm of ribbon will therefore permit an aperture of f5.6 (twice the light output reduces the aperture by one f-stop), but this assumption may not be accurate due to reciprocity failure. Tapers reduce the exposure time, but some light is lost due to absorption and heat. The time reduction is not necessarily linear: a three-ribbon taper may burn in half (rather than one-third) the time taken by a single length, for example. Construct an exposure table specific to your ribbon and reflector.

Magnesium powder

Magnesium powder produces a flash of light rather than an extended period of burning. It can be difficult to ignite as, without a good supply of oxygen, the inside of a heap of powder remains unburned.

Traditionally, magnesium powder was lit by puffing it through the flame of a spirit lamp. A variation on this theme added petrol vapour to the current of air, or used a special lamp with several heads. A very basic home-made system was a clay pipe, wrapped in cotton wool soaked in methylated spirits or rubbing alcohol and set alight. The powder was blown by mouth through the flame. Such devices were not at all safe – cave photographers aspiring to pyrotechnic photography be warned.

To burn powder efficiently increase its effective surface area. Pour powder through an acetylene flame (mix the powder with a small quantity of dry sand to help it burn evenly), sprinkle it into a metal dish of burning, alcohol-soaked cotton wool, or spread it on newspaper then light the paper.

Australian cave photographers have used a Diprotodon powder burner, named after an extinct genus of giant wombat. Designed to light huge chambers, finely powdered magnesium is gravity fed into a stream of air or butane gas and burned in a reflector. A Nichrome wire across the nozzle is heated by continued burning, and ignites more powder as it emerges. Different models exist but, in general, a rate of 1g of powder per second produces a flame over a metre long; 30s duration gives a guide number approaching 800, measured in metres with ISO 100 film. Because the

Magnesium powder burners were many and varied. Powder could be blown through a tube into a candle flame (left), or into burning alcohol in a commercially manufactured lamp. Both methods were used in early cave photography

---

Preparing flashpowder

Formula 1: Magnesium 4 parts, potassium perchlorate 3 parts, potassium chlorate 3 parts
*A predictable, rapid-burning flash. Finely powder the chemicals **prior** to mixing*

Formula 2: Magnesium 1 part, potassium nitrate 1 part
A rapid-burning flash, supposedly less explosive than some other formulae

Formula 3: Magnesium 5 parts, barium nitrate 7 parts, sulphur 1 part, beef suet 2 parts
A long-duration, slow-burning flash. Mix the chemicals, knead into warm suet and roll it into a sausage shape. Light the centre. The formula uses large quantities of magnesium more predictably than other formulae

Formula 4: Magnesium 7 parts, potassium chlorate 3 parts
A powerful flash, roughly double the intensity of formula 1

Touchpaper: Soak absorbent paper in strong potassium nitrate solution, dry and cut into strips

---

flame is continuous, photographs based on an exposure meter reading can be taken at any time while the Diprotodon is lit.

The duration of a magnesium powder flash partly depends on the quantity of powder that is used. The flash is not as fast as flashpowder, but substantial amounts can be burned within one or two seconds – far faster than magnesium ribbon. The data given for Diprotodon, with that for magnesium ribbon, provides a valid starting point for experiments. However, in common with magnesium ribbon and flashpowder, doubling the amount of powder does not necessarily double the light output.

Flashpowder

Flashpowder was the 1880s answer to problems of artificial light photography as it provided an easily ignited, high-intensity light source. A variety of formulae were developed, all based on magnesium powder mixed with a chemical oxidising agent to enable large quantities to be burned in a predictable manner. Flashpowder is more controllable than magnesium ribbon and produces highly intense flashes which are well suited to large chambers.

Flashpowder is an explosive mixture; its use has led to several fatalities. While its separate components are safe, the mixture is not. If the powder becomes damp discard it; drying moist flashpowder causes the chemicals to clump together and the mixture becomes more explosive. Keep flashpowder dry until the moment of use, and do not leave it uncovered in humid cave air while waiting for the picture to be prepared. Treat all forms of magnesium lighting with extreme care.

During preparation, mix the chemicals by pouring pre-measured quantities onto paper and gently shake them together or stir with a wooden spatula. Weigh out small amounts of flashpowder into twists of tissue paper and seal them inside an airtight container. Each twist gives a

Flashpowder produced so much smoke that bags were sometimes used to contain the fumes. This lamp was fired after a muslin shroud was lowered in place; other versions were hand-held

Flashpowder guide numbers

Weight (g)	1.2	2.5	6	14	30
Guide number	32	44	64	90	130

- Guide numbers are approximate and depend on the formula; these are based on formula 1
- Large quantities may not burn evenly and emit less light per unit weight
- Spread large quantities in a line and light in the middle using a fuse
- Approximate weights can be estimated using a simple balance:
  A US 5c coin weighs 5g
  A £1 coin weighs 10g
  A 49mm lens filter weighs 15g
  10g of flashpowder fills a 35mm film container

Goyden Pot (E8, B5 with flashpowder smoke)

predictable flash which, effectively, simulates the fixed emission of a flashbulb and by experiment yields a usable guide number.

Burn the twist of flashpowder in a tray or on a piece of dry stone, either by lighting the paper or using a fuse made from magnesium ribbon, blue touchpaper from a theatrical agency, or remotely with a heated wire. To avoid an explosion, spread larger quantities in a line and light it in the centre rather than as a heap. Consider safety: ensure there are no acetylene flames nearby (including your personal helmet lighting), recap powder containers immediately, do not approach a misfired pile of flashpowder for several minutes, use a taper not a match, and wear a glove when lighting the fuse. When it fires, cavers should be at least 2m away to avoid spitting particles. Magnesium burns are painful; carry a basic first aid kit.

Showcave lighting

Although bright to the eye, showcave lights are dim compared with the power of a flashgun and their effect on a picture can often be ignored. Problems only arise with mixed flash/fixed lighting if a lamp is visible and shining towards the camera, or an extended time exposure is used.

Showcave lights are often a mixture of lamp types and intensities, causing difficulties when using B because a mixture of colour casts in the photograph is produced; the garish colours in some cave postcards are not due to coloured lights, but only to the mismatch of colour temperature and film. While a single cast can be corrected using a filter over the lens, a mixture of colour casts cannot.

The brightest lights probably come from high-pressure sodium, metal halide or mercury vapour lamps. These are used in caves as the lamps remain cool while lit but, unfortunately for the cave photographer, some colours are missing from their emission spectra. In addition, it is possible that tungsten lamps (as used for room lighting), halogen lamps (similar to projector bulbs) and fluorescent lights will also be present. Each records with a different colour on film; tungsten and halogen lights produce a warm colour and metal halide a cold cast, for example (see p.166).

If a single type of lamp is involved and can be identified, its cast can be corrected. Exact correction filters are not always available, so colour correction gels – similar to filter sets used for photographic colour printing – are used; large gels are cheaply available from theatres, where they are used to filter spotlights. If the light sources are mixed and you have permission from the showcave owner, filter each lamp individually. One benefit of mixed lighting is that a warm colour cast from one lamp can help correct the blue or green cast from another. A mixture of tungsten bulbs and mercury vapour lamps or fluorescent tubes, if their effects overlap, may make the picture more acceptable.

Mixed light sources can be ignored when photographing in black and white. This picture, in Endless Caverns, Virginia, was taken with a mixture of showcave lights in the background and flash (E2, B6)

Showcave lights

Light	Cast	Correction filters
High-pressure sodium	Yellow	80B + 20C
Metal halide	Blue-white	40M + 20Y
Mercury vapour	Blue	60M + 30Y
Tungsten/halogen	Orange-red	80A (blue)
Fluorescent	Green	30M *or* FLD

Correction filter values are for daylight-balanced film

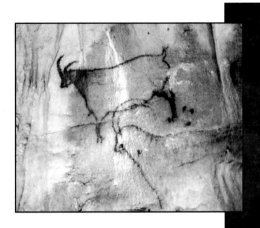

Showcave lighting

Showcave photographs which would not be viable in colour, due to the cast that is created, may be taken in black and white. Flash photography is not permitted near the cave art in the Grottes de Cougnac, France (above), but resting the camera on a railing and using the dim tungsten light was sufficient to record the figures on film. The Twin Domes (right) and the Big Room in Carlsbad Caverns (below) were taken with a tripod-mounted camera using the showcave lights.

Showcave lights are ideal for taking photographs in black and white, such as in the Cueva del Nerja in Spain, but filtration is needed to match the characteristics of colour film

All electronic lighting changes colour with age and voltage: decreasing the mains voltage by as little as 10 per cent (the approximate difference between 120V and 110V, or 240V and 220V) causes an appreciable warm cast on film. Unless an extremely accurate colour balance is required the effect – at its worst with vapour emission lamps or cine lights – is normally ignored, but it illustrates the difficulties of accurate filtration.

Accurate lighting is best achieved using standard cave photography techniques; flashguns are more predictable than showcave lights. When showcave lighting cannot be avoided, perhaps because the owner requires its use for a publicity photograph, avoid placing a person in a prominent foreground position. A colour cast on formations may be acceptable, but the same effect on a face is not: use a silhouette, or light a person with a supplementary flash.

Excellent photographs can be obtained using showcave lights and black and white film, in particular of large chambers with a tripod-mounted camera. An automatic camera makes the exposure calculation easy, but bracket the exposure and take reciprocity and colour into account. Red-rich colours, often found in cave mud or iron-stained calcite, cause exposure meters to underexpose and, without compensation, large areas of white calcite may appear grey. Increase the estimated exposure by one f-stop to compensate for the reddish light of tungsten or sodium lamps.

Luminescence

Some minerals absorb high-intensity, short wavelength radiation such as ultra-violet (UV) light and emit it as a longer, visible wavelength; the effect is termed fluorescence. Once UV radiation ceases the fluorescence stops, but some minerals continue to emit radiation. This is termed phosphorescence (though sometimes the continued afterglow is also – incorrectly – referred to as fluorescence). Both effects are present in caves as calcite can fluoresce during, or phosphoresce after, exposure to the high-intensity light from a flashgun.

Cavers sometimes fire a flash at a formation from close quarters, then open their eyes to see the afterglow. The colour they see depends on the crystal structure (in particular its trace impurities) and the energy it has

---

Fluorescence and phosphorescence

Differences in the colour and intensity of emissions from fluorescing and phosphorescing calcite produce a wide range of results. Use the following data as the basis for experimentation and bracket all exposures:

Aperture: Wide open, or f4 if slight depth of field is required
Film: ISO 400 or faster (the following data applies to ISO 400 film and an aperture of f4)
Light-to-subject distance: 30cm
Fluorescence: 90 seconds with a 6V UV security light, or set the camera on auto and −1 compensation. The background may appear blue with this imperfect light source and require subsequent analysis to identify the fluorescing components
Phosphorescence: Approximately 30 flashes with a guide number 30 flashgun, covering the lens during each flash

---

This formation in Dan yr Ogof was photographed using electronic flash to record its setting (left, E7). An ultra-violet light source was then used in total darkness with the camera shutter locked open on B. The resulting photograph was computer enhanced to remove the effects of direct exposure by the light source, which was impure, and reveal the areas of fluorescing calcite

absorbed: calcite's emission ranges from green to blue-green, and lasts up to ten seconds. If the intensity of light is high enough, phosphorescence can affect normal cave photography. In 1952 Tex Helm, photographing in Carlsbad Caverns with over two thousand flashbulbs, reported that phosphorescence affected his calculated apertures.

Phosphorescing calcite can be photographed with a tripod-mounted camera on B, using multiple flashes to build up an exposure. The flash itself must not expose the film, so between each flash cover the lens with light-proof material such as several layers of black velvet or darkroom blind material. With the shutter open the sequence is: cover the lens, fire the flash, uncover the lens while the calcite phosphoresces, cover the lens, and repeat the cycle. Practise the technique of covering and un-covering the lens in the dark. Successive exposures on the same piece of film build up the image, though there is a diminishing effect when large numbers of flashes are involved as reciprocity failure occurs.

True fluorescence can be photographed using a continuous UV light source. Small, battery-powered security lights or actinic fluorescent tubes used by aquarists, if mains electricity is available, are suitable. Theoretic-ally, a UV filter over the lens is required to prevent the UV light from affecting the film directly, but modern coated lenses are poor UV transmitters and few problems arise.

These theoretical methods are far from infallible. Phosphorescence, though clearly visible to the eye, does not record well on film and a large number of flashes at close quarters are required. An extremely powerful flashgun will help; those made for underwater photography are usually highly powered and portable, though bulky. For the best chance of success use a fast film, a wide aperture, a powerful flashgun and concentrate on a small area of calcite. Experiment with exposures and, if necessary, extrapo-late these to photograph larger areas such as a calcite-draped chamber.

The cave diver was lit with an electronic flash (E8) with the backlighting provided by a car headlight attached to a 12V battery

It is possible to take a photograph of phosphorescence using a single flash, for example with a fast colour film of ISO 1000 (which can itself be uprated during processing). When only one flash is involved the phosphorescence can be synchronised with the shutter, even though the flash is not fired with the shutter open.

Focal plane (FP) flashbulbs were made to take flash pictures at speeds faster than 1/60 second. They emit light at a constant intensity for a relatively long time, so that the film is exposed by what is effectively a constant light source. To avoid the light which is output during the initial build-up of intensity from affecting the film, FP bulbs are fired before the shutter is released using the FP synchronisation setting. If an SLR's FP setting is used with electronic flash the photograph will be totally black because the flashgun will have ceased to emit light before the shutter opens. This 'fault' gives an advantage when photographing phosphorescence: the electronic flash fires, *then* the shutter opens and admits light from the afterglow. With a powerful flash and fast film, full synchronisation is retained and the picture is taken using a tripod but without the need to cover and uncover the lens.

Take care when interpreting the photographic results. If areas of mud can be seen in the picture, they must have been lit by stray light from a flash or helmet light; if these areas are blue this is probably due to an imperfect UV light source which is also emitting other wavelengths. The pictures can still be used; areas of different colour can be analysed by computer, comparing their densities with a piece of unexposed but processed film and then stripping out the stray light from the digitised, blue channel. Areas of 'normal' lighting are probably caused by an imperfect cover over the lens during the flash.

For both fluorescence and phosphorescence, run a series of test exposures to take into account the wide variety of calcite emissions which may be present. It is helpful, in all these types of pictures, to take a photograph under 'normal' lighting to provide a record which can be used to compare the fluorescing areas with the actual shape of the calcite (see p.168).

Other light sources

Experimenting with unusual light sources underground depends more on what is convenient and available than any technical reason why it can or cannot be used. Butane gas camping lanterns yield interesting results. Candlelight is particularly appealing and, with enough candles, remarkably bright (see p.167); it is certainly an underrated light source. Candles have been used in caves to make long-duration, close-up exposures using extremely small apertures, producing an outstanding depth of field.

Continuous light sources enable the photographer to see exactly what is being taken. Checks can be made that lighting is even, and long exposures of an hour or more can proceed while exploration takes place elsewhere. Other sources of light will no doubt come to mind; if conservation is not an issue and they are considered safe to use underground, try them out.

SPECIAL EFFECTS

The light sources suggested in this chapter are intended as pointers towards further experimentation, including developing new techniques for electronic flash and flashbulbs. To paraphrase a quotation, cave photography is the mother of invention.

Synchronised flash using slave units can leave a caver's helmet light appearing dim or unlit because it is not as bright as the flashguns. This picture was taken in West Kingsdale Master Cave using experimental lighting. The main illumination is provided by a flashbulb (B5), with an electronic flash to simulate a helmet lamp.

The circuit and flash tube from an Instamatic camera were mounted in the empty shell of a helmet lamp; connectors enabled the easy attachment of an external battery and slave unit. Tests showed that the flash was too bright for the power of the backlight, so to balance the flashes a neutral density filter was fitted behind a white plastic 'glass'

Modifications to lighting techniques and equipment may be required in confined spaces or for special effects. For example, a sealed flash and slave unit on a small piece of wood enables backlighting in a tight, water-filled passage where an assistant cannot operate. A flashbulb hanging below a raft, attached to the shore by a piece of string, helps light the far side of a lake. For underwater effects use a bulb with no reflector to obtain wide, even lighting.

Some cave photographs appear unnatural because they are taken with helmet lights switched off during long exposures, or because the helmet light is swamped by the flashes and appears dim or unlit in the photograph. Experiment a little. The flash tube from a small Instamatic-type flashgun will fit inside an Oldham or Wheat lamp case, with the circuit, batteries and a slave unit mounted on the helmet. Control the flash intensity by placing tracing paper, white plastic or a grey gelatine filter under the helmet light's glass; the effect can look extremely natural.

Consider mixing colour casts from different sources. The warm, golden light from an acetylene flame against the blue tinge of an electronic flash gives a striking effect, while the colour balance between a clear flashbulb and acetylene is a close match. Choose the combination of lights with respect to the film's characteristics with care.

In short, the essence of good cave photography is to rise to a challenge and, rather than feeling that existing techniques and equipment cannot produce the photograph you envisage, find a way to *make* it work. After all, this is how modern systems were developed – by experimentation. Solving problems is the only way in which cave photography will advance its boundaries. Break the rules and see what results. Imagination and determination are the keys to success.

Unusual angles are important when searching for a 'different' photograph. These stalactites were photographed in the Grottes de Cougnac in France using an electronic flash

Chapter ten
EXPEDITION PHOTOGRAPHY

Looking up from 30m depth, daylight streamed past us. An underwater photographer's paradise, green rays through clear water, yellow torchlight from divers drifting down, stalactites hanging from sheer walls. I knew the 17mm lens should include the whole scene, but I'd lost the viewfinder; somewhere, it lay in the silt at the bottom of the shaft. I held out the flash on a boom arm, aimed the camera without knowing what I was framing, and hoped for the best.

Stargate, Bahamas

E XPEDITIONS require photographic documentation for publications, lectures, sponsors, and scientific and personal use. Photographic techniques are the same during an expedition as for a day's caving, but with different complications. Preparations, modifying equipment and photographic processing in a harsh environment are all more difficult or impossible.

Expeditions may be small and involve only a handful of friends, or be large, complex and highly organised. The nature of the expedition (diving,

A huge daylight shaft in Royal Arch Cave in Chillagoe, Queensland

deep exploration, reconnaissance of a new area . . .) and the terrain (jungle or arid karst, town-based or camping accommodation . . .) will vary greatly. These factors dictate much of the required preparations, and also whether a designated expedition photographer (or, at least, someone charged with organising a photographic record) is required, or if every member of the team will take photographs in their own right. Equally, a small group of friends caving together in foreign climes – or even a different state in the US – will need to make many of the same preparations as members of a large expedition. Whatever the case, planning ahead is all-important and this chapter discusses some of the specific photographic issues which should be considered.

Initial preparations

A designated expedition photographer may have to arrange equipment and film for the expedition as a whole. This requirement is particularly relevant when approaching sponsors.

Good expedition coverage is not restricted to underground photography; surface photography is important to help set the scene. Fundraising events, lectures and publications require full coverage of every facet of the

expedition, so document its day-to-day running as well as the more obvious fruits of exploration. Faced with a campfire at night or stars seen through a cave entrance, could you determine the exposure? Different destinations demand different approaches; dense jungle cover might require a fast film while a polarising filter is often useful in open terrain – the list of minutiae is endless.

Some team members may choose to photograph their own specialist subjects, such as cave life or archaeology, but the expedition photo-

Be prepared to photograph the expedition's day-to-day activities – such pictures will be invaluable for lectures and reports. These photographs illustrate part of the Andros Project, a cave diving and scientific expedition to the Bahamas. Freight, including a jeep and boats, is loaded into a container (top) and saltwater samples taken from blue holes are being analysed (above).

Even if there is no product to photograph it is sometimes possible to include a sponsor's name in pictures, such as with the record of core samples from marine and inland blue holes (right)

grapher should nevertheless be prepared to tackle any subject which arises. Think about the situations which might occur and the type of pictures you may need to take – if there are any techniques you are unsure of read a standard photographic textbook and practise what you learn before departure.

Adequate preparations for expedition cave photography involve one or more of the following topics, some of which interrelate, but all of which should be addressed before leaving home:

- Equipment
- Consumable items
- Contracts and agreements
- Sponsorship
- Shipping and transport
- Maintenance

EQUIPMENT

Time for cave photography is restricted, so it is even more important than when caving near home that equipment is reliable and techniques are efficient and fast. With limited consumable items such as flashbulbs and batteries, you may not have the luxury of repeating shots and bracketing. This is no place for experiments in the hope that a picture will result.

It is sensible to use tried and tested cameras and flashguns, but additional back-up equipment in case of failure is essential; it is unlikely that there will be a convenient repair shop nearby. Check flashgun guide numbers and fully test new gear before leaving. Spare items of equipment enable you to continue working in adverse situations, when breakages or losses occur.

There are usually several cavers taking photographs during an expedition but, equally, there may be restrictions on the weight or volume of gear that can be carried; backpacking in a jungle requires minimal equipment,

The floor of Kitum Cave in Kenya is pock-marked with animal tracks and piles of guano (right, B7), while deeper into the cave a recent roof fall (E8, B8) has significantly changed the access route for the cave's main visitors: elephants

not bulky, redundant spares. Discuss and agree beforehand if and how some items can be shared. Extra flashguns for specific shots, for example of a large chamber, might be taken from a pool of equipment.

Slave units have revolutionised cave photography and are extremely reliable, but even the best electronic design can fail. Pack a sturdy tripod and know how to use it; open flash techniques are dependable and require little equipment.

Cameras and lenses

Manual cameras are essential for continued underground work, although some automatic SLR cameras have a mechanical B setting and a single, flash-synchronised shutter speed which allows flash photography even if the batteries and sophisticated circuits have failed. Automatic compact cameras are ideal for surface photography and to record day-to-day life at the expedition base. Many are small and, being easily accessible in a waist-mounted pouch or pocket, are easy and fast to operate where unpacking a rucksack would be inconvenient. Consider taking both types of camera to use as the situation dictates.

There are advantages in using two manual cameras underground. Design a support which will carry both cameras alongside each other on a tripod. Using B for at least one camera (the other can fire a slave, for example), two pictures can be taken with a single set of flashes, saving time and resources. Exposures can be on different film stock, producing a print and slide, or be at different apertures to bracket the shot.

For surface work, a good quality zoom lens in the 70–200mm range is ideal for photographing distant karst features and local people without undue intrusion. An extreme wide-angle lens is ideal for landscapes which place the rest of the photographs in context.

Transport

Consider how cameras and flashguns will be carried underground, especially if baggage limitations mean that a compromise over equipment has been made. An Ortlieb drybag is light and extremely useful and, when fitted inside a tackle sack, is perhaps the next best thing to a waterproof hard case.

Search for items which can be purchased locally and might help to solve specific problems. Plastic food boxes with snap lids help protect cameras from water, and zip-lock bags form excellent stand-bys (to make leaks immediately visible use a double set of bags with a strip of coloured tissue between them). Think of ways around difficulties.

A wide-angle zoom lens is invaluable for precisely framing subjects on the surface when it is not possible to change the camera position, as here at the Devil's Coach House at Jenolan, New South Wales. The circle indicates a figure, included for scale

Processing

Setting up a field darkroom enables exposures to be checked during the course of the expedition, and allows time to retake any failed photographs. In any case, repeat important photographs – even, for vital shots, on a different film as it is not unknown for an entire roll to be lost or damaged.

Processing E6 films in the field is relatively easy, only requiring at its most basic a developing tank and processing chemicals. In addition, a changing bag is needed to transfer the film to the tank, a means of measuring the chemicals and bottles for storing them, and a thermometer

Minimal equipment is required for a field darkroom, set up here in an outbuilding on the island of Andros (the room was only used at night, avoiding the need for a blackout).

Processing films is even easier and well within the range of any expedition which has a good supply of clean water; exposures can be checked and important pictures repeated when necessary

and watch to determine processing times. A darkroom is not needed, although a good supply of fresh, clean water is essential. For printing in the field a simple enlarger, developing trays and a blackout are required. Although this may seem a bold step, a makeshift darkroom is easy to construct and the added materials need not be bulky; locally purchased black plastic is ideal for covering windows and, if all else fails, field processing outdoors is often viable at night – it is a misnomer that perfect darkness is needed when proof prints are all that are required. A method of heating chemicals may be needed in cold climates, although in the tropics E6 film can often be processed at room temperature.

If postal services are trustworthy and the expedition is a long one with storage problems, processed and unprocessed films can be sent home. If conditions are humid pack film in polythene bags, suck out the air, seal the bag and keep it cool. Unprocessed cassettes are easier to store than processed film, but if you are processing film and there is a chance to give the locals a slide show, take slide mounts with you.

CONSUMABLE ITEMS

Even if consumable items such as film and batteries will be available locally, it is safer to take everything with you. Film in many parts of the world is expensive or of dubious quality; in hot or humid countries storage may be suspect and unusual film types or speeds, other than the ubiquitous ISO 100 colour negative film, are often not available. Cheap, locally purchased carbon-zinc batteries, intended for transistor radios, may be incapable of powering an electronic flash.

Film

Photographs are needed to promote the expedition by means of displays, lectures and publications – and, of course, to supply sponsors with photographs after the expedition has closed and help obtain new sponsors who might support a return. Transparency film suits all these requirements, as slides can be projected or made into prints, and are easily duplicated for all expedition members.

However, transparencies are not ideal for all publications. Black and white film virtually always produces a better quality monochrome print than one made from a colour slide: shoot at least a few photographs in black and white. Equally, a good colour print is cheaper to produce from a negative rather than a slide. It may also yield a good black and white copy which is highly useful for promotions and sponsors. There is therefore no hard and fast rule, but record key subjects on more than one film type.

The entrance shaft to Märchenhöhle (Fairy Tale Cave), Namibia, lit with daylight plus a weak, directional fill-in flash (above: E1). The formations were lit with a single flashbulb (left: B6) plus a fill-in flash (top left: B4, E2)

Melidoni Cave, Crete (E2)

Films in the ISO 100 to ISO 200 range are good for general use. Slower slide films are useful for close-up and scientific recording. Large underground chambers, forests, jungle and predominantly overcast weather may demand faster films. Be prepared; anticipate what conditions will be present. Take more film than whatever maximum amount you think you will need – running out of film halfway through an expedition, in the middle of a desert or jungle, is not good planning!

Batteries

Taking spare batteries adds bulk and weight and may not be feasible. Estimate the number of flashes from a fresh set of batteries, allowing for fewer flashes when they are cold. Depending on the flashgun, a fresh set of alkaline batteries might produce between 50 and 100 full-power flashes.

Rechargeable batteries may not be viable, as mains electricity or a generator is needed for the charger. However, some expeditions have or can arrange these facilities. Solar-powered chargers are an alternative, but check the charger's efficiency – some commercial units are extremely poor and may not save much space or weight compared with taking additional, disposable batteries.

Do not overlook the obvious: fit a new camera battery before departing, and take plenty of spares together with a suitable coin for undoing the battery cover. Camera batteries can fail faster than expected, both because of the number of films being taken and changes in temperature.

Flashbulbs

Flashbulbs are unchallenged for output in large chambers, but may be limited in number due to restrictions in transport or availability. Large bulbs such as the M22B are often the first choice for expeditions, but there is little point in using expensive and bulky bulbs where an electronic flash or smaller bulb would suffice. Many AG3B bulbs can be packed into a small space: a box of 200 takes up a mere 140mm × 140mm × 80mm, the same volume as two or three M22B bulbs. Flashbars and flipflashes offer an alternative because the bulbs can be fired individually or together; a bank of bulbs equates with a single M22B.

Flashbulbs are extremely valuable for expedition photography, but the nature of the cave ultimately dictates how useful they are. In many circumstances, other than for the largest passages and chambers, there is no reason why a coherent system of electronic flashguns should not accomplish the same ends.

CONTRACTS AND AGREEMENTS

Large expeditions may use a contract covering such matters as copyright, sales of photographs and payment for materials. Even if this does not exist, an expedition photographer is wise to seek agreements with colleagues in order to avoid later difficulties.

Photo teams

Cave photographers sometimes forget that their passion is not always shared by other cavers. In the field a multitude of objectives – surveying, exploration, science – may be more popular than cave photography. Without cooperation, photographs will not be produced. The need for assistance, which will benefit the expedition as a whole, must be made clear before leaving: teamwork is essential in all spheres. A few cavers willing to form a regular photographic team are an invaluable asset; try to foster this ideal.

Explaining how to use photographic equipment while in the field wastes valuable time, as this could have been accomplished before leaving home. At a suitable venue conduct at least one session in a cave, even if it is to convince everyone that cave photography's notoriety is unfounded. Ensure that equipment is working correctly and that techniques are efficient for

---

Photographic agreements

This list is intended to form the basis for discussion; there are many other factors which could be included. Photographic agreements should take into account whether the expedition or the photographer is paying for materials. Agreements may differ according to the size of the expedition and whether there is a formally recognised photographer, or if all members are taking pictures and equally share the responsibility for supplying sponsors. Not all expeditions require a formal agreement, but make sure the relevant issues have been considered.

- The agreement applies to all photographers and photographs taken during the expedition [or only those taken underground]
- All photographs are copyrighted to the photographer [or expedition]. The expedition is granted the right to use all photographs for a period of [one, two or three] years after the close of the expedition
- Photographs taken by any member of the expedition will be available to other members for personal use at the cost of materials
- The photographer will be credited in all published material [in the form of expedition name/photographer name]
- The photographer [or expedition] will retain the first [insert value or percentage] of any fee received for each article or sale of photograph to any publication/other use
- After the [insert number] years, all rights and fees received revert to the photographer

The concept of a fixed fee or percentage of sales paid to the photographer takes into account photographic expenses and the effort involved in writing and selling articles or photographs. Examples include 66% to the expedition for underground work and 33% to the expedition for incidental, surface photographs; underground photographs require the assistance of other cavers, while surface views do not.

One of the entrances to Porcupine Blue Hole, Bahamas. This particular expedition's contract shared all income from photographs equally between the expedition and the photographer for two years or until all debts were paid and the expedition account was closed, whichever was soonest

that important day, or you run the risk of people always being too busy to help during the expedition itself.

Contracts

Formal contracts and agreements provide a focal point to clearly state expedition aims, and help avoid subsequent dissent. There are no hard and fast rules, but photographic copyright, payment for film and processing, income from publications, insurance and provision of photographs for sponsors should be covered.

There are two extremes. Large expeditions which cover all photographic expenses might expect to retain all the revenue from publications, while an individual on a small expedition who has personally paid all costs might expect to keep any receipts to offset expenses. A self-funded photographer should not be expected to provide pictures to expedition sponsors on behalf of all team members or, equally, to pass all income to the expedition. Such extremes ignore the effort which printing, duplicating and selling a photograph entails, apart from the matter of initial funding. A proportional division of money, weighted for the expedition or photographer according to the circumstances, is sometimes the best solution. Look for a middle ground. It is reasonable that in each case a time-limited agreement should be made, after which all photographic rights revert to the photographer. Sadly, financial matters can sour the outcome of a successful expedition: discuss these and make any necessary agreements before departure.

Copyright

Copyright exists in any work – including photographs – from the moment it is created and is owned by the person (normally termed the author) taking the picture, unless a written agreement states otherwise. Copyright cannot be claimed by default; it is impossible for a magazine, by reason of publication, to claim copyright of any material without a signed agreement. It is not necessary to register a photograph to claim copyright as this is an inherent right but, for added international protection (particularly in non-Berne Convention countries) use the copyright symbol ©, together with the photographer's name and year of production, on the mount or rear of the photograph.

Some countries, including the United Kingdom, recognise additional 'moral rights'. This gives a photographer the legal right to a credit and, if the moral right is exerted before a photograph is published in books, the right that the picture is not cropped or manipulated. While copyright can be sold or assigned (either permanently or for limited periods as part of agreements such as an expedition contract), a moral right cannot: it is inherently the photographer's alone. Moral rights can be exerted or waived, but not sold or assigned to a third party.

It is normal for expedition photographs to be credited to the photographer alone, to the photographic team, or to a combination of these and the expedition. For example:

Photo: John Smith/Africa Caves, 1997

Photo: © John Smith, 1997

SPONSORSHIP

Sponsorship carries both advantages and disadvantages. Many expeditions apply for and receive formal recognition from a national caving or grant-administering body, and may seek commercial sponsorship in the form of funds, equipment or services. Post-expedition reports should, properly, credit these sources. In the case of commercial sponsorship, expedition members may be expected to supply photographs showing equipment in use. Failure to do so will jeopardise future approaches made by other expeditions.

This picture contains a number of sponsors' products and is ideal for general use in reports and lectures. However, it is unsuitable for advertising use by sponsors as the picture contains other logos and equipment. Supply sponsors with pictures which prominently display only their product and logo

Assess whether an agreement to supply a sponsor with potential advertising material accords with the time and effort involved in taking the pictures. A trade price discount costs a sponsor very little, but it might take days to fulfil an expedition's obligations. If time is included in the equation, the price of taking a particular picture on a man-day basis may be financially too high and it is better to not accept some proposals than to involve team members for frustrating hours setting up a specific photograph. Be selective in what the expedition accepts and commits you, the photographer, to supplying. Check that the standard mail order price from a discount supplier is not as cheap. Sponsorship is invaluable, but not at any cost: it may be worth paying slightly more to avoid taking on additional responsibilities. Even if individuals are paying for their own film, it is reasonable that the expedition divides the cost of sponsorship photography between all members rather than burdening the photographer alone.

Once sponsorship is accepted there is a clear obligation on the expedition (and, in particular, the photographer) to supply pictures in return. All members will have benefited and should be prepared to help. The objectives must be clearly understood. Find out what the picture will be used for: are prints or transparencies required; should space be left for an advertising logo? Logo space can make the difference between a magazine cover or relegation to an internal page. Advertising pictures may need room for overwriting. Consider the client's potential uses for the photograph.

Sponsorship

- Be clear in your requirements and what you can realistically offer in return
- Be selective: a single large sponsor is better than a number of small ones
- Ensure sponsors' products do not clash
- Make a checklist of specific photographs for reference in the field
- Estimate the film required and check who pays for materials
- Take your responsibilities seriously; ensure others do too

Make a checklist of products which must be photographed, and ask sponsors for additional promotional material such as stickers and t-shirts bearing the company name or logo. Estimate the film required – allowing for repeat pictures and several versions of each shot – and add this to the total stock you have already calculated. Take a set of pictures at the start of the trip to show new, clean gear in a suitable setting, ticking off the photographs as they are taken. Ensure that there are no competing products in view; an excellent photograph of an oversuit is useless if a rival's suit or a prominent logo appears in the background.

Potential sponsors are frequently asked to donate products for expedition use, and expect something in return. Find an angle which offers the sponsor publicity, beyond a mere mention in the expedition report. Donating a camera to a local school after the expedition, backed up with a suitable photograph, is the basis of a good story. Stating such intentions when applying for sponsorship can enhance your request.

SHIPPING AND TRANSPORT

Bulky equipment may be shipped ahead of an expedition or, to the limit of weight allowances on aircraft, taken with you. Cameras, film and other delicate or irreplaceable items should be transported as hand luggage, with flashbulbs and spare batteries in the hold; too many expeditions have encountered the frustration of previously shipped cargo being delayed by customs until the expedition is over. Remove batteries from flashguns and other electrical equipment, but keep some available to demonstrate to security personnel that the equipment (especially home-made items) is safe and operates as it should.

Pack items to avoid the worst effects of vibration and dust, especially if overland travel is involved. Clearly label any items packed and sealed for communal shipment so that they are easy to locate. Check import regulations and, to avoid attempts to charge duty on exported goods when returning home, take photocopies of receipts for cameras and expensive items which clearly show they were purchased elsewhere. Insure cameras; a small premium may extend an existing policy to worldwide cover.

X-ray precautions

All items transported by air, particularly hand luggage, may be subjected to security searches and X-ray examination. Notoriously, X-rays cast a shadow of solid objects onto film or cause a general fogging and loss of contrast. Although machines are labelled 'film safe' (sometimes with an upper speed proviso of ISO 3200), their effects are cumulative: the more times film is X-rayed, particularly with older, high-dosage machines, the more it is affected.

Fast colour films are more susceptible to damage than slow black and white ones. Although X-ray damage is unlikely – it reportedly takes around ten passes with high-dose machines to fog ISO 400 film – a hand search removes any risk. Security staff in many airports will refuse a hand search, but some will oblige. In the USA, Federal Aviation rule 108.17 states that a hand search must be granted on demand. Check in early if you intend to take advantage of this: officers may wish to open every film package. Whether you take a hand search or not, always carry film in your carry-on luggage as high-dose X-rays may be used on bags placed in the hold.

MAINTENANCE

When far removed from specialised help, maintenance becomes doubly important in order to keep equipment in working condition. Visit a servicing agent for tips on dealing with common problems (some repair centres run specialist courses) and take relevant pages from a service manual. Service cameras before an expedition, particularly with temperature and humidity in mind.

Temperature

Modern cameras use oils which will not freeze until temperatures drop to around –30°C, although the grease on some cheap lenses makes the iris control sluggish. Under extremely cold conditions batteries may fail; a nicad cell may deliver only 60 per cent of its normal capacity at –20°C, and can be damaged by charging at below –10°C. In the cold keep a spare set of batteries next to your body. Extreme cold stiffens film, making it brittle and hard to wind on – do so slowly, without forcing.

Heat is more likely to be a problem to expedition photographers than cold. High temperatures cause sensitive materials, especially exposed film, to deteriorate. Keep film cool and away from direct sunlight. To avoid

---

An expedition checklist

Check that:
- Equipment is fully serviced
- Film is of the right speed, type and quantity
- Acceptable conditions are agreed in the contract
- Expedition members will help with photography
- Unnecessary duplication of equipment is avoided
- Freight is arranged (if required)
- A list of agreed sponsor photographs has been drawn up
- A checklist of additonal items to be purchased locally has been drawn up

Take:
- Cameras, flashes and slaves
- Back-up photographic equipment
- A sturdy tripod
- Film, flashbulbs and spare camera batteries
- Alkaline/rechargeable batteries (with charger)
- Containers for transporting cameras underground
- Promotional material from sponsors
- A list of camera numbers and photocopied receipts
- Maintenance tool kit (screwdrivers, cotton buds . . .)
- Silica gel, containers and polythene bags
- Processing equipment (if required)

Tool kits

The following items are useful for cleaning, repairs or maintenance:

- A changing bag (to remove film from cameras in daylight)
- A set of small screwdrivers, both flat and cross-head
- Cotton buds for cleaning glass surfaces
- Lens brush, cleaning fluid and cloths
- Pencil eraser for cleaning battery contacts
- Spare lens and body caps
- Spare filters
- Silicone grease (for O-ring seals)
- Swiss army knife
- Solder with a flux core (a pointed metal bar heated in a flame will suffice as a makeshift soldering iron)
- Short lengths of wire and electrician's PVC tape

Entering Porcupine Blue Hole, Bahamas (daylight)

condensation, allow refrigerated film time to warm up before opening the container. In extreme conditions, such as desert, cool film by draping a wet cloth over the film bag and allow it to evaporate, or open the bag to cool at night but insulate it during the day.

Film is designated as either 'professional' or 'amateur' stock . Professional film is intended for immediate use and is in prime condition when sold; other films 'ripen' and produce their best colours after a period of several weeks. By using fresh amateur stock rather than professional films, the effects of heat deterioration can be delayed slightly, but this is no substitute for keeping film cool.

Heat can affect cameras with liquid crystal displays, causing them to go temporarily blank – a good reason to use an older, manual camera.

Humidity

Moisture is easily absorbed by film, causing it to swell and stick to itself, which prevents re-winding. Warmth and moisture provide ideal conditions for fungal growth, and gelatine in the film's emulsion layer forms an excellent food substrate. Lens coatings suffer from the same problem, the fungal bloom growing across internal surfaces.

Avoid problems by unpacking film only when it is required and removing exposed film from the camera as soon as possible. Short rolls of film can be used and removed more frequently.

Keep film, cameras and lenses dry using moisture-absorbent silica gel. In the tropics store cameras and, especially, film and lenses in a polythene bag, having sucked out as much air as possible, with a quantity of silica gel crystals. Silica gel is blue when dry, turning pink when exhausted. Heat pink crystals over a camp stove or in an oven at 200°C to drive off moisture and regenerate the silica gel; overheating turns crystals black, and these should be discarded. Seal the dry silica gel in a small container, such as a transparent bottle or film canister (so that colour changes can be seen). Store the container with a solid lid, changing it for one with holes in when in use.

As a guide, 25g of desiccant (about one film canister in volume) can absorb the moisture from fifteen rolls of 35mm film, but greater quantities are normally used to speed up the process. Any dried material – for example tea leaves or rice – will help to absorb moisture if silica gel is not available.

Chapter eleven
UNDERWATER, STEREO AND VIDEO PHOTOGRAPHY

Play the game. Throw the dice, move your counter around the board and take the consequences. Discover new formations, move forward six spaces; forget your wetsuit, return to start. Light goes out, miss a turn. Cave with a novice, miss two turns. Break a leg, miss three turns. Cave with a photographer, miss ten turns. It's a much maligned hobby, is cave photography.

BCRA caving conference

U NDERWATER, stereo and video photography in caves increasingly attract interest. This chapter serves to aid cavers beginning work in these specialist areas, and indicates some of the basic techniques and pitfalls. Further information lies outside the scope of this manual, and can be found in standard texts.

UNDERWATER PHOTOGRAPHY

It is self-evident that a caver must be fully conversant with both caving and cave diving before taking up underwater photography; unless diving has become second nature the additional discipline of photography is not an area for experimentation. The safety of assistants – other divers – who are acting as models or firing flashes is paramount: do not ask a diver, however competent, to leave a diving line to place a flashgun or to undertake a potentially dangerous operation.

Equipment

A totally sealed, waterproof camera such as a Nikonos is ideal, though other makes are available (see p.8). Before buying a camera consider its lens quality, flashgun availability (some are specific to one camera only, and are expensive), whether there is a manual override, and that the camera is waterproof to the required depth. Some 'weatherproof' cameras are restricted to a depth of 3m or, at most, 10m. Check the extent of the viewfinder image while using a diving mask as, with a greater distance between the viewfinder and your eye, not all of the image may be visible.

The lens is vitally important. It is a lucky cave photographer who dives in a crystal clear, warm sump with no trace of suspended particles. To reduce the camera-to-subject distance, and therefore the amount of water and sediment, a wide-angle lens is essential. Due to diffraction, a 35mm underwater lens is the equivalent of a 50mm lens in air and is considered

Virgin Blue Hole,
Bahamas (daylight)

a 'standard' lens. This is only just acceptable in clear water. Wider lenses, such as a 28mm or 15mm, are expensive, although worth the cost. A 16mm wide-angle adaptor lens and matched viewfinder, such as made by Sea & Sea, is a good alternative. Extremely wide-angle lenses enable work at close range, yet still encompass a field of view which can contain a diver.

One or more powerful, underwater flashguns are required. Although they may bear a high guide number, the effective power of any flash is reduced underwater: light intensity drops by about a half for every 30cm of water between the flash and subject. Commercial guns are expensive and large, so some photographers mount a standard electronic flash in a waterproof container or use flashbulbs. Flashbulbs are waterproof, and a bulb gun's circuitry can be cheaply and easily sealed in a box or with resin. Ensure the battery is new or fully charged; cold water quickly decreases its effective power. Devise a system for holding the flash and collecting used bulbs, which will float if they are released inadvertently.

Take advantage of diving activities to take surface shots, as here in Noxon Park Iron Mine (E8, B5). Reflections from diving masks (and spectacles) can be minimised by tilting the caver's head slightly downwards with respect to the flash position

Underwater flashguns are fitted with a short, often coiled cable which connects to the camera's proprietory fitting. Ensure that the fitting is still in use, as some second-hand models – both camera and flashgun – bear obsolete connectors.

Integral cables are reliable and allow a flash to be held at arm's length. Making a cable longer is unwise and potentially dangerous underwater, as well as causing inconsistent firing. Longer cables do, however, allow

Sediment in water, arising from the floor or disturbed by divers' bubbles, reflects light back to the lens even more than humidity does in air (E8). Move the flash position as far from the camera as possible to reduce this problem

Bidet Blue Hole, Bahamas (daylight)

other divers to fire flashes and appear as silhouettes in the photograph, the cable looking like a diving line.

If you wish to experiment, restrict the cable length to about 3m – enough to place the model in the picture with a wide-angle lens. Even better, fire remote flashguns with slave units. Visible light penetrates water better than infra-red wavelengths. A full-spectrum sensor makes the slave more efficient, but diving lights may trigger the slave. In addition, the trigger flash itself, because it is normally mounted near the camera, can produce enough back-scatter from particles in the water to affect the picture.

Basic techniques

Red wavelengths of light are absorbed by water more readily than the blue part of the spectrum. When the combined flash-to-subject and subject-to-lens distance is more than about 3m a significant colour shift occurs, resulting in a blue colour cast. Note that this is not linked with the intensity of daylight or with depth – it is purely due to the distance which light travels through water. The colour shift can be corrected by using a warmer light source, such as a clear flashbulb, or with a magenta filter over the flash or camera lens. Kodak manufactures a specialist magenta-rich slide film for underwater use. Extreme wide-angle lenses, because they allow the photographer to move both camera and flashgun closer to the subject, help keep the flash-to-subject-to-camera distance within manageable limits and avoid unacceptable colour casts.

During 'normal' cave photography a flashgun fired near to the lens produces a misty, low-contrast photograph because light is reflected from condensation in the humid air. The problem is infinitely worse underwater, where silt and air bubbles produce large, out-of-focus blobs. Again, this is minimised with ultra-wide lenses as there is less water between the lens and subject (although backlit silt can add dramatic effects to the photograph).

The front flash must be removed from the camera, by either holding it at arm's length and firing it via a cable or firing it remotely using a slave unit. With a wide-angle lens in clear water it is viable to hold the flash at arm's length. Aim the flash at 45 degrees to the subject, and avoid lighting the water between the lens and subject. If an inbuilt flash is not used, in dim light the camera shutter may lock to prevent underexposed pictures; cover this flash with PVC electrician's tape to eliminate its effects.

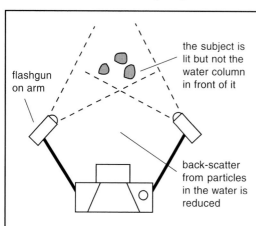

flashgun on arm

the subject is lit but not the water column in front of it

back-scatter from particles in the water is reduced

Avoiding back-scatter

Back-scatter occurs when particles of mud reflect light back to the camera lens. Aim flashes (or video lights) so that the edge of the beam passes just in front of the subject, avoiding illuminating the water between the subject and the lens; this principle holds true for single flash or, as here, two flashguns on arms.

Stargate, South Andros,
Bahamas

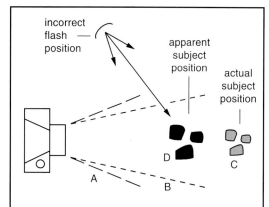

incorrect flash position

apparent subject position

actual subject position

D

C

A

B

Estimating distance underwater

The angle of view of a lens in air (A) becomes narrower underwater (B). The eye is fooled into perceiving objects as being larger and therefore 25 per cent closer than they really are; in this diagram the formations at (C) appear to the diver to be located at (D). Inexperienced photographers often aim the flash at the subject's apparent position, leaving the real subject unlit. Aim behind the apparent subject position, or use a pencil-beam light on the flash to help locate it.

Vision is distorted and distances are fore-shortened by refraction in water, making objects appear 25 per cent closer than they really are. Without experience, estimating true distances and accurately aiming a flash is, in particular, extremely difficult, resulting in lighting a position too close to the camera. Some commercial flashguns are fitted with a 'spotter light', a thin beam which helps the photographer aim the light. A pencil-beam torch attached to a home-made flashgun fulfils the same function.

Communication

Communication between divers can be attained with careful, clear planning before entering the water. Practise techniques on a simulated 'dirt dive' or in open water before venturing into a cave. A sump with easy access enables divers to surface between shots to discuss difficulties and the next picture.

One of the most difficult aspects to master is lining up a remote flash with a diver and the camera: there are three elements moving in three dimensions to contend with. Movement of any of the three is likely to be imprecise, and certainly harder to coordinate without good communication and a clear understanding of the objectives by everyone concerned.

The nature of the sump, water clarity and the ability and help of team members all influence the techniques required, but it is imagination and dedication from the small fraternity specialising in underwater cave photography which increasingly yields visually outstanding pictures.

STEREO PHOTOGRAPHY

The human brain perceives depth by comparing differences between the separate images produced by each eye; the more the images are alike the more distant the object. Stereo photographs consist of two pictures taken a few centimetres apart and mounted side by side. These are viewed so that each eye can see only one image, simulating the different scenes which each eye would have originally observed – the brain interprets the view as a three-dimensional picture. Effectively, the slight differences between the images fool the brain into 'seeing' depth.

The technique is not a new one: the earliest cave photograph, taken in 1865, was a stereograph. Specialist two-lens cameras were manufactured and today's enthusiasts use old models such as the Stereo Realist. This uses standard 35mm film but yields pictures which are almost square, alternative frames being part of the same stereo pair. Other photographers construct home-made cameras by combining two existing bodies. Slide film is best processed and returned uncut, leaving the photographer to complete the mounting; prints and slides must be mounted with care to place the closest object level with the imaginary stereo window.

Using standard cameras

Stereo viewers were commonplace in the latter half of the 1800s; this viewer dates from 1895.

The card is an example of the millions produced and shows guides holding magnesium burners at Jenolan, New South Wales. The two central figures are Jeremiah Wilson, the first caretaker at Jenolan, and 'Voss' Wiburd. Wilson explored local caves between about 1880 and 1896, while Wiburd began work as a guide in 1885, aged nineteen. Information such as this is useful when dating old photographs

Specialist cameras are not essential for stereo photography. Two views separated by about 8cm, the approximate distance between the centre of human eyes, can be taken using a single camera and lens.

Standing with your legs slightly apart, take a photograph with your weight on one foot, then sway and shift your weight to the other foot for a second exposure. The procedure is easily practised at home until the technique has been mastered. For more exact work make a tripod-mounted bar or rack which allows a camera to be moved a set distance between exposures, or fixes two identical cameras side by side. A single camera requires separate flashes for each part of the stereo pair, but with two cameras a single exposure can be made using B.

Because the two photographs are mounted and viewed as one, each must receive the same exposure and lighting to avoid conflicts within the images. Cavers in the pictures must remain still, and flashguns must be fully recharged between exposures to ensure consistent lighting. Using two identical flashguns, one for each picture, reduces the time between images as they do not have to be recharged. It is also important to use off-camera flashes rather than a flash mounted on the camera. Because the

subject is static but the camera has shifted position, a camera-mounted flash will cast slightly different shadows which interfere with each other when viewed in stereo. By using a separate flash or flashes the shadow remains in the same position in each image.

The two photographs must be absolutely level and compatible with each other. Line up the centre of the lens (use the middle of the focusing screen in an SLR camera) with a specific point in the picture; do not

601. On the way to Jenolan Caves, N. S. W.

E7, B4

E2, B5

Stereo views

These stereo pairs, of Ogof Ffynnon Ddu, were taken with a single hand-held camera which was moved between exposures, demonstrating that stereo pictures can be taken with minimal equipment. The pose and lighting angles must be kept identical; a camera-mounted flash would cast different shadows from the two positions, so flashes must be fired remotely. Moving parts of the scene will appear differently in each image and may therefore be indistinct in the stereo view; condensation from a caver's breath is a common example, although flowing or falling water may be enhanced by the effect (see top photograph, this page).

The problem of movement is overcome by using a specialist two-lens camera which makes both exposures at the same time from a single set of flashes. Obviously, this eliminates many difficulites but it also removes some areas of experimentation. For example, normally the scene remains unchanged but the camera is moved between exposures. If a caver (but not the camera) moves laterally, the resulting stereo photograph appears 'flat' and two-dimensional with the caver standing out in 3D.

The illusion of depth is produced by differences in the images: the greater the difference, the more depth is perceived. Increasing the distance between the two camera positions therefore increases the apparent depth. These photographs were taken further apart than 'normal', producing 'hyper stereo' pairs (the depth is exaggerated). The 'correct' separation between the two lens positions is considered to be 1/30 of the camera-to-nearest-subject distance: a subject 3m from the camera requires a theoretical separation of 10cm.

Working with prints means that a slightly larger area than required can be photographed, the results being cropped for mounting and viewing. Transparencies do not allow the same degree of freedom, although

E8, B4

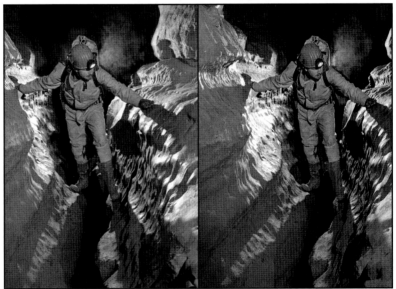

E2, B5

specialist stereo mounts allow some masking. To view a pair of transparencies in stereo, use a specialist viewer or a pair of small, 'daylight' viewers (these are usually made of plastic with a lens at the front and a frosted screen at the back). Attach them side-by-side with tape, with the lens-to-lens distance adjusted for viewing so that each eye can see the relevant image.

A special viewer is normally used with stereo photographs, but they can also be 'free-viewed'. This takes a little practice but, while there are several methods to try, once the technique is learned it becomes increasingly easy to put into use. The trick is to separately focus on one image of the pair with each eye, effectively 'looking through' the photograph but focusing on it. To view the pictures on this page, make a crude stereo print viewer. Place a long piece of card between the images, physically separating them. With good lighting on each, view the stereo by looking down the card so that it is impossible for either eye to see the other image. The historical picture on p.201 can also be viewed in this way.

True free-viewing dispenses with the card. Hold the book upright at arm's length while looking into the distance, bring the pictures into your field of vision and refocus your eyes. Effectively, your eyes are focused for a near distance but are 'aimed' for a far distance. You may need to move the page towards you to help focusing, but more distant images (because they are smaller and cause less strain on what you are requiring your eye muscles to accomplish) are easier to free-view. It is to aid free-viewing that the pictures are presented here at this size. Eventually, with practice, a 3D image will snap into focus between the other two. Persevere: the effect is worth it.

A Stereo Realist twin-lens camera in Llygad Llwchwr (E8, B4)

use the edge of the viewfinder, as the picture will be offset relative to its sister. Carefully cropping and mounting prints can correct or mask some errors, but this is less viable when preparing full frame transparencies for projection – it is better to get it right in the camera than to correct faults later.

The technique of swaying from one foot to another can yield excellent results; it is fast, easy, and worth experimenting with.

Apparent depth

Increasing the separation between lenses makes the images progressively different. The brain perceives depth by comparing the image from each eye; the greater the difference, the closer the object appears to be. An increased separation (producing 'hyper' photographs) therefore exaggerates depth. Photographs taken too close together diminish the 3D illusion.

A range of subjects lying at different distances from the camera give the best impression of depth in the resulting stereo photograph, but require a small aperture and good depth of field. In '2D' photographs backgrounds are often deliberately placed out of focus to isolate the subject; this is not necessary in stereo photographs so keep everything sharp and well lit to make the best use of the 3D effect.

Mounting stereo photographs is an art in itself, where fractions of a millimetre can make a profound difference. A poorly executed or mounted stereo image has notorious effects: focusing on the picture is difficult and headaches result. If the image, or part of it, projects 'through the window' (in front of the plane of the page) rather than receding into the distance, adjust its mounting; if focusing is difficult, check that the images are not left–right reversed.

VIDEO PHOTOGRAPHY

Even with the attendant problems of providing a bright, continuous light source, underground video photography has become popular. A different aspect of caving, which includes movement and sound, can be captured. However, the topic of moving pictures, both cine and video, could demand its own manual and the information given here is only intended as a basic aid for a competent cave photographer moving into the field.

Cameras

Manually operated, clockwork cine cameras are traditionally the first choice for underground work as they are robust and not as susceptible to moisture as electronically operated models. However, for amateur use, the high cost of film and processing means that video is the only choice.

Video tape is cheaper, requires less light than cine film, and the quality of output is increasingly excellent. The remainder of this chapter therefore concentrates on underground video rather than cine.

There are several formats and sizes of camera to choose from and, as with 35mm still photography, automatic models are more common than manual ones. As film is not involved, conventional photographers might be excused for confusion over specifications. An ISO rating is not appropriate, for example. The equivalent is the minimum illumination required for recording, measured in lux; use a camera capable of recording at 3 lux or lower. Sensitivity can be increased by amplifying the signal (video gain), at the expense of picture quality ('noise' is introduced, the equivalent of increased grain but which may appear as horizontal streaks across the recorded image).

Filming for a television broadcast in Ogof Draenen, using a Hi-8 video in a commercial waterproof housing (E8, E5)

The sampling rate of the camera's CCD (charge-coupled device), usually 1/60 or 1/90 second at its slowest, is the equivalent to shutter speed. The camera's size and weight (including a spare battery), sound quality and an ability to override automatic features should be considered. Manual control of focus and aperture is essential to avoid the camera unduly reacting to highlights or silhouettes. A good zoom lens with a wide-angle of 8mm or better is needed.

Video picture resolution relies on lens quality, the number of pixels produced by the sensor, and the frequency range of the tape which stores the image as a magnetic signal (the bandwidth). The quality of the signal on tape is influenced by the way it is recorded. Hi-8 and S-VHS systems record separate signals for black and white and colour information, and normally produce a better quality picture than VHS and video-8 systems. In addition, the camera is usually physically smaller.

The colour of the filming light should be sampled before shooting to set the white balance. This means that whatever colour the video light actually produces, it will be interpreted as white. The white balance is often set automatically but, for in-cave use, manual adjustment is useful.

Modern cameras often have unwanted features which are controlled by small buttons that can allow mud and moisture to enter the camera. If such designs are unavoidable, protect the camera with a housing. Commercial housings may need modification for use underground. Remote (plug-in) control features help to make home-made housings cheaper and easier to construct, as the switches can be wired through the casing. Cover unused controls with, and operate them through, cling film or PVC tape. A washing-up glove, either complete or using single fingers, can be built into home-made housings to access and operate controls.

Lighting

There is a direct relationship between light intensity and the rate of battery drain: brighter lights have a shorter duration. Several low-wattage lamps may prove more useful than one large one, allowing a lower consumption when shots which require less light are involved. Carry plenty of spare nicad or sealed lead-acid batteries for the planned trip.

Obviously, as much light as possible over a long a period of time is needed. A 6V, 10W bulb can last for up to 4 hours; the same battery might only power a specialist 50W video lamp for 10 minutes. Time home-made lights until the light begins to yellow, indicating a voltage drop and the end of their useful running period. Allow a few seconds for lights to attain their correct colour temperature before beginning filming, and turn off lamps immediately afterwards to conserve power.

Techniques

A transmission-quality Betacam at Porth yr Ogof

When planning shots, remember that working in confined spaces is extremely difficult. For example, automatic cameras adjust for changes in light and sound levels but some models are not sophisticated enough to cope with a caver giving a commentary while crawling towards the camera in a confined space. Manual control of both sound and aperture may be required to overcome problems of fixed intensity light sources combined with a moving subject, or for special effects. An assistant to operate a separate sound recorder may be an asset.

Write a script and edit hard; do not be tempted to retain footage because it 'came out and looks good' if a similar shot has already been used. If it does not add to the story, remove it. The lack of a storyline turns hard-won film into an uninteresting sequence that will only be viewed by those involved. Decide in advance exactly what shots are required, use battery power wisely, and even a single trip underground will be extremely productive.

Video tips

Most video techniques are no different underground from on the surface and reading a standard text is advised. Assuming that technical ability with the camera has been mastered, the most common mistakes made while producing a film are:

- Not using a tripod, resulting in irritating, unsteady shots
- Overuse of zooming (altering the focal length during a shot)
- Panning too fast (moving the camera too quickly across the subject)
- Unedited or poorly edited film
- A lack of linking shots (such as feet walking, close-up pictures of formations or hands gripping rock, all of which help assemble the story during editing)
- Poor continuity (for example, a different caver in the film or models using a new colour of oversuit on successive days)

Chapter twelve
COMPOSITION

It was seven hours since we had seen daylight, yet we had been taking pictures within fifteen minutes of the entrance. Changing at the car, other cavers couldn't understand where we'd been for so long. The trick is, lighting angles and composition play as much a part in cave photography as passage characteristics. You don't need distant depths to create a picture: you need a willing team and imagination.

Bridge Cave

E VEN when all the technicalities of cave photography have been mastered, a photographer is still faced with decisions: once *how* is understood, *what* becomes important. Most problems can be tackled in more than one way; there is no right or wrong method of making a cave photograph.

Note the distinction: a cave photograph is *made*, not taken; pictures do not lie around waiting to be picked up and carried off. Cave photographs must be created. The photographer controls the technicalities: the aperture, type of flash, angle of lighting. . . . What remains is the composition: which elements produce a pleasing photograph, and which do not?

ELEMENTS OF COMPOSITION

Good composition requires that a number of factors are balanced, including colour, tone, what is included or excluded, and where and how a caver stands and poses. The interplay of these, and other elements, determines whether the picture is outstanding or consigned to the waste bin.

The subject

Photographs contain one or more subjects; the photographer controls how many, where they are placed and how much importance is attached to each. One subject normally forms the centre of interest, with other elements supporting it; a simple arrangement is easier to control and more likely to succeed. The photographer must arrange the composition and lighting so that the viewer's attention is directed where required and, often, a picture stands or fails on whether this is successful.

It is important to identify *why* the photograph is being taken: is the subject a caver crawling in mud, or the mud in which the caver is crawling? Is the objective the creation of a moody, atmospheric photograph, or to record the fine

The Canal, Little Neath River Cave (B5)

detail in a scientific specimen? The function of the picture will help to determine how lighting should be used and where elements of the picture are placed with respect to each other: will the caver or the mud form the largest part of the picture? Know *why* the picture is being taken.

Foregrounds and backgrounds

For a photograph to be successful the main subject must stand out from its surroundings, so the subject must have a different tone or colour tint from the background. 'Tone' refers to the effect of light and shade within the picture. In black and white, areas of similar tone blend together. In colour photographs two areas of colour, even if they are the same tone, remain visibly separate. In all pictures a silhouette against an unlit passage is lost to obscurity, unlike a dark caver against white calcite (tones remain separate). In colour photographs a blue oversuit against a muddy background is visible, but in black and white these tones may merge.

The subject's characteristics are therefore the controlling factor; they determine what the background's tone or colour must be for the subject to stand out. If, inherently, there is insufficient contrast between the two,

changing the lighting can sometimes introduce a clear separation between them. Avoid distracting, light-coloured areas in the background. Out-of-focus highlights, perhaps from water droplets on a dark background, are particularly intrusive and easily missed when composing the picture. Check for distracting highlights by placing a caver's helmet light at the flash position and move the flash or camera to eliminate any problems which this identifies.

Isolating a subject against a black background can be highly effective and need not be a silhouette. Side lighting should be minimal and must be carefully controlled. The flashes in these pictures in Ogof Ffynnon Ddu (above: E7, B4) and Little Neath River Cave (E3) were shielded to provide a narrow, directional light

Foregrounds also affect the photograph: an overlit foreground distracts from the subject, while dark areas can help to concentrate attention where it is required. A silhouetted formation or caver can add scale without intruding on the main subject. Use shields to control which parts of the scene, both foreground and background, are lit.

Focus, critically, on the main subject and exclude light from other areas which might distract. There are obvious exceptions: you may *wish* an out-of-focus effect in part of the picture, for example a close-up picture of speleothems with a caver in the distance. Ensure out-of-focus effects are obviously intentional; any which are *just* out of focus look like a mistake and destroy an otherwise good picture.

To summarise, maintain a difference in tone or colour between the main subject and the background, check there are no intrusive elements or

Beyond a Choke in Ogof Draenen. The caver has fired a flashbulb aimed away from the camera and picked out the passage shape. The backlight (B5) has been angled upwards to add detail to the roof, but enough light reached the figure to separate it from the dark background

out-of-focus areas – especially if they contain highlights – and do not overlight foregrounds. Isolating the main subject against a black background can produce an exceptionally strong composition.

Colour

Careful use of colour influences mood and is an important part of composition. There is often a single, predominant colour such as brown mud or grey rock. Strong photographs can be built on this by adding a single, contrasting colour such as a caver in a red or yellow oversuit: red colours stand out strongly while blues are more subdued.

When viewing a well-composed photograph the eye is drawn to one spot first before roaming around the rest of the picture. A subject of

Unusual angles help add variety to compositions, such as in Ogof Ffynnon Ddu (B6). Here, although there is a good diagonal design running through the picture, there is a tendency to first look at the figure and then the light area of water. The viewer's eye is distracted and led out of the main part of the picture

contrasting colour or different tone helps direct this interest where the photographer wishes. Faces, especially eyes, are crucially important.

The lightest area of a photograph, whatever its colour, always attracts attention. This is helpful if it is part of the subject, but is a distraction if the lightest area is in the surroundings. An overexposed rock or other white area draws the viewer's interest; as a generalisation, control areas of highlights and make the main subject the brightest colour or lightest area (or, if the main subject is a silhouette, ensure that it lies against a light area or strong colour). When planning a photographic trip, check on helmet and oversuit colours. A white helmet, in particular, can be extremely distracting as it draws attention away from the nearby face; switch helmets or oversuits with anyone wearing white. By preplanning the colours you will work with, many problems are eliminated before they occur.

Composition is, in the final analysis, a very personal matter. Make up your own mind what pleases you; study published photographs for compositional rules and use of colour and tone. Turn to a new page in this or any other book and, for an instant, sweep your eyes across a picture you have never seen before. By only glancing at it you have time to register shapes and colours, not detail. How easy was it to spot the main subject? Do you remember a light or brightly coloured area? Was a person present? What design does the composition reveal? In a striking photograph your glance will register the main elements; in a well-composed picture the most apparent should be the main subject. If nothing registered, take another look at the photograph: is it a memorable one, or is it weak?

Analyse what is important in pictures, and apply your decisions to your own compositions. Are they poor, or could they be improved with better

The Tesla Coil, Breezeway Cave, Colorado (B5). The formations have acted as natural reflectors, providing enough light to bring out details on the front of the caver

lighting or printing to help concentrate the viewer's interest; was there a better way of composing the picture? Simple compositions are often the strongest, so use carefully considered lighting angles and flashgun intensities to eliminate distractions.

Black and white photography

Not all colours translate well to monochrome. For example, red and orange appear darker than expected on black and white film. A bright red oversuit against a dark background is stunning in colour, but in black and white photographs it can appear as black-on-black. Blue against a mid-tone background can produce a similar effect.

When a slide is reproduced in black and white the pattern continues; similar tones merge, detail is lost and contrast increases. To demonstrate

Some subjects, in particular silhouettes, work extremely well in monochrome. Ogof Ffynnon Ddu (B5)

This caver in Ogof Ffynnon Ddu (E8, B5) is wearing a wetsuit made with red and blue panels. Photographed in black and white these have darkened considerably; experienced cave photographers use a modified lighting angle or exposure to allow for this.

Further comparisons of how colour translates to monochrome appear on p.170

the effect, alter the settings on a television set or computer monitor to display a colour picture in monochrome. How easy is it to tell the difference between the colours of snooker or pool balls in black and white? If the tones are similar and the colours are unidentified, then black and white photographs will not separate these colours unless they are lit to create a difference in shade and highlight.

Yellow is an ideal colour for an oversuit as it is striking in both black and white and colour photographs. Because red oversuits and helmets darken when photographed in black and white, a light background or strong side lighting is needed. These colour restrictions require careful, sometimes imaginative lighting.

Using a coloured filter alters the tonal range of a black and white photograph. Filters lighten tones of their own colour: a red filter lightens red, blue lightens blue. There are, however, associated problems. The

A yellow filter was used to darken the blue sky, increasing the contrast around the clouds, above the entrance shaft to the Gouffre de Padirac in France. A polarising filter would have the same effect in colour by deepening blues

opposite (complementary) colour is darkened: a red filter darkens blue-green colours and increases contrast. Because filters absorb light (red filters absorb blue and green but transmit red, for example) the exposure must be increased to compensate, either with an increase in flash intensity or by opening the aperture and losing depth of field; such exposure adjustments may be severe and some red filters demand the equivalent of two f-stops of additional light.

These factors make filtration appear impractical, but experimentation is worthwhile. Calcite often contains reds and other warm colours due to iron impurities, and therefore appears darker than it should in black and white photographs. A yellow filter helps reduce contrast and lightens these colours, in turn making printing easier. A pale yellow filter is sometimes useful in colour photography as it helps control exposures of white calcite without introducing an appreciable colour cast.

The rule of thirds

Before the invention of photography, painters developed rules of composition; artwork which conformed seemed pleasing to the eye and, in a later era, photographers accepted the same strictures. An understanding of classical composition can help when making fast decisions but, in reality, such 'rules' are only guidelines.

The rule of thirds divides a picture into nine parts using imaginary vertical and horizontal lines. A subject placed on a 'vertical third' or a horizon on a 'horizontal third' is more interesting to the viewer than one which lies between the lines; a subject on a 'third line' creates emphasis, while a subject centred in the picture is too symmetrical and splits a photograph into two parts. A main subject placed on any of the four intersections is considered to be extremely strongly positioned, while two subjects which each occupy a third can be distracting.

An empty area within a composition can strengthen other parts of the picture and throw additional emphasis onto the subject. For example, a black void adds mystery and depth; a small figure surrounded by a large chamber is awesome. A vertical photograph with a caver on a top third intersection, looking downwards into darkness, emphasises the drop below.

The illusion of movement is enhanced by using thirds: a caver walking or looking into the centre of a photograph is more acceptable than a caver looking outside the frame or about to step outside its boundaries. This concept of leaving a space to 'move into' is considered an important one in sports photography.

These rules were made to be broken, and many excellent photographs do so. With a suitable use of space a subject looking out of a picture can create a disturbing image in the viewer's mind;

intersecting thirds

The rule of thirds

Imaginary vertical and horizontal lines indicate the positions where a viewer's interest is maintained. The strongest composition results when a subject is placed at an intersection, avoiding symmetry but creating a pleasing use of space.

The caver, in Carlsbad Caverns, New Mexico, is perfectly placed on an intersecting third (E3, B6)

a good photographer manipulates the picture to create the desired feeling. If in doubt as to the outcome of a particular composition, take two or more versions and compare the results. Which worked the best? Which invokes the most feeling, is the most atmospheric?

An instinctive understanding and use of the rule of thirds helps create strongly composed photographs. Successful rule-breaking photographs are eye-catching *because* they break the rules, so learn them well – but never stop experimenting.

Shape and line

A photograph can be broken down into compositional components by considering it as a series of shapes and lines. For example, straw stalactites or a caver on rope produce vertical lines, a pool of water a horizontal one, a crouching figure as a square or triangle. These shapes can be combined with the rule of thirds to create strong compositions, for example a straw on a vertical third with its tip on a lower third line.

Diagonal shapes and lines, imaginary or real, direct the viewer's eye where the photographer wishes and imply depth, drama and a sense of movement; diagonals work well with action photographs. A caver on a lower third intersection looking at a formation on an upper third introduces an imaginary diagonal line which strongly ties the two subjects together. A shadow cast from a strong flash can produce a receding line leading down a passage, or introduce a diagonal to a wall. Meandering curves, perhaps the course of a streamway, draw the eye through a sinuous S-shape

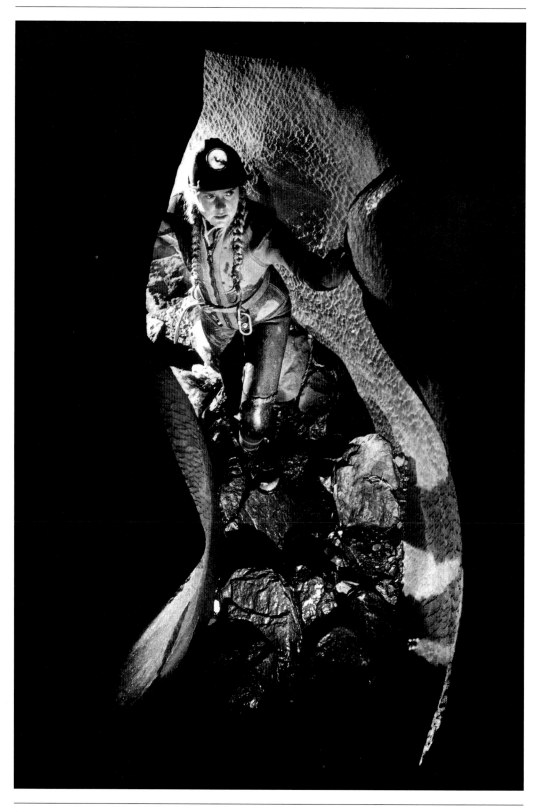

The curving lines of this passage in Poulnagollum, Co. Clare (opposite), and the circular phreatic tube of Bakerloo Straight in Dan yr Ogof both demonstrate the power of shapes in moulding strong compositions.

In Poulnagollum the caver was posed to accentuate the passage shape. The front light was concealed within the picture and fired by slave from the top of a pile of rocks (E1), while the backlight (B6) was held in position by another caver.

Bakerloo Straight is notoriously difficult to photograph well due to the black limestone making silhouettes hard to light, appearing as black-on-black. Water was carried a reasonable distance and thrown over the walls before taking the picture. When the flash was fired (B5) this produced highlights on the walls. By wetting the caver's back and standing still for a few minutes, enough condensation formed in the air for the flash to pick out the figure from the background

towards the main subject. Circles also direct the eye; a circular passage with radiating lines creates an impression of depth.

The orientation of the photograph is important. A 35mm camera can be used vertically or horizontally: which will suit the subject? Would the composition be better served by altering the shape of the picture by cropping to a square or letter-box? Will large areas be left empty when a camera is horizontal, or can a vertical shape accentuate the subject? There are no hard and fast rules and, certainly, there is no reason to always retain the shape of the film or printing paper for every picture.

Using different camera orientations a selection of implied, compositional lines and shape ensures variety is maintained throughout a series of pictures, something vital to consider when putting together a slide show. It is, however, easy to over-analyse a photograph to the point where comments and conclusions are ridiculous. A good analysis takes care, thought and time – but, if you apply the 'rules' to your existing pictures, you might be surprised at what you discover.

Adding mood and interest

Too many elements or colours are distracting and make photographs unnecessarily complex. When creating a moody, atmospheric picture, limit the number of flashes, subjects and colours. Overlit photographs generate little feeling of 'being there'; a cave is a dark, mysterious place and unlit areas add to that mystery. There are advantages in minimal lighting and a major part of cave photographic composition lies with recognising what *not* to light.

Elements of composition

- Identify the purpose of the picture, the main subject and supporting elements
- Orientate the picture, upright or horizontal, to suit the subject
- Avoid distracting objects and out-of-focus highlights
- Make good use of contrast and colour
- Move closer to the subject for emphasis
- Allow space for the subject to 'move into'
- Include a suitable scale
- Use, but be prepared to break, the rule of thirds
- Consider how colour and tone is translated to black and white
- A yellow filter can help to retain tonal detail in black and white photographs
- Avoid overlighting

The caver in Pollskeheenarinky, Co. Tipperary, is situated on an intersecting third (above: B8 fired by the caver, E4) while the caver in Upstream Passage, Ogof Draenen (opposite: B5), is central in the composition. Here, the upright shape of the picture accentuates the height of the waterfall, which lies on a vertical third. In addition, diagonal shapes – real or implied – are considered strong compositional elements. This impression is introduced to both pictures by the tilt of the caver's head

Examine the cave photographs in this manual and elsewhere and see how many have been made with two guns (or, if more than two guns are used, as with fill-in flash techniques, how many flashes are *obviously* present). A helmet light does not light a vast area, and limiting the numbers of flashes can simulate the feeling of being underground. Learn the techniques of cave photography, experiment, then concentrate on lighting scenes in an unobtrusive manner. If a technique is immediately apparent, such as revealing dual flash positions when two shadows are cast in different directions, it is probably overdone.

There are several techniques which help a composition hold a viewer's attention. A caver's face (particularly the eyes), an unusual viewpoint, lighting from an unexpected direction and highlight areas all create an immediate centre of interest. A high vantage point adds perspective – a feeling of depth – and often introduces a diagonal line through the photograph, especially with the use of a wide-angle lens and a prominent foreground subject.

It is not always possible to place either the camera or flashguns at the perfect position to create a particular effect. Bear in mind the range of

E8, B5

E8, B5

B4

E8, B5

E2, B5

Working in one area

It is very easy to decide upon a destination within a cave and head for it, blinkered, without pausing to explore the photographic possibilities along the way. By working within a limited area you learn to recognise alternative viewpoints and may discover a picture that, at first, had been discounted.

This location in Ogof Ffynnon Ddu was chosen because heavy rain had produced a small waterfall on the corner of a side passage. The first, more distant views were mediocre but, by changing the camera and model's position to concentrate attention on the caver and rockwork, using a bulb to accentuate the falling water, a worthwhile picture eventually emerged from the series.

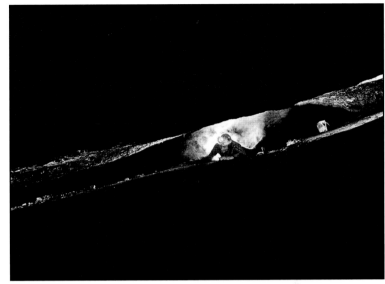

A bedding plane in Poulnagollum, Co. Clare, lit with electronic flashguns (E3, E7) and a flashbulb (B5), all fired by infra-red slaves. The shape of the passage is set off by the black surround and, compositionally, would not be as strong if the picture was cropped to include only the bedding plane

options: in any given situation, which techniques will produce a satisfying photograph? What are the alternatives? There are few cave passages, even in the most mundane 'sacrificial' cave close to an overused entrance, which with imagination and the right technique cannot yield a good picture.

THE PHOTOGRAPHIC TEAM

By the time the technicalities of cave photography have been mastered and composition has become the most important factor you will, with luck, be supported by a regular team of cavers. Members will begin to suggest ideas as they learn your techniques: build upon their input.

The complete team will not be involved in every picture, and inactive cavers soon become bored and cold. Find ways to occupy everyone, all the time – if you wish them to join you for a future trip. Take some snack food; eating something gives assistants something to do while you are setting up the next shot and adds to the general enjoyment of the trip. Above all, work quickly and efficiently: if you look as if you know what you are doing it helps inspire confidence in cavers who are freely giving their time and effort to help.

Models

Few cavers are relaxed or appear natural when given an instruction to 'stand there and fire a flash'; the majority require directions on how and where to stand. A model's pose will, almost above all other factors, make or break an otherwise perfectly exposed and executed photograph.

Interpreting verbal instructions can be difficult: show what you want by example. Take the caver to the right position and demonstrate what is required. A static pose *can* appear dynamic, but an action photograph of

a caver walking down a streamway, splashing up water, is far more appealing. A moving figure is difficult to deal with using B, but with slave units a short-duration, synchronised electronic flash prevents blurring.

When arranging a model first decide the position of the caver and the basic pose. Sitting and kneeling are often the easiest and most natural poses to set up, while standing poses can be static or 'walking' even when there is no running water or a climb to add an 'active' element. When arranging a walking pose ask the caver to 'move through' the picture, stopping them when it appears realistic. Always put cave conservation first and never ask models (or assistants) to do something they are unhappy about, such as standing too near to a drop. On pitches, clip into a safety line. Listen and respond to comments. Is the caver comfortable in doing what you have asked? As the photographer you are in charge of more than just shooting a picture.

Begin with the basic composition: will the caver be 'on a third', or in the centre of the photograph? Is there a specific place where the caver must look, such as a formation, the point where a handline is tied off, or the next handhold on a traverse? These factors determine the basic position and direction the caver faces. Avoid cavers looking out of the picture as, unless there is a deliberate attempt to create an off-centre image, a self-contained composition is generally stronger.

With standing poses, work upwards when arranging the picture: feet, shoulders, hands, head.

Feet, if placed properly, control the body's orientation. Turn the model so that both feet are aimed to the side, then move the nearest foot so that it points towards the

Static poses

Static, standing poses are often the hardest to deal with and, without careful directions, cavers often stand with their arms at their sides, posing squarely to the camera (top).

In the middle photograph the caver was asked to stand at an angle of 45 degrees to the camera, facing the wall, then turn one foot and the head towards the camera. This immediately introduces a better composition.

A similar pose was used for the final photograph, but with the caver turned around. He is now facing out of the picture and the composition is not as satisfying. Always consider the shape of the final photograph and whether it will be cropped (as these have been at the top and bottom) before the picture is taken. Cover the right-hand side of the lower photograph: the caver is once again 'looking into' the scene and its composition is improved.

All photographs: E8, B4

A flashbulb backlight (B5), aimed directly at the camera from behind the caver, has produced highlights on the walls and accentuated the passage shape of the Ogof Ffynnon Ddu streamway. The foreground has been lit with a shielded, narrow beam from an electronic flash (E1). The composition is central and breaks the 'rules', but is nevertheless successful.

The poor pose in the first photograph (left: E8, B5) is improved by turning the caver and placing a hand under a shoulder strap. However, the viewer's attention is divided: is the subject of the picture the formations in the foreground or the caver? Moving the camera closer to the now-crouching caver, who is looking at the flowstone, produces a more compact, coherent composition

camera. This throws the weight slightly onto the back foot and produces a natural pose with the shoulders on a diagonal; avoid a static, square-on appearance. Professional models earn huge fees on the basis of the way they stand and look; analyse advertising photographs for the position of models' feet relative to their pose.

Some cavers find difficulty in knowing what to do with their hands. A 'prop', such as a tackle sack, gives a caver something to hold and makes the pose more natural, for example with one hand tucked under a shoulder strap while walking. Set up an activity: rigging a rope or opening a camera box – there is always one available. A silhouetted caver firing a flash with two hands, elbows sticking out, is almost a cliché; create a different outline using a slave flash held in one hand, leaving the other to hang free.

Finally, control the orientation of the head. A slight tilt makes an enormous difference as it influences the helmet light's position (especially important in silhouettes) and, even if the eyes are not visible, the direction of sight is implied and a diagonal is introduced.

Before pressing the shutter, is there anything that can be improved? Tidy any hanging straps or dishevelled clothing which will cause distractions. In a crawl, clench a fist as if pulling or holding, rather than allowing it to lie flat on the ground. Remove spectacles if they will catch light from the flash and produce intrusive highlights, or tilt the model's head downwards to avoid the worst of the problem. Check for shadows across the face from the peak of a helmet or nearby formation. Anticipate

Directing a pose

This series of pictures (all E8) was taken in a crawl. In the first photograph the head-down caver is crawling directly towards the camera and there is little to interest the viewer. In photograph (2) the head has been raised, adding interest as the eyes are visible, but the pose is still exceptionally static.

To add interest, a prop – a tackle sack – was used and the camera angle changed to the side. This introduced a diagonal shape to the composition. In photograph (4) the caver was asked to lie down lower and grip the floor, rather than leaving her hand flat on the ground.

Finally, the viewpoint (and the diagonal) was strengthened with a lower camera angle and by raising the model's head to look in the direction of travel. Complicated lighting set-ups and exotic locations are not vital in order to produce interesting pictures.

Posing a model

- Indicate the direction to face and what to look at; demonstrate by example
- Decide on the basic pose: sitting, kneeling or standing
- Consider the model's safety and cave conservation
- Place the feet; standing with one foot nearer the camera looks natural
- Use a prop when necesary
- Give clear instructions on where to put hands
- Place shoulders at an angle to the camera; avoid 'square on' poses
- Tilt the head to add interest to the pose
- Check for stray shadows and reflections from a helmet peak or spectacles; ensure clothing is tidy
- Anticipate the outline of a silhouette: is a tackle sack a bonus or intrusion?
- Final check: feet, shoulders, hands, head

the shape of a silhouetted caver: is a tackle sack well placed, or will it confuse the outline?

Some cavers never feel comfortable in front of a camera. Their help is nevertheless appreciated and a willing model who is not natural in a photograph can still appear as a silhouette. Never turn away an enthusiastic assistant, and always show your gratitude with a copy of the picture; it is something unobtainable elsewhere and will be much appreciated. A well-trained caver who knows how to follow instructions and use your equipment to best effect is like gold dust. Nurture any such person: they're worth it.

In short, make a final check covering every element: framing, focus, shutter and aperture; foreground, background, lighting and shadows; feet, shoulders, hands, head.

More than in any other chapter in this manual, the 'rules' and ideals presented here are subjective; with regard to composition they can only be personal opinion. It is not important whether you, the cave photographer, agree with what is written here: it is enough that you use the information as an aid. Consider what you are trying to achieve; head towards your personal goal using the 'formal' elements of composition which are of help, and discard the rest. Composition holds no right or wrong, only what pleases and what does not. Simplicity in lighting and design is often the best approach but, whatever the composition, if you can control the outcome of a photograph and convey the desired mood to the viewer, the picture is certainly a success.

The angle of the conservation tapes in Galería Garimpeiros in Ogof Draenen adds a strong diagonal to the composition, aided by the direction of the caver's gaze. As it was not possible to hide an assistant behind the model without crossing the tape, the backlight was propped up on the camera box and fired using a slave (E8, B5)

Chapter thirteen
ASSESSING YOUR WORK

My results are really awful – always! All the slides are black, with little points of light for caver's helmet lamps. I don't worry, though – the flashguns were cheap and I use outdated film, so it doesn't cost much when I waste it.

Comment by a novice cave photographer

P HOTOGRAPHS should be assessed in order to learn from mistakes and capitalise on successes. By identifying difficulties and their causes, corrections can be made the next time that situation occurs.

Photographic problems arise from a number of sources, compositional as well as technical, and are sometimes difficult to identify. An unexpected experimental result might lead to further research while, to avoid future complications, difficulties with an established technique or equipment (was the flash too weak, the aperture wrongly calculated, or is the camera synchronisation faulty?) demand an investigation.

Careful assessment is needed to identify an error, understand its cause and then correct it the next time you are underground. While taking pictures, in particular experimental ones, write down data in a waterproof surveyor's notebook and match it with the resulting photograph. Analyse your results to continue learning and improving.

IDENTIFYING ERRORS

A weak subsidiary lamp (top left) can be angled across the camera to help to indicate the viewfinder limits

Use transparency film for tests and experiments which will set parameters for future exposures. Mistakes on slide film are immediately apparent because they are not masked by subsequent processing.

Check for obvious errors first. Was the framing accurate; was the composition acceptable or could it have been improved with a different camera position? A tilted photograph is easy to take when hand-holding a camera in the dark – more so when lying on your side or twisting your head to see through a low, tripod-mounted viewfinder.

If a problem arises, work on a solution. For example, it can be difficult to see the limits of the picture when the edges of the viewfinder are in total darkness, and therefore it is impossible to accurately check the exact composition of the photograph. Shining a dim light across the viewfinder makes it visible, but if the light strikes the lens it causes flare so it must be turned off before taking the picture. In turn, this can cause camera movement and loss of the carefully prepared composition – the very thing you were trying to attain. There is often more than one solution to a problem – in this case, making use of an assistant or moving the light away at the last moment is easier than turning it off.

Breezeway Cave, Colorado (B6). The vast bank of helictites forms a giant reflector which has helped to fill in details in shadow areas

Errors commonly result from exposure variations. In practice, some error is masked by the film's latitude and viewers will not notice slight discrepancies in the texture, colour or tone of rock walls: there is no specific feature that a viewer can use as a reference point. The colour and tone of a face, however, is well known and even slight overexposure is unacceptable. If a face is overexposed but the surroundings appear perfect, remember that your perception will have a wider range of acceptance with dark areas than with faces: the face *must* be correct, whereas the background need not be perfect. A common cause of overexposure arises from an automatic electronic flash exposing for the background. Moral: expose for flesh tones, at the expense of darker, surrounding features.

Visible defects can originate from a number of causes, and some effects may mask problems arising from unrelated factors. This makes some errors difficult to identify but, with care, many causes can be eliminated by considering the in-cave situation and using your notes on exposures. Build up a reference set of 'failed' photographs, clearly labelled with the identified cause; failures are valuable learning aids and can help determine the solution to a recurring error. Take note of unexpected effects; these might lead to a new technique. It is a mistake to believe that everything in the cave's unique environment causes 'problems'; just as high humidity with a flash near the camera can ruin a picture, it enhances backlighting. Capitalising on such features may help to produce a new and unique photograph but, above all, budget for a lot of film: it is the best way to learn. Practise, then practise more – if necessary, outdoors at night using different flash positions in readiness for that perfect underground exposure.

Equipment, technique, exposure and processing all affect the picture's success. The following tables include observable errors in broad groups such as colour cast and contrast control. Effectively, as well as offering possible solutions, the tables contain a series of tips: if a potential difficulty is noted and understood, the error can be avoided.

No two cave photographers approach the same problem in the same way. Learn from your mistakes; build on the specific techniques you are satisfied with until you develop your own, distinctive, style. It must be added that there are so many interrelated parameters which can affect the final photograph that no set of tables can ever be complete; these are merely suggested causes and solutions, which should be considered alongside the relevant chapter in this manual.

ASSESSING ERRORS

Basic errors

Visible effect	Possible cause	Suggested correction
Photograph not level	Low tripod or restricted space caused tilted head and camera	Keep head directly behind viewfinder to decrease risk of tilted photographs
	Difficulty in deciding when tripod-mounted camera is level	Fit a small spirit level in the camera's hot shoe or to the tripod head
	Camera moved while hand-held on B; there was a delay between opening the shutter and firing the flash. With no reference point in the dark, the camera wavered	Use a rock or passage wall as support for hand-held cameras
		Check manual flash firing and that test buttons are easy to operate. Ensure the command to fire is clearly heard and understood
Picture is blurred (sometimes linked with light trails from helmet lights)	Camera moved during exposure; 'camera shake'	Use a tripod when daylight is involved; a steady hand is needed with the slow production of light from flashbulbs
	Effect is sometimes confused with condensation on lens	See section on low contrast (p.234)
Movement within picture area is blurred	Flashbulb duration does not freeze motion	Use electronic flash to freeze movement, or reduce movement in the picture
	Part or all the scene is lit with daylight (photo 1)	Reduce exposure time by using a faster shutter speed (and wider aperture)
Main subject is unsharp (photo 2)	Poor focus, accentuated by a wide aperture and narrow depth of field	SLR camera: focus on a helmet light at the subject position – when the light appears to be at its smallest it is in sharp focus. Compact camera: estimate or measure distances more accurately

1. Shutter speed too slow to freeze movement

2. Poor focus. Highlights are poorly defined. Only the areas lying within the zone of focus are sharp

A moving subject is sharp but the surroundings are blurred (typically in an entrance picture)	Camera movement forms a blurred image where there is ambient light, but a moving subject (e.g. caver) is frozen by an electronic flash	Restrict camera movement; use a tripod to ensure background cannot blur; use a different aperture (effectively a different flash/daylight lighting ratio) to make the shutter speed faster and decrease the risk of blurring

Basic errors (continued)

Visible effect	Possible cause	Suggested correction
Picture is grainy and poorly defined	Fast film or poor processing	Use a slower film with finer grain; underexposed colour prints are noticeably grainy
Photograph is totally black	Incorrect flash synchronisation	Use the X setting
	Film incorrectly loaded	Check film is correctly loaded by winding on and watching the rewind knob turn
Half (or other proportion) of photograph is black	Flash synchronisation incorrect; shutter speed too fast	Check for sync failure and correct shutter speed. Use 1/30 second or slower for flashbulbs

Exposure errors

Visible effect	Possible cause	Suggested correction
Subject or complete photograph is too dark	Underexposure	Use faster film, open the aperture, use more flashes or reduce flash-to-subject distance
	Wrong flash synchronisation speed with flashbulbs	Using a shutter speed faster than 1/30 second wastes part of a flashbulb's output and affects exposure calculations
	Two or more automatic flashguns used	Use manual flashguns so that the light from one is not detected by the sensor of another
Subject or complete photograph is too light	Overexposure	Use slower film, close the aperture, use fewer flashes or increase flash-to-subject distance

3. Flash E8 is lighting the foreground and figure, with flash B7 on the background. The flashes overlap and have overexposed the face and arm

4. Foreground too light: use a shield to make the flash more directional. Cropping the print would improve its presentation

Both an electronic flash and bulb are used, but only the bulb has lit the photograph	Wrong flash synchronisation. FP sync fires flash before shutter opens and thus electronic flash is completed before shutter opens or bulb begins to burn	Use the X setting at 1/30 second or slower
Most of scene is correctly exposed, but areas such as a caver's face are overexposed	Local overexposure: light-toned areas are easily overexposed, while the same error in dark areas is not as noticeable	Avoid automatic flash; calculate apertures using guide number of a manual flash and flash-to-subject distance. Use a film with more latitude
	Overlapping flashes (photo 3)	Alter placement of flashes, or add further flashguns to produce more even lighting

Exposure errors (continued)

Visible effect	Possible cause	Suggested correction
Light areas such as faces are correctly exposed, but background areas are too dark	Insufficient or poorly placed supplementary flashes	Use additional or more even background lighting or replace it with side lighting which evenly illuminates both the background and the subject
Different areas are unevenly lit; lighting is patchy or some areas are overexposed	Flashgun incorrectly placed	The flash must be equidistant from subjects to avoid over- or underexposing different parts of the scene
	Two or more flashguns incorrectly placed	Space existing flashes to avoid overlap, or add flashes to fill dark regions between lit areas
Foreground too light but subject correctly exposed	Flash incorrectly aimed (photo 4)	Aim flash slightly upwards, shield foreground or move flash nearer to subject (and alter aperture to match)
	Ultra wide-angle lens used	Use a narrower angle lens to exclude foreground when flash position and direction cannot be altered

6. Electronic flash is directional. This vertical picture was lit with the flash reflector held horizontally. Orientate the reflector to match the photo format

5. Reflective surfaces (water, wet rock) can produce distracting highlights. *Left:* Intrusive droplets of water and an out-of-focus straw stalactite. *Right:* Reflections on the surface of water

Part of picture unacceptable

Visible effect	Possible cause	Suggested correction
Distracting highlights or colours in background	Highly reflective areas, in particular droplets of water, can produce out-of-focus highlights (photo 5)	Change camera position or composition to exclude the problem area. Check reflections using helmet lights from flash positions. Use shields
	Caver operating backlight is visible, particularly when firing flashbulbs	Flashbulb reflectors throw light over a wide angle and light easily spills onto the person firing the flash. Hold flash at arm's length to reduce the problem
Poor texture	Excessive front lighting	Use side or 'grazing' lighting angles to accentuate subject's texture by adding shadows
Texture good, but part of photograph overexposed	Side lighting too oblique, giving excessive exposure to the part nearest the flashgun	Change the angle of lighting. Add a reflector or fill-in flash. Fire flash across long axis of photograph

Part of picture unacceptable (continued)

Visible effect	Possible cause	Suggested correction
Corners of photograph are unexpectedly dark	Uneven lighting. The extreme edges of a flashlit area may have more than one f-stop difference in intensity compared to the middle of the area	Test the flash. Use a narrower angle lens, increase the flash-to-subject distance, or diffuse the flash
	Electronic flash poorly aimed (photo 6)	Electronic flashguns are very directional. Take care when aiming. Hold flashgun vertically for upright pictures and vice versa
	Lens partly obscured by additional filter or by an incorrectly shaped or positioned lens hood causing cut-off (photo 7)	Ensure filter used as a transparent lens cap is removed before taking picture. Match the shape of the lens hood to the angle of view of the lens

 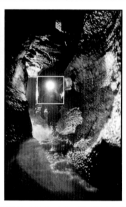  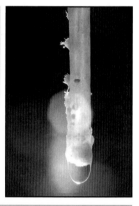

7. Cut-off (darkened corners) from a filter used on a wide-angle lens at Pomongwe Cave, Zimbabwe

8. Helmet light too bright relative to flash intensity

9. Flare, showing shape of camera iris

Visible effect	Possible cause	Suggested correction
Helmet light (or flash) in picture appears too large or is surrounded by a 'halo'	Excessive moisture in the air	Aim light away from camera, use a dimmer light or work with helmet lights off
	Halation. Uncommon with modern film, halation is due to light sources bright enough to cause reflection within the film	Aim light away from camera, use a dimmer light or work with helmet lights off. Reduce exposure. Use a different film stock
	Overexposure	Helmet light too bright for exposure duration (e.g. when using B). Reduce exposure time or make helmet light dimmer (photo 8)
Passage surroundings 'dull' and lack brilliance or detail	Insufficient reflection from muddy walls or rock	Increase reflection by wetting walls; add backlighting
Red eyes in subject	Flash too close to camera	Move flash to *minimum* of 0.5m from lens axis; use a 'red-eye pen' to correct defective prints
Shaped areas of flare	Light striking lens at an angle produces an aperture-shaped flare (photo 9)	Prevent direct light striking the lens. If flare is unavoidable, diminish its effects using highlight areas, or place flash in the exact centre of the picture

Part of picture unacceptable (continued)

Visible effect	Possible cause	Suggested correction
Dark and light fringes to subject	Subject has moved between flashes; fringes are due to background receiving different lighting	If flashes are not fired at same time ensure subject is static. Slight fringing can occur if subject moves when a bulb and electronic flash are fired by slaves (photo 10)
Light trails	Light source moved during exposure (typically on B)	While shutter is open all lights must be static; turn out lights or ensure they are stationary
	Light trails formed although there was no movement of subject, because the camera was moved while shutter was open	Fault is typical of hand-held camera on B, giving parallel light trails from two or more light sources (photo 11). Check shutter is not sticking open

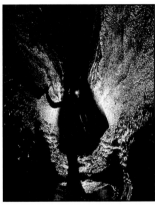

10. Movement between flashes: note dark fringe above arm and light fringe below

11. Parallel light trails caused by movement of camera while shutter was open

12. Silhouette on dark background

Silhouette unclear

Visible effect	Possible cause	Suggested correction
Overexposed area near silhouette (e.g. passage wall or area near feet); main area of picture correctly exposed	Aperture is correct for main area, but foreground is overexposed due to incorrect use of flash or poor choice of type of flash	Tilt flashgun slightly upwards or away from nearby areas. Use a narrower angle of flash by modifying the reflector or use electronic flash in place of flashbulbs. Use a shield
Poor silhouette of caver firing flash, but foreground correctly lit by second flash	Distance between caver and background too great	Change composition to decrease the caver's flash-to-background distance. As foreground is correctly exposed, do not adjust the aperture or this flashgun's distance
	Background has insufficient lighting	Add an additional flash to increase lighting on background. Adding a backlight can help separate the subject from the background by introducing highlights and rimlighting
Backlit silhouette does not stand out from background (photo 12)	Insufficient moisture or dust in the air, giving a black-on-black silhouette with poor rimlighting	Add more backlight or use a wider aperture. Some mines are drier and better ventilated than caves and a successful technique in a cave may not transfer directly to a mine. Silhouettes in streamways may be easier to produce due to high levels of moisture

Silhouette unclear (continued)

Visible effect	Possible cause	Suggested correction
Unacceptable dark shadow on waterfall	Backlight throws shadow (e.g. of silhouetted caver) onto waterfall	Stand caver within or in front of backlit waterfall
	Caver, lit with electronic and bulb flash, has moved during exposure	Electronic flash freezes movement. The bulb flash then casts a slightly different shadow which, with a moving subject, appears as a dark rim in the photograph. Avoid movement while using flashbulbs
Passage shape/ background not completely lit	Electronic flash too directional	Use a flashbulb or fire several electronic flashes at different angles

Contrast problems

Visible effect	Possible cause	Suggested correction
Low contrast, milky or misty photograph	Flash too close to camera (photo 15)	Move flashgun to 0.5m *minimum* distance from camera
	Excessive water or dust in air	Avoid foreground light; work with side light and backlight only
	Frontlit subject	Use side lighting and backlighting
	Photographer's helmet light too close to lens	Turn off or redirect light before taking photo-graph. Use an assistant's light to aid framing
	Flare from light source within photograph	Avoid helmet lights or flashguns aimed directly at lens. Check accurate line-up of backlight with subject
	Filter or lens misted up; highlights spread into shadows (photo 16)	Allow time for lens to equalise with the cave temperature; do not cover lens with a hand or damp material when using B
	Filter dirty or scratched	Keep filters clean; light scatter on the glass reduces contrast
	Fill-in flash too powerful	Increase lighting ratio to give a 'modelling' effect
	Flare from light source outside photograph	Shield light sources or use a lens hood matched to the lens' angle of view
	Overexposed with low contrast	Reduce exposure (photo 13)
	Underdeveloped negative: highlight detail good but lacking shadow detail	Extend development time; check for developer exhaustion and dilution (photo 14)
	Black and white print has 'flat' (low contrast) appearance	Increase paper grade; increase development time or exposure. Developer exhausted or temperature too low. A negative which lacks shadow detail is underexposed. A negative which contains shadow detail but lacks contrast is underdeveloped

13. Overexposed negative: good shadow detail but low contrast highlights and mid-tones

Contrast problems (continued)

Visible effect	Possible cause	Suggested correction
Picture harshly lit; contrast too high	Electronic flash too close to subject; side lighting too pronounced; effect is often coupled with local overexposure (photo 17)	Increase flash-to-subject distance; a flash which is too close makes exposure differences between different parts of the same subject more pronounced
		Use a larger flashgun reflector or soften the light source by bouncing it off reflective material
		At close range, cover electronic flash with translucent material to diffuse it. Use a flash-bulb in a large reflector to 'soften' light
	Overdeveloped negative: highlight detail lacking but good shadow detail	Reduce development time; check developer dilution
	Black and white print too contrasty	Decrease paper grade; decrease development time or exposure. A negative which is dense but retains shadow detail is overexposed. A negative which is too contrasty may be overdeveloped (grain structure will be large)

14. Underdeveloped negative due to chemical exhaustion

15. Flash too close to camera has lit condensation from photographer's breath

16. Condensation on the lens 'softens' photographs; highlights spread into shadows

17. Flash too close to caver (note lighting gradient and harsh light on figure)

Incorrect colour

Visible effect	Possible cause	Suggested correction
Blue colour cast in slide	Tungsten slide film exposed with electronic flash, blue flashbulbs or showcave lighting	Only use tungsten film for special effects or with showcave tungsten lighting
Some areas blue, others are reddish	Mixture of flashbulb and electronic flash lighting	Flash colour balance is not the same; use one flash type only (backlight colour imbalances are usually less noticeable)
Pink colour cast in slide	Gross overexposure may produce a pink tinge in highlight areas in some slide films, e.g. a daylight-lit entrance	Reduce exposure or increase fill-in light to balance light sources. Use a different film type. Film may be outdated or faulty

Incorrect colour (continued)

Visible effect	Possible cause	Suggested correction
Black areas in colour prints are recorded as brown; other colours are incorrect	Print overexposed, but negative is good. Poor processing due to automatic machine printing exposure; the machine assumes photograph is evenly lit rather than containing large areas of black	When print is made, request the lab bases its exposures on highlights at the expense of shadow detail. Expose the first frame on a roll with an evenly lit daylight subject containing a selection of colours, including flesh tones. This gives a test print for the machine operator
	Black and white prints made from chromogenic film in a C41 process	Some machines are not properly fitted with chromogenic correction filters; sepia prints are produced. Ask for a reprint
Red colours too dark in black and white prints	Film is not equally sensitive to all colours	Avoid red oversuits (yellow is better); deliberately overexpose reds or use a pale yellow filter to lighten the tone
	Print made from a colour slide	Use a yellow or orange filter to lighten red colours when making an internegative (but blue colours will darken). Overexpose and underdevelop negative to reduce contrast increase due to copying procedure

NB: Incorrect colours arising from poor technique may be partially or totally masked in colour prints, as corrections can be made during processing. Transparency film is more critical

Test series, processing and scratches

Visible effect	Possible cause	Suggested correction
Non-parallel/curved scratches in photograph (photo 18)	Scratches produced during processing or handling	Check storage methods. Handle film with greater care. Have film inspected by the laboratory

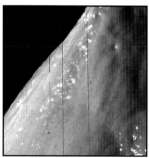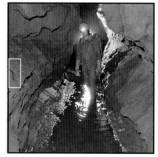

18. Parallel and curved scratches. These are normally dark on a slide (left) and light on a print made from a negative (right)

19. Hair in shutter track (shown here in a section taken from an upright photograph)

Parallel/straight line scratches in photograph (photo 18)	Grit in camera or damage to film cassette	White, parallel scratches in prints (black or blue on slides) are probably caused in the camera. Avoid changing rolls underground. Polish the pressure plate in 35mm cameras before closing the back (a paper backing protects roll film). Keep cassette light traps clean. Thoroughly clean and service camera

Test series, processing and scratches (continued)

Visible effect	Possible cause	Suggested correction
Colour cast in all pictures	Poor processing, printing, or an imbalance between film sensitivity and light source	Ensure lighting matches the film's sensitivity. See also the section on incorrect colour (p.235)
All exposures of a test series are unacceptable	Insufficient bracketing of exposures	Increase number of f-stops (and intermediate settings) during bracketing
	Tonal variation too great to be recorded	Tonal range may be beyond the film's capabilities. Use a film with greater latitude or reduce the tonal range
Hair or thread on every photograph (photo 19)	Loose thread on blind of focal plane shutter; hair or thread caught in shutter track; hair trapped under filter	With lens removed and back open, wind on slowly and check both sides of blind; service camera. Check track with shutter on B; remove hair. Hair on filter will be unsharp or unseen on film, but will reduce contrast

MANIPULATING IMAGES

It is part of the nature of cave photography that not every image is successful. Often, it 'almost' worked as planned. These 'failures' can sometimes be salvaged, at least partially or to the extent that an important record photograph is usable. Other pictures can be improved by darkroom work or by using simple, but nevertheless important, techniques such as cropping.

Cropping

Cropping consists of altering the shape of an image, whether by covering parts of a transparency so that only a selected area is visible, or cutting or covering a print. It is an accepted photographic technique that is used to produce a variety of shapes in a set of photographs or to remove potentially intrusive highlights or other areas lying near the edges which attract the eye away from the main subject.

Cropping from the top and bottom to produce a wide, narrow picture has strengthened the composition by concentrating interest on the caver and heaps of guano in Ogof Draenen (E8, B5)

When cropping, either remove one side or two opposite sides of the picture; it is considered bad practice to remove two adjoining sides. Adjacent sides are cropped to retain the original proportions of the photograph while removing extraneous details, but a smaller area of the negative is then used which requires greater enlargement to produce a print of any given size, thus reducing its quality.

To find the best shape for a print cover it with two L-shaped pieces of card, then mark and cut the print. Slides can be cropped by masking them with aluminium cooking foil: cut a narrow strip, fold it in two (a folded edge is both straight and stiffer than a cut edge) and place it over the film. Hold it in place by closing the slide mount. Correct misaligned verticals by twisting the slide in its mount and concealing the now visible edge of the frame with foil.

In the darkroom

Producing your own prints, interpreting and coaxing the most out of a negative to turn a pre-envisaged scene into reality, is as challenging as taking the original picture. Printing is obviously a valuable skill but, as darkroom techniques are found in any darkroom manual, they are not

Pictures taken in crawls or rifts can often be improved with careful printing as any uneven lighting can be smoothed out. This crawl in Ogof Draenen (E8, B5) has been printed to concentrate interest on the caver by lightening the central part of the photograph and darkening the edges

Extensive dodging and burning in (lightening and darkening selected areas) has enhanced details in the water and rock in this picture taken in West Kingsdale Master Cave (B5)

repeated here. However, it is worth considering the specific advantages which you will gain if you set up a home darkroom and take the time to learn how to manipulate photographs:

- Overexposed areas can be removed or partially corrected by 'burning in'
- Edges of prints can be darkened, helping to hold a viewer's interest in the centre of the print
- Contrast can be controlled by using different b&w paper grades
- Slight colour casts can be corrected
- Variations of exposure can be evened out

Darkroom work is not limited to making colour or black and white prints; it is possible to create overlays and masks to improve or alter the reality of photographs, to repair damage such as scratches and processing marks, and to combine more than one image to form a composite or sandwich (see p.172).

Digital imaging

The rise of digital (or 'electronic') imaging will ultimately have a huge effect on cave photography. Video has pointed the way into low-light photography with automatic exposure control, and digital 'still' cameras are increasingly treading the same pathway. As technologies improve, digital cameras may permit future cave photographers to take pictures with fewer difficulties and less powerful flashguns, though it will be many years before conventional silver-based film is completely superseded.

Photographs contain a range of colours and tones which can be scanned and converted into a digital format and stored as a computer file. Given a good original, the scanning resolution determines the quality contained in the image file which, if necessary, can be remade into a photograph. The trade-off lies with the file size – high-resolution scans produce large

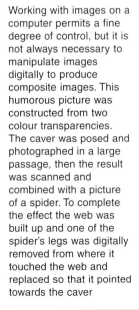

Working with images on a computer permits a fine degree of control, but it is not always necessary to manipulate images digitally to produce composite images. This humorous picture was constructed from two colour transparencies. The caver was posed and photographed in a large passage, then the result was scanned and combined with a picture of a spider. To complete the effect the web was built up and one of the spider's legs was digitally removed from where it touched the web and replaced so that it pointed towards the caver

The photographs show the mosaic ceiling in Buckeye Creek Cave in West Virginia. The small silhouette (B5) shows the marks extremely well, being lit in relief, but the fill-in flash (which adds detail to the figure; E8, B5) flattens the image. The two photographs were combined using a computer to create an picture which displays the best of both originals

files that require a fast computer and plentiful storage space. While an entire set of the *Encyclopaedia Britannica* can fit onto a single CD-ROM, the same storage space only holds eight 35mm slides scanned to the theoretical limit of photographic quality, or 100 slides in Photo-CD format.

Each image on a photo-CD is represented by five files. These range from a low 'thumbnail' resolution suitable for identification purposes to a high resolution which has sufficient quality for manipulation or publication (although a 'standard' file cannot produce a full photographic quality duplicate transparency; a 'professional' scan is required for that purpose).

Manipulation might involve repairing a scratch, correcting a colour cast or localised exposure errors, or removing unwanted details by cloning an acceptable part of the picture and copying it over an unacceptable one. The possibilities for altering an image are endless.

This photograph was taken in Bridge Cave (B6). A print was made in the darkroom, enhancing detail in the caver, who is only lit with light reflected from the water. Unfortunately, the negative was badly scratched in the camera.

This damage was repaired using a computer, in this instance an easier exercise than the more conventional technique of 'spotting' – using a brush and photographic dyes to spot out the white lines. Only extreme purist photographers would object to this use of digital manipulation.

However, other forms of alteration may not be approved. Was it acceptable to remove a sponsor's name from the cave diver's helmet in the picture at the top of p.197?

The question is not whether such technology *should* be applied to cave photographs; it already has been and will continue to be used as a tool like any other. As the technique gains in popularity, books are appearing which detail specific software and equipment; *how* to manipulate an image is outside the scope of this manual. However, it is worth asking to what extent digital imaging should be used in cave photography.

The digital imaging 'manipulation scale' runs from correcting minor defects to significantly altering a picture. Is it acceptable to change the size of a formation, or place a caver in a passage which that person has never visited? At least one advertising agency has added a product to a caving photograph without the permission of the caver involved. Would you be happy shown using equipment you have never trained with? Few people would worry about repairing an image which has been damaged during processing, but doubts might arise over gross alterations to reality.

It must be said that cave photographers have been manipulating images in the darkroom for many years and their techniques are accepted as standard; a great deal can be accomplished during printing with dodging, burning and the use of lith overlays and negative masks. Colour transparencies are also susceptible to alteration. Digital imaging may be doing no more to change reality than conventional techniques, though manipulation via a digital route is often faster, sometimes (though not always) easier and is more likely to be undetectable. What is important is intent: concealing the fact that a radical change has been made is more serious than displaying an obviously false image, constructed for amusement. Before altering reality, consider the outcome: how ethically acceptable is it? There is a vast difference between removing information from an image (darkening intrusive highlights or the corners of a print, something which could be accomplished as part of a standard darkroom technique) and adding false details such as additional stalactites to an image. The integrity of the image, as well as the photographer, is important. What is certain, in this fast-changing technological world, is that embracing the concept of digital imaging and considering its implications is the only viable approach to take.

THE FINAL STEP

It's over: you've spent time and energy and have the pictures you worked towards. The first priority is to supply copies of the best photographs to the cavers who helped you take them; involve your team in your work. But, what then do you do with your pictures? . . .

Slide shows

Variety in any slide show or lecture is advantageous. Practise the talk and be selective about what is shown. Use slides to illustrate your words, talking through them, rather than showing a picture and talking about it.

Genesis Gallery in Little Neath River Cave (B5)

In the river entrance to
Dan yr Ogof (E1, B4)

Maintain interest by changing the type and sequence of photographs: leave slides on the screen for varying intervals, and intermingle different lighting techniques and scenes. Avoid a dark moody picture followed by a very bright one or vice versa as, when shown in quick succession, this is disturbing to the viewer. A series of passage shots is enlivened by interspersing them with close-ups or cavers in action: introduce changes in emphasis. Be ruthless, and leave out 'almost identical but really good' photographs from bracketed series. Do not be tempted to put in a poor picture as it is the only one available; reshoot the photograph or do without.

It is surprising how cavers and non-cavers perceive cave photographs; there is often a distinct division between what is liked by the two sets of people. Cavers, accustomed to cave images, are more used to high-contrast, dramatic silhouettes than non-cavers. While appreciated by cavers, a silhouette, even a mediocre one, often elicits additional praise from non-cavers and it is worth including several in any slide show.

Exhibition and competition

Speleo-photo competitions offer an excellent route to improving skills. Many national caving organisations run an annual convention or conference which includes a photographic competition or salon; make contact and become involved. There may be several sections, such as colour slide,

The cascades in Dan yr Ogof (left: E2, B6) and after a visit to Ogof Cynnes. When selecting photographs for slide shows or to support articles, include a variety of shots – silhouettes, action, faces – to maintain interest

colour or black and white print, a portfolio of images judged as a set, exploration, cave life, humour, experimental and so on. There will certainly be a category for your area of interest.

When selecting your entry you are forced to analyse your pictures in a critical manner, and later to make comparisons with other photographs on display. Winning is less important than entering the best pictures you can produce; be proud of your images and let others see them. You will collect advice; you do not have to accept it – make your own decisions based on constructive criticism. Do you agree with the judges? They are expressing an opinion based on experience, but your own ideas may be as valid as theirs. Equally, do not be blind to suggestions – after all, you entered to learn and, hopefully, will always continue to do so.

That *you* think about the pictures is of ultimate importance. If you pick up ideas of where improvements can be made, or new techniques which you might try, go caving and discover what yields the best results. Photo salons are a means of seeing other work and showing cavers what you are doing: it is a learning situation to be made use of however possible.

Publications

Opposite: The route to Top Waterfall, Ogof Ffynnon Ddu (B4)

The caving press is also a competitive arena: photographs form article illustrations, record certain caves or newsworthy events, or stand alone as an artistic work. In each case the editor will look critically at your work and decide on the magazine's needs – and whether you can supply them. The standard will vary: a small club newsletter may apply different criteria from a national journal. Submitting pictures may be unsuccessful at first, but you will gain experience and eventually see your work in print if you listen to comments and advice along the way.

From the editor's point of view, photographs may or may not be in short supply (the competition for a cover illustration can be fierce), but they will never be considered for use unless they are sharp and correctly exposed. Technically, they must be perfect. An ink-on-paper print does not have the same tonal range as a photographic print, and far less than a slide. This means that areas of similar tones may merge together when printed in a magazine: the tonal range is collapsed and detail may be lost in either highlights, shadows, or both. Editors are sometimes forced to reject pictures for seemingly obscure reasons. Talk to the editor and find out what is required; help is normally forthcoming, within the confines of available time.

In this specialist market, colour reproduction may be limited to the cover and the picture must take the magazine title, logo or advertiser's name into account. The photograph's composition must leave space for this to appear without cutting off a crucial part of the composition. Usually, an upright photograph is needed for a full cover 'bleed' (a photograph which

This picture, taken at the end of The Chasm in Ogof Ffynnon Ddu (B5), has proved popular as a competition winner. As there is space at the top for a magazine logo, it has also been used as a cover illustration

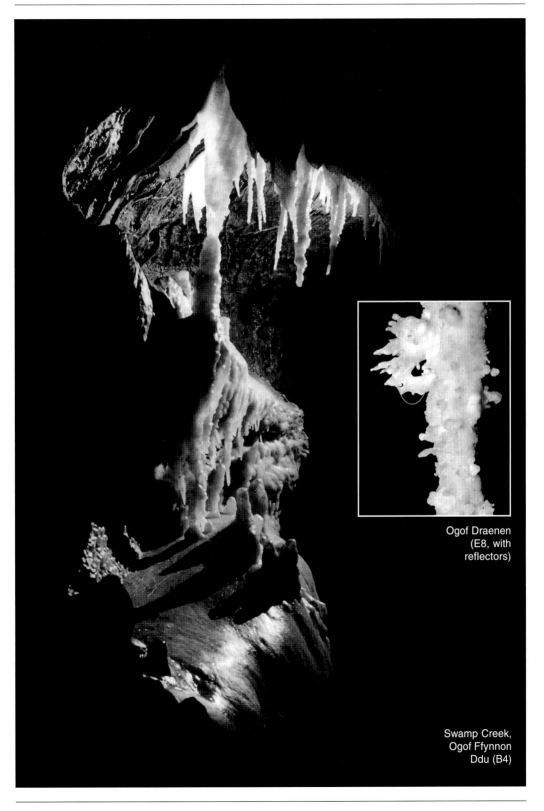

Ogof Draenen
(E8, with
reflectors)

Swamp Creek,
Ogof Ffynnon
Ddu (B4)

Lamb & Fox Chamber, Ogof Draenen. Five flashes were fired: (B2) by the caver, a backlight (B5), a light to add the highlights seen along the caver's back (E4), and two electronic flashes fired towards the wall and floor from the lower left corner

reaches the edges of the page; effectively, it is partially cropped as the original would extend beyond the page area). A 35mm format picture does not have the same proportions as standard paper sizes: unless it is used as an inset, the long dimension of the picture will be shortened and this must be taken into account. Project a slide onto a sheet of paper, perhaps with the magazine logo drawn on, to check how much cropping will occur if the editor chooses your picture.

Before submitting slides, assess their suitability. If possible, match the photograph to its use: black and white prints for monochrome reproduction, colour for colour. Slides are normally preferred to prints for colour reproduction. A photograph of a caver with a red oversuit against a rich, black background will possibly be rejected by a caving magazine which only reproduces photographs in black and white; superb as the original is, it will not look flattering as a black-on-black print. Estimate what it will look like by holding the slide in front of a piece of white paper, viewing it using reflected light – the tonal range is depressed and it more closely represents how it will appear in print. If a picture passes your tests or you think it might be suitable for publication, send it to the editor with a caption and a stamped addressed envelope for its return. You have nothing to lose and everything to gain.

Chapter fourteen
A TOUCH OF HISTORY

I opened the leather case to find a jumbled heap of unprotected, age-yellowed glass plates. Some were broken; many were stuck to each other in a final emulsive embrace. Unsalvageable, lost to posterity, twenty priceless turn-of-the-century negatives of Mendip caves were dropped into a waste bin.

Conservation work in a museum

F OR over 130 years caves and caving have been documented by photography and the discipline has, on several occasions, been instrumental in promoting photographic advances; in 1865 magnesium was developed as a photographic light source with experimental photographs taken in the Blue John Caverns. The acceptance of flashbulbs as a replacement for flashpowder was linked to underground photography, without considering technical innovations such as the caver-designed,

The Cave Diving Group celebrated fifty years of underwater activity in 1996, staging dives in Wookey Hole using period equipment. Photographs such as this (E8), which document modern day events, will become part of tomorrow's spelean legacy

infra-red slave units of today. The resulting pictures from all the ages contain information that is invaluable to the speleo historian and provide a visual record of techniques and days long passed.

The same is true of photographs taken today: in years to come, these images will be sought after by new generations of cavers. Sadly, however, photographs are often poorly documented and there is no doubt that without proper care these will be (and indeed are being) damaged and destroyed – caving club archivists take note. How important or diligent you are depends on what you consider your pictures to be worth, not necessarily in monetary terms but in terms of their historical content or sentimental value.

RECORDING INFORMATION

Photographs must be stored so that they are accessible and specific pictures can be readily located for slide shows, exhibitions and study. There is little point in taking photographs if they are not used and seen, or of archiving historical material if it cannot be found and studied without risk of damage.

The storage system must allow expansion to accommodate additional pictures. Old photographs often bear no date or site; many photographers of yesterday remain anonymous and, as with their work, their details are

Showcave entrances

Historical photographs of cave entrances are often of interest as these areas are susceptible to change. These pictures depict, clockwise from top left, Goatchurch Cavern during its brief period as a showcave (photo: F.G. Jenkins, *c*.1921), Swildon's Hole (H.E. Balch, *c*.1902), Kent's Cavern (William Spreat, *c*.1865), and Peak Cavern's ropemaking industry (John Latham, *c*.1870).

It is vital, for future historians, to record information on the print when it is first made. The left-hand photographs, showing the remains of the 1812 saltpetre works in Mammoth Cave, Kentucky, were taken by Ben Hains in 1892. Information on photographs which were commercially available is relatively easy to track down, but it is more difficult or impossible for personal photographs.

No details accompanied the right-hand photograph, taken outside what was then known as Easter Cave at Jenolan in New South Wales. The group of tourists was probably photographed by the resident photographer, J. Rowe, in 1896 or 1987. Inevitably, without annotations on the print, the names of the people have been lost to time

lost. It is impossible to overstress the importance of accurately recording information about an image, including the date, location, subject matter (with identifiable cavers named) and the photographer's name plus any relevant additional facts.

Write the details on the slide mount or the reverse of the print, so that the data cannot be separated from the image. Use a soft pencil with a light pressure when writing on prints, so that the impression does not transfer to the front. Many photographers add a record number which ties in with a card file, catalogue listing or database; this can include a code representing the site, type of picture or the date it was taken. If possible, use a number code as this can be extended and subdivided with greater ease than letter-based codes.

TYPES OF PHOTOGRAPHIC MATERIAL

Most photographic material is identical in structure: there is a base support coated with a light-sensitive layer of silver salts embedded in gelatine (three layers are used for most colour material, the silver salts being replaced by dyes during processing). When a photograph is taken the silver is exposed to light in a controlled manner, then the latent image is processed to make the silver which has reacted to light visible and to remove unexposed silver salts, making it insensitive to further exposure to light. The main stages in black and white processing are development and fixing. Problems at a later date can arise due to imperfections in the process, including deterioration of the support material, the processed silver or the gelatine carrier, or the presence of contaminants which were not removed from the print after fixing.

To determine the best method of storing photographs first identify their type, which may also give an indication of their age. Pictures (excluding ink-printed reproductions) fall into the following categories:

- Negatives: glass-plate or celluloid, in both colour and b&w
- Black and white prints: fibre-based paper or resin-coated plastic
- Colour prints: modern material or older, hand-coloured b&w originals
- Transparencies ('slides' or 'reversal film'): celluloid-based or lantern slides on glass
- Cine film: nitrate or celluloid-based
- Digital data: scanned from a conventional silver-based image or created using a digital camera

FACTORS CAUSING DAMAGE

Cave photographs, whatever their nature, must be preserved to avoid deterioration due to:

- Physical damage, for example from harsh handling
- Poor processing leading to degradation, for example due to trapped chemicals reacting to light or releasing damaging contaminants
- Poor storage conditions

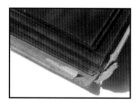

This set of cave-related glass plate negatives was beyond redemption. The plates had been stored, in contact with one another, in damp conditions and had fused together

The first factor is obviously controllable; photographs must be protected during storage and more valuable images copied for study or publication, rather than continually handling the original. Cover individual slides with an archival sleeve. If a glass plate or lantern slide is broken, tape it between two sheets of plane glass to preserve it.

The quality of processing is under your control, either in your own darkroom or by your choice of laboratory: go elsewhere if the standard is low. Make copy prints of historical material. If accidental damage or loss occurs, the image is safeguarded. It may not be possible to prevent deterioration which began over one hundred years ago.

Poor storage is the greatest threat to photographs. Given that material can be safeguarded against harsh handling, and copies can be made to record fading data in historical photographs, controlling storage conditions is crucial to preserve images for the future.

There are four environmental conditions to guard against:

- High temperature
- Incorrect humidity
- Light
- Chemicals, solvents and other pollutants

To protect photographs to the full, expensive equipment is required to monitor and control every aspect of storage. Pictures can be sealed in the dark at a constant humidity in cold storage but, realistically, this makes them inaccessible and impossible to use from day to day. The factors of expense and viable access often limit archival approaches, especially as the various categories of photographic material react at different rates or in different ways to environmental factors. It is nevertheless possible to counteract the most damaging aspects of the environment.

Temperature and humidity

Temperature and humidity interact to cause photographic deterioration. Low temperatures provide the best storage conditions, even to the extent of deep-freezing film. However, the changes in humidity when photographic material is restored to room temperature can induce other

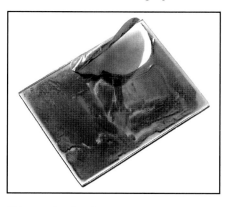

problems. For normal storage a constant, cool temperature is recommended.

High humidity causes the gelatine layer of a photograph to swell and, at 'room' temperature, provides perfect conditions for fast fungal growth. Glass mounts trap moisture and must not be used for archival slide storage; even small amounts of moisture are sufficient to bond film to glass during projection.

Contrary to popular belief, totally dry conditions are also unsuitable. Low humidity (for example, from using silica gel as a drying agent) causes gelatine layers to shrink and crack, especially on glass plates.

This negative has been kept too dry. The emulsion has cracked and peeled away from the glass plate

Light

Light probably causes more damage, especially to colour dyes, than any other factor. A colour print made from a negative (as opposed to a reversal print made from a slide) fades rapidly in light.

Colour slides, of any make, are extremely vulnerable to light damage, while black and white material is more stable. Ektachrome is less sensitive than Kodachrome to heat and will fade less during projection, but Kodachrome is better for long-term, cool storage. Kodak uses a 10 per cent decrease in the density of yellow (or magenta) dyes in a slide as an indication of fading. This can occur in as little as two years, even in the dark, if temperatures are too high. Only one hour in a slide projector can have the same result, as the slide is subjected to both heat and light during the process. This can be cumulative time, for example sixty slide shows of one minute each has the same result as a single showing of one hour. Glass slide mounts increase the problem as trapped moisture swells the gelatine layer, sometimes unevenly, causing it to stick to the glass as it warms up.

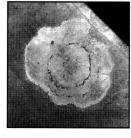

Store all photographs in absolute darkness, restrict projection of colour material, and do not leave slides on a light box when it can be avoided.

Moisture and warmth are ideal conditions for fungal growth, as here on a negative of Wookey Hole. All photographs, including transparencies, are susceptible to fungal attack

Pollutants

Check the quality of storage containers for possible pollutants. Gases such as sulphur dioxide cause discoloration in prints. Solvents are released from paint and glues used to manufacture chipboard and plywood, and these can react with a photograph's silver content to produce a 'silvered' image (see p.169). PVC slide sheets and some plastic boxes also release solvent fumes as they age; if they smell of plastic they are not of archival quality. Avoid storing photographs in containers made from any of these materials.

RECOMMENDED STORAGE

The recommended conditions for storage of all photographs are:

* Cool temperature, 10°C to 15°C
* Controlled relative humidity, 25% to 35%
* Absolute darkness
* Archival storage media

Archival storage media is expensive. Acid-free paper or polyester envelopes and lignin-free conservation board storage boxes are suitable for prints and glass plates, and non-PVC slide wallets or sheets for slides.

Many slide boxes, used by the processing lab to return slides to the photographer, have a transparent lid. If these are used for storage, keep them in the dark. An ideal system uses archival quality sheets in a metal filing cabinet, which is dark and does not release pollutants.

Given a cool temperature, controlled humidity and no light, modern transparencies can be stored for many years without damage, but colour dyes will inevitably fade. The most stable photographic material is a toned, well-washed black and white, fibre-based print.

As an experiment this transparency, taken in Wookey Hole in 1977, was placed in a slide box with a transparent lid; three months' exposure to light was enough to produce the faded band across the top

Digital storage

Advances in technology make it possible to scan images, including cine film, and store them in digital format on magnetic media or CD-ROM. There are both advantages and disadvantages in this.

As a means of safeguarding an image, high-quality scanning and storage can yield full photographic quality without loss of information. The cost per image is relatively low, and storage conditions are easy to maintain. However, magnetic media (including computer disks and video tape) degrades over time and an eventual total loss of data is certain. CD-ROM storage (using Photo-CD format) is cheap and offers long-term storage, but copies of the disk should be made to protect against the possibility of loss or damage. Photo-CD files do not hold sufficient detail to recreate a 35mm slide at full definition without using a professional format.

The fear is often expressed that the hardware and software required to access the images may not be available in the future. There may be grounds to support this but, even with the pace of technological change, photographic digital *information* should be transferable given the hardware to read it and, although it is time consuming, the data can be transferred to a new medium with no loss in quality. Optical disks are considered archivally stable for at least 40 years, and good quality CD-ROM disks for 100 years, although all plastic-based products must be considered suspect as they may suffer degradation.

All copying techniques, whether photographic or digital, should be considered as adjuncts to, not replacements for, correct archival photographic storage.

CINE FILM

Pollutants also affect cine film, but older films made with a nitrate base are more difficult to preserve as they are inflammable and more unstable than celluloid. Nitrate-based film was used until 1951 and decomposes in five stages: amber discolouration and fading, then the emulsion becomes sticky and the film turns brittle, gas bubbles form and gas is released before, in the fourth stage, the film softens and then finally decomposes to powder.

Nitrate film is sometimes difficult to identify. It is usually only found in 35mm format and contained in metal tins; if it has a pungent smell it is

nitrate. There may be edge markings indicating the manufacturer plus the words 'safety film' or 'nitrate', but these may have been transferred from a nitrate negative to a safety film positive. If the film is silent (there is no optical sound track running the length of the film) and there is no gap between the sprocket holes and frame, it is probably nitrate. In addition, varnished safety film can look like nitrate stock. To positively identify nitrate film clip a frame from the film (not the leader) and light it with a match. Nitrate film flares and leaves a little ash, while safety film curls and smoulders.

Nitrate film is dangerous when it is decomposing. The film can spontaneously ignite at temperatures below 50°C and, for reasons of safety, must not be projected or posted; it is illegal to carry it on public transport in the UK. To prevent gases building up, do not keep nitrate film in a sealed metal container. The only means of conservation is to have the film copied onto modern stock by a professional, specialist company. Thankfully, comparatively few caving films are known to exist on nitrate film, but any that are located should be copied as a matter of urgency.

Store nitrate film in an open canister. The short length on the right, from which the single frame is taken, is part of a 1950s British Screen Tatler newsreel; the location of the cave is unknown. Clear captions are essential to help future historians

An archival database and repository for caving films is based at Wells Museum in Somerset. No copyright transfer is involved, and both original material and video copies (with the copyright owner's permission) are welcome. The usefulness to future historians of recording film production details, regardless of whether they are amateur or professional standard, cannot be overemphasised and this information is welcome even if the film itself is not lodged at the museum.

CONCLUSION

How often have jokes been told about cave photographers, those much-maligned people who dare to venture underground and spend an era setting up a picture while other cavers, in boredom, shiver in the cold? It cannot be denied that cave photography takes time, but there is no reason why this should become an undue burden.

Every photographer will remember a trip during which everything went wrong: flashguns failed, cameras jammed, time ran out before you were finished. However, with careful preparation these problems can be minimised and your assistants given an enjoyable time underground; without that care you will soon run out of help. Your team is part of the photographic process; ignore its members at your peril. Never take things for granted and, like a good craftsman, don't blame others for your mistakes: were your instructions clear, was the shot too ambitious? Was the lighting overdone? Like children who should be seen and not heard, multiple sources of light might have been used but they should not be obvious. The vagaries of sunlight are not involved: you, the photographer, are in total control.

Or should be. You should know when to continue working at a theme when you *know* there is a golden opportunity waiting to be exploited –

just as you should know when to abandon a picture which, try as you might, is not working and will not yield a result.

As you gain experience at working underground, photographic technique will become second nature. Once technical quality has been learned and mastered you can truly concentrate on composition and strive towards that decisive, original image which stands out from all others. Stamp your badge upon your pictures, develop a new technique or equipment. Follow in others' footsteps, but demand individuality through your photography.

Luck? Yes, there are lucky breaks but, just as the quality of a gardener's spade does not raise wonderful flowers from seed, your camera does not make a picture. You do. Cave photography is a discipline unlike all others, from the dedication and effort it takes, to the rewards it offers. Take up the challenge and turn the outcome into something which is yours, and yours alone.

Left: Ogof Ffynnon Ddu (E2, B6)
Opposite: Longwood Swallet (B6)

BIBLIOGRAPHY

ARTICLES on cave photography appear regularly in the caving press or as a chapter within a larger volume. This bibliography is restricted to specialist guidebooks and manuals.

Many national and international caving organisations, including the British Cave Research Association (BCRA) and the National Speleological Society (NSS) of the USA, organise an

annual conference where the work of cave photographers is displayed and photographs are entered in a speleo photography competition. Contact the BCRA at BCM BCRA, London WC1N 3XX, UK and the NSS at 2813 Cave Avenue, Huntsville, AL 35810-4431, USA.

Since 1984 the photographic section of the NSS has published a biannual newsletter, *Flash*, and in 1995 an independent quarterly journal, *Underground Photographer*, was established. Contact the editors at 40 Buckingham Road, Petersfield, Hampshire GU32 3AZ, UK.

ALABART, Fèlix & RELANZÓN, Iñaki. 1995. *Fotografía del Mundo Subterráneo*. Espeleo Club de Gràcia, Barcelona, 160pp
Well-presented manual, in Spanish

AUDY, Igor. 1988. *Fotografování v Podsemí*. Ceská Speleologická Spolecnost, Prague, 32pp
Guide, in Czech

BAPTIZET, Alain. 1981. *Cineaste des Cavernes*. SAEP, Colmar, 139pp
Guide to cine photography, in French

BOCCA, Umberto. 1990. *Speleofoto*. Via dalla Pazza Folla, Cassolnovo, 96pp
Guide, in Italian

CALLOT, François-Marie & Yann. 1984. *Photographier Sous Terre*. VM, Paris, 263pp
Well-illustrated manual, in French

DÉRIBÉRÉ, M. 1952. *La Photographie Spéléologique*. Prisma, Paris, 48pp
Concise, well-written guide, in French

HOWES, Chris. 1987. *Cave Photography. A practical guide*. Caving Supplies, Buxton, 68pp
Guide, in English

HOWES, Chris. 1989. *To Photograph Darkness*. Alan Sutton, Gloucester, 352pp
The history of underground and flash photography, in English

MARTEL, E.A. 1903. *La Photographie Souterraine*. Gauthier-Villars, Paris, 70pp
The first guide specifically devoted to cave photography, in French. Reprinted 1989, Laffitte, Marseille

PRANDO, Edo. 1982. *Fotografia Speleologica*. Il Castello, Milan, 84pp
Guide, in Italian

STODDARD, Sheena. 1994. *An Introduction to Cave Photography*. BCRA, London, 32pp
Guide, the fourth in the *Cave Studies* series, in English

The 18m entrance pitch to Juniper Gulf

PHOTOGRAPHIC AND CAVING GLOSSARY

angle of view: The maximum angle contained within the *field of view* of a lens, determined by its *focal length*. Short focal lengths, eg. 35mm, have a wide angle of view and are termed *wide-angle lenses*.

aperture: An adjustable opening in the lens, controlled by the iris, through which light passes to reach the film and indicated by the f-number or *f-stop*.

aperture priority: An automatic exposure system. The photographer chooses an aperture and the camera selects a matching shutter speed. See also *shutter priority*.

APS: Advanced Photo System. The film cassette is smaller and lighter than 35mm. Cassettes can be changed part way through; they are auto-loading, allow a mixture of image ratios on one roll, and permit electronic information storage.

ASA: See *ISO*.

automatic flash: An electronic flashgun with a sensor which detects light reflected from the subject. When enough light has been received for a correct exposure the flash output is quenched automatically, hence the alternative term 'computer' flash. See also *thyristor*.

B setting: 'Bulb' or 'Brief'. A camera setting that allows the shutter to be locked open for an indefinite time using a *cable release*. See also *T setting* and *open flash*.

backlit: The effect of placing a flash immediately behind the subject, aimed towards the camera.

BCRA: The British Cave Research Association, organiser of an annual caving conference which includes a Photo Salon competition for cave photography.

bracketing: Taking multiple pictures using different exposures, usually altered by one or two f-stops from the calculated exposure.

burning in: A printing technique. Additional light is used in a selected area, darkening it when printing from a negative. See also *dodging*.

cable release: Attached to a shutter release, a cable release is used to lock open a camera shutter on B or to avoid camera shake when the camera is mounted on a tripod.

CD-ROM: A compact disk storage medium for digital information, including electronically scanned photographs.

chromogenic film: Black and white negative film based on colour negative technology, conferring good *latitude* and ease of processing.

close-up: Photography at close range, by definition between about one-tenth life-size ($\times 0.1$) and life size ($\times 1$). In this manual the term close-up encompasses the term *macro*.

co-axial cable: See *pc cable*.

cold shoe: Flash support point on a camera which has no electrical contacts. Synchronisation with the shutter is achieved with a *pc cable*.

colour temperature: A measurement of the colour composition of a light source. It is derived from the temperature (measured in kelvins) required to heat a pure iron bar so that it emits the same colour as the light source. Colour films are sensitive to specific colour temperatures, typically daylight at noon (5,500K).

compact camera: A term loosely applied to viewfinder cameras, designed to be lighter and more compact than an *SLR* camera. Usually fully automatic, some have manual overrides.

compensation: Exposure correction, usually indicated by (for example) +1 or –2 f-stops, the degree which the *exposure meter* is being overridden. The system is used on automatic cameras to override settings.

Compur shutter: See *leaf shutter*.

computer flash: See *automatic flash*.

contrast: The degree of separation of tonal values (areas of different density or colour) within a picture. High contrast means that there is a clear separation of tone, and vice versa.

cut-off: The metal rim of a filter may intrude into the field of view of a wide-angle lens, causing cut-off (darkening) in the photograph's corners. Do not stack filters on a wide-angle lens.

dedicated flash: A highly accurate *automatic flash* system requiring a 'dedicated' flashgun. Sensors built into the camera body detect light reflected from the film during the exposure.

dense: An overexposed *negative* or underexposed *transparency*. See also *exposure* and *thin*.

depth of field: The portion of the image which is considered to be acceptably in focus, extending in front of and behind the position of sharpest focus. Depth of field is dependent on *focal length* and *aperture*, as well as the lens-to-subject distance. Given a fixed lens and subject distance, the aperture controls the depth of field. Small apertures produce the greatest depth of field. Typically, one-third of the depth of field is in front of the position of sharpest focus, and two-thirds are behind. In close-up photography the two zones are roughly equal.

diaphragm: See *iris*.

diapositive: A positive image on transparent film; a *transparency*.

DIN: Deutsche Industrie-Norm, a German system of indicating the sensitivity of film and the equivalent of *ISO*. The scale is logarithmic, each additional DIN 3° indicating double the film speed. For example, the series DIN 18°, 21°, 24° represents the progression ISO 50, 100, 200.

dodging: A printing technique where light is selectively prevented from reaching the paper. The area becomes lighter (negative printing) or darker (slide). See also *burning in*.

electronic flash: A flashgun producing a short-duration pulse of light when a high voltage is discharged through a xenon tube; a strobe (US).

emulsion: The layer of light-sensitive chemicals coating *film*, photographic paper or a *plate*.

exposure: Production of a latent image (an unprocessed image) on the light sensitive emulsion layer of film by permitting light to reach it. This is controlled by the camera's *aperture* and *shutter* speed. An underexposed picture is dark (an underexposed *negative* is referred to as 'thin'; in *transparencies*, 'dense') while an overexposed photograph is light, or 'burned out' (in negatives, referred to as 'dense'; in transparencies, 'thin'). Incorrect exposure results in a lack of *contrast* and detail in some or all highlight or shadow areas.

Opposite: Ogof Ffynnon Ddu (front light E6 in an alcove, shielded from the figure; backlight B5)
Inset: Llygad Llwchwr (E2, B5)

exposure meter: A device for measuring the quantity of light falling on a subject or entering a camera's lens, in order to calculate or control an exposure. Also known as a lightmeter.

f-stop: Also known as an f-number, an f-stop relates to the *aperture* of a lens. 'Fast' lenses have a wide aperture and a low f-number. A scale of f-stops is typically: f2.8, 4, 5.6, 8, 11, 16, 22. At each f-stop increase, the light admitted into the lens is halved (larger f-numbers indicate smaller apertures).

field of view: The area covered by a lens; the subject area included in a photograph.

fill-in flash: A secondary flash which adds light to shadow areas not lit by the main, or key, flash. The lighting ratio is the ratio between the intensity of the key flash and the fill-in flash.

film: Light-sensitive material which, when exposed to light, forms an image (either as a positive *transparency* or *negative*). Film is made from a transparent base material covered with a sensitive layer of emulsion.

filter: Optical glass, fitted to the front of a lens for protection and, if tinted, to alter colour balance.

flare: Bright, degraded areas of an image due to reflection of light within a lens, caused by direct light striking the lens. Flare causes a loss in *contrast*. All lenses and filters flare to some extent; this is reduced by an anti-flare coating on the glass surface.

flashbulb: Aluminium (only bulbs made during the first years of manufacture used magnesium) in a 50 per cent oxygen atmosphere enclosed in a glass envelope. Two terminals are connected with thin wire that becomes hot when an electric current is discharged through them. This fires an explosive paste which ignites the aluminium, releasing a flash of light.

flashgun: Equipment (*electronic flashgun* or *flashbulb* gun) which produces a flash of light.

flashlight: North American term for a hand-held light (a torch in Europe).

flashmeter: An electronic device for measuring the intensity of a flash at the subject or camera position, producing a reading calibrated for the aperture and film speed in use.

Clockwise from top left:
Calcite formations in
Gilwern Passage, Ogof
Draenen (E8); Ogof
Ffynnon Ddu (B4); White
Arch Passage, Ogof
Draenen (B1, B5); Ogof
Draenen (E4); Piccadilly
in Ogof Ffynnon Ddu (B5)

fluorescence: See *phosphorescence*.

focal length: The distance between the optical centre of the lens and the film plane when the lens is focused at infinity. This relates to the *angle of view* covered by the lens. A 'standard' lens for an *SLR* camera is 50mm. More popular in cave photography is a *wide-angle lens*, usually 35mm or 28mm. *Compact cameras* have fixed focal length lenses of around 40mm.

focal plane: The sharpest point of focus and the plane in which the film lies. A focal plane shutter is located just in front of the focal plane. A focal plane (FP) flashbulb produces a long-duration flash to allow flash synchronisation at higher speeds than normal.

format: The size and shape of film. Common formats are 110 cartridge-loading film (Instamatic cameras), 35mm full and half-frame (most compact and SLR cameras), 120 roll film (giving 6cm × 6cm, 6cm × 4.5cm, or 6cm × 7cm medium format images), and sheet film (4in × 5in and above for large format cameras).

formation: A structure found in caves, normally based on calcium carbonate in the form of calcite. See *speleothem*.

frontlit: Effect of lighting from the front.

grain: The pattern of chemical granules in a processed film, dependent on the film's construction, sensitivity and processing.

guide number: A number representing the power of a flashgun or flashbulb, determined by multiplying the flash-to-subject distance in metres or feet with the aperture required for a perfect exposure at a specific film speed. Although a guide number can be found for any film speed, the standard (allowing comparisons between flashguns) is for ISO 100 film. This is normally measured using metres in Europe but elsewhere may be measured using feet.

helictite: A cave formation growing in an eccentric manner, apparently in contradiction to gravity.

hot shoe: Flashgun attachment point on a camera. The flashgun synchronises with the camera's *shutter* via electrical contacts.

infra-red: Part of the electromagnetic spectrum beyond visible light. Used to trigger *slave units* as it is not detectable by normal film.

iris: Part of a lens, also known as the diaphragm, which controls the size of the *aperture*.

ISO: International Standards Organization. Film sensitivity is rated according to an ISO scale; the higher the number the more sensitive (or 'faster') the film. The ISO designation replaced the ASA (American Standards Association), but is numerically identical.

key flash: The main flash of two or more, used as the basis for exposure. Other flashguns may provide *fill-in flash* or backlighting. Also known as the key light.

latitude: The ability of a film to yield an acceptable image when over- or underexposed. Fast films have more latitude than slow ones.

leaf shutter: A design of shutter within a lens. Found in older cameras and modern medium format lenses, it enables electronic flash to synchronise at any shutter speed. Also known as a Compur shutter. See also *focal plane*.

lens: The means of focusing light onto *film*. Fixed focus lenses only focus over a fixed range, dependent on the *depth of field*. Other lenses can focus on objects at different distances. See also *focal length*.

lens hood: An attachment to the front of a lens which shields the front glass from any non-image-forming stray light which might strike from the side and cause *flare*.

light tent: A structure, made of a translucent material, used to enclose an area around a subject. A flash fired through the material produces a soft, diffuse light, useful for photographing close-up subjects.

lightmeter: See *exposure meter*.

macro: Production of a photograph with a magnification between life-size (×1) and ten-times life-size (×10). See also *close-up*.

negative: A 'reversed' black and white or colour image on film, used for subsequent printing onto photographic paper.

NSS: The National Speleological Society, which organises a Photo Salon competition during its annual convention in the USA. The journal *Flash*, devoted to cave photography, is published by an NSS group.

Indiana Highway,
Ogof Draenen (B4)

O-ring: A rubber ring, O-shaped in cross-section, used to waterproof underwater cameras or containers. Seated in a groove, the O-ring distorts under water pressure and increases the seal. The ring should be kept supple with silicone grease.

open flash: The technique of using B in total darkness with the shutter locked open with a *cable release*. Flashes are fired, not necessarily at the same time, to expose the film before the shutter is closed.

orthochromatic film: A film insensitive to the red part of the visible spectrum, particularly older types of black and white film. See also *panchromatic film*.

overexposed: See *exposure*.

panchromatic film: A film sensitive to all visible colours, a term particularly applied to modern black and white film. See also *orthochromatic film*.

parallax: The image seen through a non-SLR viewfinder and the image formed on the film are slightly different. This difference is caused by parallax and can produce an error in composition, particularly in *close-up* photographs.

pc cable/socket: A cable and socket system which synchronises a flash with a camera's *shutter*. Sometimes referred to as a co-axial or sync cable.

phosphorescence: Calcite, and some other minerals, can absorb short wavelength radiation such as ultra-violet light from a flashgun. The energy is then emitted as visible light, a process which continues until the UV radiation ceases to strike it. This effect is termed fluorescence. Some minerals continue to emit their stored energy after the UV radiation has ceased, an effect sometimes referred to as an afterglow. The afterglow is technically termed phosphorescence, although it is often (incorrectly) also referred to as fluorescence.

plate: Prior to the invention of flexible film, a glass plate carried a layer of light-sensitive chemicals which were developed to form a negative.

prime lens: A lens with a single, fixed *focal length*, unlike a *zoom lens*.

processing: Chemical development of any sensitised photographic material.

rangefinder: A device, most often used with older cameras, for determining the camera-to-subject distance.

reciprocity: Photographic emulsions are rated for *exposure* within a specified range of time, generally between 1 second and 1/1000 second. A correct exposure within this range is controlled (in darkness, where flash is required) by the intensity of the flash (which is the equivalent of the shutter speed in surface photography) and the *aperture*. Longer or shorter exposures lead to a loss of sensitivity of the *emulsion* which is termed reciprocity failure; the rule of doubling time for each halving of light intensity or closing down an aperture by one *f-stop* does not hold true for longer or shorter exposures.

red-eye: A red colour in eyes in a photograph, caused by reflection of light from the retina. The effect can be avoided by moving the flash away from the lens-to-subject axis.

resolution: The ability of a film or lens to record fine detail; technically, resolution is expressed as the number of lines per millimetre which are distinctly recorded in the final photograph.

rimlit: The brightly lit margin of a backlit subject.

rule of thirds: In composition, imaginary lines which divide the picture into three horizontal and three vertical parts. Placing the subject on the intersection of the lines gives a strong composition.

scrim: Gauze or other material which partially covers a flash or video light to decrease intensity in part of the scene, for example where one area is closer to the flash than another.

sharpness: 'Sharpness' in a photograph is subjective, being based on the viewer's perception. Technically, it initially depends on the quality of the lens and the film's *resolution*. The image is also affected by focusing, processing, magnification and its content. In cave photography, *backlit* and *sidelit* photographs can appear sharper than *frontlit* photographs (even though they may not actually be as sharp). Electronic flash produces distinct shadows and increases apparent sharpness.

shutter: Device within a camera body or lens for controlling the duration of time that light is permitted to reach the film. See also *focal plane* and *leaf shutter*.

shutter priority: An exposure system where the photographer chooses a shutter speed and the camera automatically selects a matching aperture for a correct exposure. See also *aperture priority*.

sidelit: Effect of lighting by placing the flash to the side of the subject.

slave unit: An electronic device which detects a visible or *infra-red* pulse of light emitted by a flashgun and fires a second flash. Slave units allow synchronised, multiple flash without the requirement for a connecting cable between the guns and camera.

slide: See *transparency*.

SLR: Single Lens Reflex. A system of viewing through the lens using a mirror and pentaprism, giving exactly the same image in the viewfinder as will reach the film.

speleothem: Cave formations, such as *stalactites*, *stalagmites* and *helictites*.

SRT: Single Rope Technique. A system of moving up or down a rope to ascend or descend a shaft.

stalactite: A *formation* growing downwards from the cave roof.

stalagmite: A *formation* growing upwards from the cave floor.

standard lens: A lens of 50mm *focal length* for 35mm *format* cameras. The 'standard' lens was originally intended to 'see' the same area as the human eye. A focal length nearer to 35mm is a closer approximation.

stop down: A contraction of *f-stop*, a reference to closing the *aperture*.

straw stalactite: A thin stalactite; soda straw in North America.

strobe: Alternative term for *electronic flash*, especially in North America.

sync cable: See *pc cable*.

synchro-sunlight: Outmoded term for daylight combined with fill-in flash, as used in cave entrances and now normally called *fill-in flash*.

T setting: Camera setting to allow 'Time' exposures by holding the shutter open; one press opens the shutter, the second press closes it. Operates in a similar fashion to the *B setting*, without requiring a *cable release*. Found on older models and some modern medium format cameras.

tackle sack: A bag used for carrying rope or other caving equipment (UK); a cave pack, gear bag or gear sack (US).

telephoto lens: A lens with a *focal length* longer than 50mm.

thin: An underexposed *negative* or overexposed *transparency*. See also *exposure* and *dense*.

thyristor: A component in an electronic flashgun which retains unused power in the capacitor after a flash has been automatically quenched. See also *automatic flash*.

tone: The *contrast* between light and dark areas or between different colours. A tonal range may be limited (for example, have few mid-tones, such as a silhouette photograph) or a full range of tones (where all details are present). Different colours may not record with their anticipated brilliance in black and white photography: reds record with darker tones than expected.

torch: A hand-held light (UK); a flashlight (US).

transparency: A positive image on a transparent base material; 'slide film', used for projection. Also referred to as a diapositive or reversal film because processing produces a positive rather than a negative image.

TTL: Through The Lens. A term usually applied to exposure systems which measure light reaching the film through the lens, as opposed to being measured by a flashgun's sensor or separate exposure meter. TTL also indicates that the viewfinder produces its image through the lens, as opposed to *compact cameras* with a separate viewfinder.

underexposed: See *exposure*.

viewfinder camera: See *compact camera*.

wide-angle lens: A lens with a shorter *focal length* than 50mm.

zoom lens: A lens with a changeable *focal length*. See also *prime lens*.

INDEX

acetylene lighting, 163-5
ammunition box, 61
angle of view, 15-17, 259
aperture, 16-18, 119, 259
APS system, 3, 259
aquarium, 151
archaeology, 141-6, 177
ASA, *see* ISO

B setting, 6, 83-4, 90, 103, 259
back-scatter, in water, 198
background, choice, 208-10
backlighting, 92-5, 136-7, 140-1
bag, polythene, 15
   zip-lock, 62, 186
ball-and-socket head, 46-7
bat, photographing, 147-8
battery, electronic flash, 20-1
   on expedition, 189
   flashbulb gun, 34-5
   hydrogen venting, 42-4
   rechargeable, 35-6, 61, 65, 189
   temperature, 61, 194
   video, 206
bellows, 126-8
bounce flash, 24
bracketing, 69-71, 259
butane, 180

cable release, 47, 259
calcite, colour in b&w, 214
   colour emission, 178-9
camera, automatic, 3-4, 153-8
   bracing, 83-4
   choice, 1-15
   cleaning, 2, 64
   compact, 10-11, 124-5, 153-8
   flash synchronisation, 6-7, 15
   focusing screen, 125
   format, 2-3
   housing, 15
   and humidity, 195
   protection, 13-15
   SLR, 11-13, 125
   temperature effect, 194-5
   underwater, 6, 8-9, 196-7
candle, 167, 180
case, camera, 13-14
   flash, 26
   transport, 61-4
cave life, 146-52
cave paintings, 141, 144, 177
chamber, lighting, 37, 104-7,
   112-13, 189, 248
cine, 204-5, 255
   see also video

circuit diagram, bulb gun, 35, 38
   slave unit, 53
cleaning, 2, 64
close-up photography, 123-52
   depth of field, 130
   exposure determination, 130-5
   lens attachments, 125-6
   multiple flash, 138-9
   reflector, 139-40
cold shoe, 6, 259
colour, balance, 56, 235-6
   in black and white, 170,
     212-14, 236
   composition, 210-12
   flashbulb, 30, 87, 171
   incorrect, 160, 235-6, 237
   oversuit, 213
   temperature, 159-61, 259
   video light, 205
communication, 100-1, 200
compensation, 67-9, 70-1, 135,
   161, 259
competition, 243-5
composition, 207-26
condensation, in air, 82, 87, 90,
   92-3, 235
   on lens, 18, 235
conservation, of photographs,
   169, 251-5
contract, 190-1
contrast, 56, 58, 234-5, 259
copyright, 191-2
cropping, 237-9
cut-off, 232, 259

darkroom, 187, 238-9
depth of field, 73-5, 130, 136,
   261
developer, viii
digital, imaging, 239-42
   storage, 254
DIN plug, 52, 53
distance, estimation, 73, 200
diving, 196-200
documentary photography, 146
drum, screw-top, 61
drybag, 62
DX code, 156-8

entrance, exposure, 67-71, 113,
   120-2
errors, identifying, 227-37
exhibiting work, 243-5
expedition photography, 183-95
exposure, angle of lighting, 97-8
   close-up, 130-5

exposure (cont)
   compensation, 67-9, 70-1, 135,
     161, 259
   control, 3-4, 67, 70-2, 75, 154
   correct, 77, 99, 230-1
   in daylight, 67-71
   entrance, 67-71, 113, 120-2
   meter, 4, 261
   over-, 77, 98-9, 162, 230-1
   phosphorescent effects, 179
extension tubes, 126-8

f-stop sequence, 17-18
fill-in flash, 116-22
film, amateur, 195
   care, 194-5
   characteristics, 56-8
   choice, viii, 55-6, 58-61
   chromogenic, 60-1, 259
   cine, 255
   colour temperature, 159-61
   comparison, 170
   DX code, 156-8
   for expedition, 184, 188-9,
     194-5
   fading, 254
   format, 2-3
   grain, 56, 58
   latitude, 56, 58, 70, 71, 263
   nitrate, 255
   processing, 163, 187, 234-5
   scratched, 236, 241
   speed, 56-8
filter, 18, 160-1, 176, 213-14
flare, 96, 232, 261
flash, auto, 20-3, 98, 104, 154-8
   bounce, 24, 139
   on camera, 82, 153-4
   cascade, 31
   characteristics, 33, 85-7, 92,
     102
   combining types, 113
   cumulative, 107-8
   duration, 86
   fill-in, 116-22
   hidden, 108-10
   integral, 82, 153-4
   interference, 104
   lighting effects, 31, 72, 86-7
   multiple, 103-22, 138-9
   open, 83-4, 100-1
   power, 19, 85-6, 98-9
   shielding, 96, 139-40
   siting, 87-95, 104-14, 136-8, 145
   synchronisation, 6, 7, 15, 33, 34
   TTL, 22, 154-6, 266
   see also flashgun